STRESS
& THE
BOTTOM LINE

STRESS
& THE
BOTTOM LINE

A Guide to Personal Well-Being and Corporate Health

E.M. GHERMAN, M.D.

A Division of American Management Associations

Library of Congress Cataloging in Publication Data

Gherman, E. M.
  Stress and the bottom line.

  Bibliography: p.
  Includes index.
  1. Stress (Psychology)   2. Stress (Physiology)
3. Stress (Psychology)—Prevention.   4. Psychology,
Industrial.   I. Title.
BF575.S75G48   158′.1   80-69697
ISBN 0-8144-5696-0   AACR2

FIRST PRINTING   7653682

This book is dedicated to the hundreds of people throughout my life who shared their knowledge with me and contributed so unselfishly to the never ending process of my learning, understanding, and maturing. They include parents, children, teachers, friends, clients, patients, associates, and casual acquaintances. All of them added significantly to the breadth of my conscious awareness.

Foreword

Human existence has always been marked by danger, pressure, and stress, whatever the historical era. Prehistoric man was threatened by a hostile and unpredictable environment. In the Middle Ages, disease and famine were the major sources of tension. Throughout history, man has responded to the challenges of his environment in an effort to try to avoid or reduce damaging wear and tear in mind and body, serious interference with daily life, and destructive behavior toward others.

Urbanization and scientific advancement have solved many of the old problems and, in turn, created their own stressors. The sources of distress have changed from physical threats to social and psychological strains—loneliness in a big city, frequent changes of employers, marital conflict, feelings of rejection by a group, a complex job with too many things to do each day. The struggle to survive involves trying to maintain good health, emotional stability, a sense of identity, and harmonious relations.

Today man is challenged by the potentially dangerous stress and disorientation of accelerated change within the span of a single generation. Contemporary society is marked by almost continuous revolts, disruption, shifting responsibilities and priorities, shrinking durability, planned obsolescence, and nomadic work and lifestyles. This accelerated thrust has personal, psychological, and sociological consequences. It affects individuals, corporations, and society as a whole.

Mankind is forever being confronted by a multitude of crises: for example, overpopulation, environmental pollution, and world food and raw material shortages. In addition, in the 1980s, people will have to deal with continuing inflation, terrorism, the taking of hostages, and nuclear saber rattling. Americans will put increasing demands on the government for better performance at lower cost, will face the dilemma posed by health and safety advocates on advisability of some technological innovations, and will worry over a number of other very real concerns.

To exacerbate the situation, high-speed communications media overload us with information about many problems that are beyond our control and far removed from our immediate experience. This input can worsen cumulative tensions. And the subsequent development of the recession–inflation complex and high unemployment rates has resulted in new problems at all levels of industry. Increased technology, affluence, education, and leisure were supposed to improve the quality of life, but it is clear that for many people it just hasn't happened.

So the American lifestyle can be characterized by affluence and material comfort, coupled with discontinuity and uncertainty. The effects of social, economic, and environmental stressors are steadily piling up on most Americans. These effects, added to the steadily declining level of physical conditioning and good health habits and the usual stress to which an adult is subject, make Americans more prone to stress-derived disorders than ever before.

We are in the middle of a national epidemic of stress disease, as clearly shown by death and health breakdown statistics. Stress directly and indirectly adds to the cost of doing business, and it detracts from the total quality of life for a very large number of American workers.

Today, the average 50-year-old white male can reasonably expect to live to the age of 73—only nine months longer than his counterpart in the 1920s. Medical advances have largely wiped out infectious diseases such as pneumonia, which killed many of our ancestors in their early years. However, a host of once uncommon disorders have reached epidemic proportions: cardiovascular disease, stroke, cancer, and other big killers are relatively new.

These realities have created a growing concern among both individuals and organizations about physical and mental illness and how to maintain health. In response to the demands of what is frequently called the "rat race" or "corporate jungle," Americans are increasingly recognizing the need to relax and to develop positive strategies for coping with the stresses of today's world.

Stress is rampant in the maze of complex interpersonal business relationships on all rungs of the corporate ladder.

Over the years medical thought has come more and more to recognize the interaction of the mind and the body in the production of health and illness. Rather than seek the cause in a single pathogenic agent, germ, or toxin, science has shown that many factors influence the development of poor health. A compound of psychological, physical, and social environment factors interact to disrupt or contribute to a person's well-being.

An employee is first of all a human being. As such, he or she is subject to all the intrapersonal dynamics we have just mentioned. Many adults spend roughly half their waking lives in work-related activities, so it seems likely that social and psychological factors have an important influence on their health.

The tensions of work spill over into the personal lives of employees and vice versa, so that pressured individuals are caught in a vicious stress style that escalates unhappiness and conflict in many areas of life at once. Stress compounds itself as people feel stress about stress.

It is vital to break this vicious cycle at an early stage. Employers must take the time to listen to the sources of fear, anger, worry, and frustration among employees. Employers must be sensitive to basic problems that are stressful and seek ways to handle or reduce them in order to decrease or eliminate their debilitating effects. Stress overload, regardless of the source, takes its toll on the individual and ultimately on the organization.

Distressed employees suffer from inadequate attention and concentration, have memory lapses, and are generally distracted from their jobs. This malaise fractures the work team and isolates overstressed individuals as their erratic moods and behavior strain their relationships with others. It can also undermine self-confidence, leading to lower and/or poorer production by blocking initiative, persistence, and creative problem solving. Thus developing skill in the early detection, recognition, and management of human problems can help a good supervisor keep stress at a healthy functional level.

There are positive aspects to stress. It can motivate and stimulate employees to meet challenges and use their human potential. Without a certain amount of stress, reports would not get written and advertising campaigns would never get out of the planning stages. However, we are addressing the problems of stress that tip the scales and work against the individual and ultimately the corporation. It is in the self-interest of corporate management to understand and deal with stress. Good health is good business.

The corporate sector has a unique capacity to promote awareness of preventive health. Since the corporation has almost daily extended contact with a large portion of the general population (nine out of ten working people work in organizations), it is an advantageous position to provide opportunities for promoting health. Chapters 16 and 17 examine a variety of programs that corporations may wish to consider.

The problem of rising health care costs is the most immediate factor leading business to become more directly involved in health care. Some businesses are reluctant to move into the personal health arena, but there is overwhelming evidence that personnel issues cannot be ignored. Corporate health depends on a productive workforce, and stress and productivity go hand in hand.

There are budget and business systems for just about everything. Yet despite the wealth of knowledge about management and personnel practices, implementation of these guidelines often breaks down on a day-to-day basis. This in itself can produce stress.

The perception of the corporation as a key stressor cannot be dismissed lightly. Whether the perception is rooted in reality is unimportant if a significant number of employees at all levels feel the company is ignoring its responsibility to provide knowledge and assistance.

Distress can create a vicious cycle in the work environment. Managers often pass pressures from budget constraints, production quotas, and time problems on to those who work for them. Employees in turn pass the stress back by refusing tough challenges, creating difficult interpersonal relationships, delaying or stopping work, or engaging in outright sabotage.

Stress reduction programs are of considerable value in bringing the stress in the work environment under control. This guide to corporate health and personal well-being has specific objectives:

1. To explain what stress is—its multiplicity of sources, what it does to the mind and body, its "individualized nature," its potential for helpful or harmful consequences.

2. To establish a clear understanding that the key to stress management is not to eliminate stressors but to develop the ability to reduce and cope with them more effectively.
3. To provide knowledge of self-observable, early-warning signs of excessive stress.
4. To establish proper identification and handling of excessive stress in subordinates or peers.
5. To introduce the major techniques of coping and to show how they are used, when they are used, and why they work.
   Fight-or-flight decisions
   Physical activity
   Deep relaxation techniques
   Sensible diet
   Commitment to a personal stress-reduction program
6. To provide guidelines and to encourage those who need it to seek professional assistance.
   Signs that indicate help is needed
   Guidance from company medical department or personal physician
   Familiarization with the work of psychiatrists, psychologists, biofeedback therapists, group therapy

It is time to devote some of the insight and energy we bring to furthering our business and professional careers to the development of a healthy workforce. American business has played a key role in making us the first nation to achieve such unprecedented prosperity. It might also help us become the first to achieve holistic health and individual effectiveness and fulfillment.

New patterns of management show that we recognize the human side of enterprise. One outgrowth of the 1960s, the first decade to be endowed with wide-scale material affluence, is that people are not willing to spend the majority of their time and energy at unsatisfying or life-damaging pursuits. Ambition, power, and wealth are not enough. Modern individuals seek some measure of serenity and a development of their total potential. They demand that their human need for dignity, self-expression, and growth be met.

It is time for the employee and the corporation to come to grips with the stress in human life. They can learn to use stress as a positive factor, and to defend themselves against the excessive wear and tear that result in disease and mental turmoil and are reflected on the bottom line.

In my many years of intimate involvement in the industrial scene, I have had frequent occasion to review the forward-thinking efforts of those whose purpose it is to enlighten and enhance the social sensitivity and progressive contribution of the modern executive. I feel that this book illustrates an outstanding recognition of the broad dynamics of the industrial environment and a meticulous awareness of the overall stresses in daily living.

If one examines the table of contents, and indeed the contents themselves, of this notable piece of research by Dr. Gherman and his associates, one cannot help but conclude that it represents a truly important contribution to the thinking of the American business executive. It is explicit. It defines the problem. And it imbeds in its conclusions specific plans for a corporate stress management program.

J. Robert Fluor
Chairman, President, and
Chief Executive Officer
Fluor Corporation

Preface

This book contains personal and corporate approaches to dealing with stress, both positive (eustress) and negative (distress)—approaches that are designed to help you understand and cope effectively with stress-creating by-products of our urban, industrial, highly mobile American lifestyle. It is to be used as a working manual in handling stress, both your own and the stress found within your company.

The technical language of research on stress is translated into understandable guidelines for stress management that can be applied to everyday experiences on and off the job. Basic concepts are introduced and then applied to many specific situations, spanning the entire life cycle.

The book is structured to accompany an in-house behavioral intervention program to reduce employee health risks associated with a stressful lifestyle. Recognizing the intimate relationship between happiness and the state of well-being on the one hand and physical health and resistance to illness on the other, you can review the stress reduction program with the goal of improving both physical and mental health. The program is designed to educate and motivate employees to reduce their susceptibility to chronic diseases and accidents and to actualize their potentials for positive health, well-being, and effective productiveness.

For each individual, perhaps the greatest costs to health come from such self-inflicted lifestyle diseases as heart attacks, hypertension, alcoholism, and depression. For the corporation, organization and employee "burnout" costs billions of dollars each year from premature employee death, turnover, absenteeism, accidents, lowered performance, and medical expenses. Failure to recognize and deal with the stresses inherent in different vocations, working conditions, personalities, and organizational structures is as dangerous to corporate health as it is to yours.

Part I—chapters 1 through 8—focuses on the social forces that tend to cause stress. Special attention is given to the kinds of pressures you face in the work setting, the family and other group situations, and the community and world at large.

Part II—chapters 9 through 12—focuses on the nature of stress and disease—what happens in your mind and body during times of stress.

Part III—chapters 13 through 19—deals with specific techniques of managing stress. Ways of coping constructively to reduce distress are outlined in various personal and corporate situations. By growing in personal awareness of the nature of stress and how to handle it, you can improve your health and well-being and those of the corporation.

In this book, we will carefully examine some familiar questions that will serve as vehicles for you to look at your own experiences, obtain insights, and apply principles. Each person can then use the principles in ways congenial to his or her own personality, modified according to personal circumstances and problems.

In the course of your lifetime, you will come to know *about* a great many things. For example, many of you know about flying from traveling, reading, and observing airplanes. Until you are at the control of an airplane, however, your experience and related knowledge will be limited to *knowing about*. You will actually learn *how* to do only a few things. The things you know how to do well determine your feelings of achievement.

Technically, everyone has the ability to reduce stress arousal and thus prevent stress-related disease. To realize this potential, you must acquire a working knowledge about the multidimensional phenomenon of stress. And you must learn how to design and follow your own stress management system, involving a variety of techniques.

Stress is unavoidable, but it can be directed and controlled to provide the energy for health, growth, and the development of human potential.

E. M. GHERMAN, M.D.

Acknowledgments

I am compelled to acknowledge the extraordinary contribution of the late J. Samuel Bois, former president of the Canadian Psychological Society, who helped me take many quantum jumps into new worlds of understanding the nature and character of man's behavior. We joined together in our exploration of the early works of Hans Selye, chairman of the International Institute of Stress. This introduction, fortified by my meeting and coming to know Dr. Selye, germinated in my commitment to document a functional application of his monumental research in the field of stress in disease and health.

This volume could not have come into being in its present form without a prodigious amount of work and research on the part of my research assistant, Jan Kingaard. Her dedication in meticulously probing the works of the hundreds of writers and researchers in the field of stress was beyond comparison. Her effort was a continuing unifying force in bringing this work to completion.

In the early conceptual days, my close friend James L. Goddard, former commissioner of the U. S. Food and Drug Administration, added order and structure to my formative thoughts and contributed to the emerging organization of the book.

William R. Matheson, vice president, Avco Financial Corporation, provided many helpful and practical suggestions for structuring the early days of our research.

Barbara Jessen, president of the Orange County Neurological Society, contributed great insight into the neurological implications of stress.

Norman Cousins, former chairman of the *Saturday Review* and author of *Anatomy of an Illness,* evaluated the contents, affirming the breadth and application of its coverage.

Jay Reed, vice-president, Fluor Corporation, provided insight into the range of stress in day-to-day corporate activity that was exceedingly useful.

John Caffrey, former executive vice-president of Rockland College, painstakingly reviewed the manuscript.

Richard Stone, deputy corporate medical director, American Telephone and Telegraph Company, and his highly knowledgeable staff contributed importantly to the consideration of stress research in industry.

Paul Rosch, chairman of the American Institute of Stress, evaluated the content structure.

James S. J. Manuso, director, Emotional Health Program, Equitable Life Assurance Company, provided important input in the area of cost-effective justification for stress management programs.

Throughout the writing, Donald Schaeffer, professor of psychiatry, University of California at Irvine, and Louis A. Gottschalk, former chairman of the Department of Psychiatry at the University of California at Irvine, added immeasurably to my knowledge of how to identify stress manifestations early and how to manage them.

Alan D. Stewart, vice-president, Alpha Beta Company, displayed an inquisitiveness and concern about the pervasive nature of stress in business that raised important questions.

Frederic F. Flach, author and professor of psychiatry, Cornell University, is one of the few creative psychiatrists I have known. I thank him for his thoughts on coping creatively with personal change.

Throughout the many months of manuscript preparation, layout, proofreading, and repeated retyping, Judy Kuckowicz, my secretarial assistant, effectively eliminated the frustration and impatience that would have been a normal part of this effort. She was ably assisted by a calm and competent Marlene C. Bumbera.

The foregoing is only a partial list of the many—too many to name—who in their way spontaneously added substance to this volume. Special appreciation and attention are directed to those included in the bibliography.

Finally, and nonetheless importantly, I am deeply grateful to Natalie Meadow, Managing Editor of Books at AMACOM, and her associates for their forthrightness and careful attention to the contents in making this manuscript more succinct and comprehensible for the reader.

Contents

8. Corporate Social Responsibility   131

Environmental—noise, water, air, energy / Community endeavors / Personal development / Personal ethics / Organizational values

Part II   Stress and Disease

9. The Physiological Results of Stress   147

Nervous system / Reticular activating system / Sympathetic and parasympathetic systems / Endocrine system / Muscular response / Gastrointestinal response / Brain states / Skin response / Mobilizing physiological defenses

10. The Psychobiology of Stress   167

Relationship between stress and disease / Mind–body involvement / General process of habituation / Psychological variables and disorders / The psychological process of coping

11. Male and Female Psychobiological Differences   178

Biological biases / Male vulnerability and liberation / Working women and stress / Adjusting to changing roles

12. Adaptation and Contemporary Life   195

Biopsychosocial investigation / Era of radical change / Reactivity levels and adaptive ranges / Patterns of vulnerability / Adaptive skills

Part III   Managing Stress

13. Goals and Principles of Coping   207

Coping with tomorrow / Identifying stressors / Controlling events / Seeking a healthy balance

14. Perception and Communication   217

General semantics / Conscious awareness of your stress filter / Constructive thinking / Effective listening / Management of conflict / Low-stress communication

15. Understanding Yourself and Stress   239

Individual responsibility / The health checkup and professional monitoring / Achieving self–managed change / Health risks and rewards

Part I
IDENTIFYING THE SOURCES OF STRESS

CHAPTER 1
A General Overview

If a member of your staff surprises you with a call from the hospital informing you that he has been hit by a truck and has a broken leg, you know that he will recover, that the accident will probably not happen again right away, and that it was not your fault. If another employee calls in sick and reports an attack of viral flu, you know, again, that modern medical help will have him or her up and around again soon, although not back at work soon enough to infect others.

But when a member of your staff suffers a nervous collapse or a heart attack or is institutionalized suddenly for an alcoholism you did not even suspect, you will wonder what happened. You should know that these absences are caused by a common factor: stress. If you are really up to date, you may suspect that one major source of stress is work and the working conditions in your company. Stress derives from other causes and environments as well—marriage, community, and family conflicts—but even these should be of concern to the modern corporation, because the price paid for stress is lost expertise, time, productivity know-how, contacts, and many other valuable attributes of your employees.

The word *stress* comes from the same source as distress. Early fourteenth-century writings mention a man under "so hard stress that his goodness grew the less," and another one who "had some sickness or other grievance that maketh him stress." An 1883 issue of the British *Fortnightly Review* speaks of "this age of stress and transition," leaving one to wonder what the writer of a century past would think of the 1980s.

Long the subject of studies by Hans Selye, in the fields of biology and medicine, stress is now a household topic. Despite familiarity with the term, it is important to understand just what stress is and is not—and the several principal kinds of stress.

[3]

The word *stress* has long been used in engineering and physics and is now found in most languages from French to Chinese. In the sense used in this book, stress is the nonspecific response of the body to any demand made upon it. The source of stress is called a *stressor*. Popular parlance is not always so careful.

Studies of stress and its effects are now under way in more than 20 institutes as well as in numerous university departments, hospitals, and other organizations around the world. Stress has become a major problem for both individuals and institutions in an era of accelerating change, characterized by the rapid growth of knowledge and technology. Over 6,000 separate reports on stress research have been made in recent years, and the largest and most comprehensive stress documentation center in the world, at the International Institute of Stress in Montreal, Canada, houses over 120,000 volumes on the subject. This output is, in itself, a telling commentary on the central role of stress in the twentieth century.

Stress research as a recognized field of study began over 40 years ago with the work of Hans Selye, first at McGill University, then at the University of Montreal's Institute of Experimental Medicine and Surgery. Dr. Selye's work focused on defining in precise physiological terms how the body reacts to stress.

In a landmark experiment, Selye found that the adrenal glands are the body's prime reactors to stress. Stress is no longer thought to be "just in the mind"—it is a chemical reaction of the body to daily events and perceptions.

PERSONALITY TYPE

Everyone is subject to stress, but some people are more aware of it than others or are better able to handle it. Several useful theories have been developed from research done on stress and personality.

Perhaps the most significant of these personality theories, developed by Meyer Friedman and Ray Rosenman, is popularly referred to as the Type *A*/Type *B* classification. In looking for methods of predicting the effects of stressful situations on various types of people, they linked distinct personality traits to the probability of developing heart disease as one result of stress.

Characteristics of Type *A* personalities include intensive drive and ambition, aggressiveness, competitiveness, a need to get things done and meet deadlines, visible restlessness, and impatience. The extreme Type *A* person has been described as a very hard worker, a perfectionist filled with apparent confidence and resolution. A male drives himself hard and strives to gain the respect, rather than the appreciation, of others; he is seldom out sick and is on time for appointments. He is more likely to develop heart disease in middle age than his Type *B* counterpart.

Type *B* personalities, as described by Friedman and Rosenman, have an easygoing manner, are patient, are able to take time to appreciate leisure and beauty, are not preoccupied with social achievement, do not feel driven by the clock, and are less competitive than Type *A*'s.

According to Friedman and Rosenman, Type *A*'s are more likely to make the best salespeople, whereas the position of corporate president, which requires broader, more sensitive thinking, is usually held by Type *B*'s.

Personality is not the only factor affecting reaction to stress. Living habits and attitudes can help you identify where your particular stress problems lie. There is a sharp difference in attitude and behavior between people who suffer from constant stress and those who do not. Executives who are under stress report such habits as:

Taking tranquilizers
Having two or more cocktails at lunch
Using sleeping pills
Rarely having weekends for family and self
Hurried breakfasts
Heavy cigarette smoking

Stressed executives also report similar attitude characteristics:

More fear of self-expression
More boredom
More suspicion that they are not receiving
    their due for efforts
More job insecurity
More dissatisfaction with job progress
More dislike for colleagues
Greater desire to retire by age 55

THE ROLE OF PERCEPTION

Individual perceptions are important in understanding the consequences of events in our lives. Whether or not a stressor actually provokes stress depends a great deal on how a person perceives it. The perception in turn is influenced by a variety of individual differences in people, like those already discussed, and by differences in stressors, discussed below. All of these can affect both physiological and behavioral outcomes.

Stress is the physiological and psychological response to any demand made on the human organism and should not be confused with its cause, which we call a *stressor*. Stress is defined as the result of a person's response to pressure; it is not the pressure (stressor) itself. We will first examine the causes and then the effects of stress on the human organism.

STRESSORS

Stressors vary in many ways and along many dimensions. When you think of stressors, you probably think first of those that stem from the environment. These may be physical, such as a hurricane, a speeding car, or a threatening dog. Sometimes they are social, such as a demanding employer, a complaining customer, or an appointment to an active civic committee.

Stressors may appear to originate inside the person, stemming from inner drives that have been learned. There are demands you make on your own mind or body—for example, when you work hard to exceed your sales quota or push to compete in a marathon race. Another kind is operating when you bottle up your resentment toward someone who has hurt you.

Stressors often have both external and internal factors. Marriage, for example, requires adjustment to a new set of external conditions: new uses of time, new ways of relating to friends, or different surroundings as you set up your household. At the same time, the newlywed places new demands on himself or herself: new expectations, a new self-image, a new daily routine. For many people this combination of new and interrelated stressors in marriage may create intense distress. A period of adjustment may be required before they can feel comfortable with their new roles and responsibilities by learning the dynamics and value of compromise.

Whether external or internal, stressors create demands on your thoughts, your feelings, and your body. As long as you remain alert to what is happening inside and around you, you will respond unconsciously or instinctively—with stress. There is even some evidence to show that you may suffer stress without being aware of the cause, for example, when you have been subjected to constant noise, or to glare while driving.

We all face many stressors every day. When you open your eyes in the morning, you must adapt to brighter light. As you get out of bed, your body must cope with the temperature change from the warm bed to the colder air. Throughout the day, you continue to react to changing conditions, sometimes automatically. As you react to each event, or stimulus, you experience some degree of mental and physical adaptation, however slight or unconscious.

We generally tend to think of stressors as unpleasant—too much to do in one day, a death in the family, near collision with another car, loss of a job. But stressors can also be extremely pleasant: a raise, good food, a new baby, a vacation, a victory in sports.

Most people live somewhere between the boredom of those retired persons who suffer from understimulation and the tensions of air traffic controllers who are overwhelmed by more daily stressors than their minds and bodies can handle easily.

Micro-Stressors

Hundreds of different stimuli barrage your senses every minute. Most stressors in daily life are mild, requiring little in the way of physical or mental adaptation. Usually you are barely aware of these "micro-stressors"—sights, sounds, smells, tastes, temperatures, textures, lighting. Repeated exposure to such micro-stressors as constant airplace traffic, irritations of a frustrating relationship, or a meaningless and repetitious job can do considerable damage to your health. You take them for granted, not recognizing the negative effects of their cumulative impact.

Macro-Stressors

At the other extreme are severe stressors, or "macro-stressors," intense pressures such as a death in the family, a burning house, a job transfer. For some people, macro-stressors may bring about antisocial behavior or disease, especially if many such stressors are clustered together in a short period of time.

Duration of Stressors

Stressors that last a relatively short time (an auto accident, a move to another city, or a new supervisor) are "acute" stressors, which may be intense or mild. On the other hand, stressors that persist and confront you continuously over long periods of time are chronic—the din of the city, an unhappy family, the pressures of living in a foreign culture. Chronic stressors also vary in intensity. The more intense stressors exact a toll earlier than those that are less intense.

Stressors also vary in their novelty or familiarity. Facing an irritable employer every day is not pleasant; but the fact that the employer is familiar makes the situation somewhat more tolerable than if a different irritable employer had to be faced every day. The larger the proportion of frequent stressors that are novel and unfamiliar, the greater the stress you will experience.

This suggests that some degree of routine or predictability in daily life is necessary if stress is to be minimized. Research has confirmed this idea, but we should point out that too much routine can have ill effects. People whose work is very repetitive and boring (assembly-line work, for example) are unchallenged and may become demoralized. As a result they may develop such stress-related illnesses as high blood pressure and ulcers.

Controllability

The amount of control you have over changing the stressor is yet another factor in generating stress.

The death of a loved one is illustrative of stressors that cannot be controlled or changed. Other examples are the disappearance of a favorite landmark, your employer's going out of business, or the discovery that you have an incurable disease. Faced with uncontrollable stressors, a person must somehow adjust to and accept reality in order to prevent stress from becoming distress.

At the opposite extreme is the stressor that can be relieved easily. Poorly fitting shoes, a chronically "sick" car, or an incompetent employee will fit this category. You can easily reduce stress in such circumstances simply by changing or removing the stressor.

Between these extremes is a third type: stressors that are difficult but not impossible to change. Examples include a poor fit between a person and his or her job, marrying the "wrong" person, and being overwhelmed with debts.

FIGHT-OR-FLIGHT SYNDROME

Some scientists suggest that human beings, like other animals, face stressors with a primitive "fight or flight" reaction. The body is equipped with an instinctive chemical response pattern designed to supply energy in stress situations. The activity of certain glands is triggered by a threat or stressor in the environment. The stressors themselves may be quite different—our ancient ancestors were threatened by wild beasts—but the ways in which we react to them are not so different.

Each demand made upon your body is, in a sense, unique, specific. When exposed to cold, you shiver to produce more heat; the blood vessels in your skin contract to diminish the loss of heat from the body surfaces. When you eat too much sugar and your blood sugar level rises above normal, you excrete some sugar and burn up the rest so that the blood sugar returns to normal.

Each drug or hormone has such specific actions: The hormone adrenaline augments the pulse rate and blood pressure, simultaneously raising the blood sugar, whereas the hormone insulin decreases blood sugar. Yet no matter what kind of effect is produced, all these agents have one thing in common: They also increase the demand for readjustment. This demand is nonspecific; that is, the body has to adapt to a problem, irrespective of what that problem may be.

In other words, in addition to whatever else they do, all stressors to which we are exposed also produce a generalized increase in the body's need to perform adaptive functions and thereby to reestablish normalcy. This need is independent of the activity that caused the requirements to increase. The nonspecific demand for activity as such is the essence of stress.

From the point of view of its stress-producing or stressor activity, it is immaterial whether the agent or situation we face is pleasant or unpleasant. All that counts is the intensity of the demand for readjustment or adaptation. The mother who is suddenly told that her only son died in battle suffers a terrible mental shock. If years later it turns out that the news was false, well, she experiences extreme joy. The specific results of the two events, sorrow and joy, are completely different; in fact, opposite to each other. But their stressor effect, the nonspecific demand to adjust to an entirely new situation, may be the same.

It is difficult to see how such essentially different things as cold, heat, drugs, hormones, sorrow, and joy could provoke an identical biochemical reaction in the body. Nevertheless, this is the case.

ALARM REACTION

The stressors are first experienced by the nervous system, which signals the hypothalamus–pituitary–adrenocortical axis. This axis is a coordinated system consisting of the hypothalamus (a brain region at the base of the skull) and the pituitary gland (hypophysis), which regulates adrenocortical activity. This mid-brain area is the highest center of the autonomic (involuntary) nervous system, which is also the seat of all behaviors (such as eating, drinking, sexual actions, social contact, and emotions). The hypothalamus, which is connected with other brain areas as well as with the cortex (voluntary nervous system), organizes all part functionings into a single unit, the total organism, and integrates the whole of the organism into the society (the external environment).

The stressor excites the hypothalamus (through pathways not fully identified) to produce a substance that stimulates the pituitary to discharge adrenocorticotrophic hormone (ACTH) into the blood. ACTH in turn induces the external cortical portion of the adrenal to secrete corticoids. These elicit thymus shrinkage simultaneously with many other changes, such as atrophy of the lymph nodes, inhibition of inflammatory reactions, and production of sugar (a readily available source of energy).

Another typical feature of the stress reaction is the development of peptic ulcers in the stomach and intestines. Their production is facilitated through an increased level of corticoids in the blood, but the autonomic nervous system also plays a role in eliciting ulcers. Thus the glands produce the hormones that stimulate protective bodily responses.

For instance, the cardiovascular system suddenly increases the heart rate in order to pump more blood to the skeletal muscles in preparation for fighting back or running away from danger. When the caveman was threatened, this effect on the cardiac system would be dissipated by the physical act of fighting or fleeing.

Therefore, this emergency readiness was a highly functional response.

As society became more complex and abstract, however, fight-or-flight tactics became inappropriate in many stress situations. Today we no longer encounter wild beasts in our environment, but our bodies still react as if we do. Modern man cannot turn off the alarm. Instead, his high state of readiness can persist for days, weeks, or even years, doing more harm than good because it is not discharged in action. Because we do not ordinarily fight or flee under modern-day stress situations, the excess hormones that under primitive conditions would have been useful now frequently build up to toxic levels in our body.

Stress becomes distress when the stress response is too intense and/or lasts too long. When the delicate internal balance among your physical systems goes awry, it leads eventually to a lowered resistance to illness, a breakdown of body functions. The result can be a "stress illness." In light of this theory, it is no wonder that people suffer from chronic diseases in our stress-filled society.

RESISTANCE PERIOD

After the initial alarm reaction, the body moves into the resistance period. Here the body attempts to return to its normal balance by coming to grips with, or adapting to, the cause of stress. These physical changes are the same whether the cause of stress is a mental problem, a disease, or even a passionate kiss. If the stress can be overcome, the body repairs the damage that was done, the physical signs of stress disappear—heart beat and respiration normalize and muscles relax—and resistance to the source of the crisis is released.

EXHAUSTION STAGE

The resistance period may last for some time. After long and continued exposure to the same stressor, to which the body has become adjusted, eventually adaptation energy is exhausted. If it is not ended by a satisfactory adaptation to the cause of stress, the body enters the exhaustion stage. The signs of the alarm reaction appear, but now they are irreversible and no longer helpful.

In effect, the body has used up all its adaptation energy. It just can't cope any more. Your supply of life energy and your ability to withstand stress are like mineral deposits; once you have drawn on them and used them, they are gone. If you pick a high-stress career or lifestyle, you spend your portion quickly and age faster. You may then be a prime candidate for an early coronary, migraine, ulcers, asthma, or ulcerative colitis—or perhaps a collision on the road; stressed people are more accident-prone.

Thus tension produces physical wear and tear on your body. And the longer the tension continues, the greater the bodily damage may be—including death.

Stress is not to be avoided. In fact, by definition, it cannot be avoided. To be free of stress is to be dead.

In common parlance, when we say someone is under stress, we actually mean under excessive stress or distress, just as it is commonly understood that when we say someone is running a temperature, we are referring to an abnormally high temperature. However, we know that some heat production is essential to life.

Similarly, no matter what you do or what happens to you, there is a demand for the energy necessary to maintain life, to resist aggression, and to adapt to constantly changing external influences. Even while fully relaxed and asleep, you are under some stress. Your heart must continue to pump blood, your intestines to digest dinner, and your muscles to move your chest in respiration. Even your brain is not at rest while you are dreaming.

While recognizing the usefulness of stress in our lives, most medical researchers now believe that the chemical effects of stress within the human body are causative factors in most contemporary health breakdowns and are linked to many other mental and physical disorders. Although you must probably tolerate a certain amount of discomfort from minor stress in modern living, it is clear that chronic stress prolonged beyond reasonable bounds can precipitate a major health breakdown.

PREVENTIVE ACTION

More and more attention is being focused on the opportunity to prevent excess distress from accumulating by teaching health personnel techniques of stress management. There are strong indications that stress-related disorders are greatly reduced when people understand how stress occurs, what it does, and how they can cope with it. But understanding requires in-depth training, reinforcement, and practice.

This working manual concentrates on teaching you to analyze and control your own stress reactions. It may incidentally help you to become less stressful to others and to learn how to recognize distress in subordinates, but the key is learning to help yourself.

MANAGING STRESS

Stress management is essentially a personal skill, to be used by and for an individual. The ability to cope with stress is not a typical supervisory skill to be exercised on subordinates. "Coping" cannot be done by someone else; it must be internalized as a part of each individual's personal makeup.

Each person has a slightly different bodily response to stress, ranging from neck tension, to teeth clenching, to queasiness, to frowning. Once you learn to map your own profile of muscle tension, you can use these bodily responses as early-warning signs of the onset of stress. After you learn to identify your stress signals, you are able to act immediately to ease the tension with an instant of relaxation.

Know the warning signs, whatever the cause. When tension is allowed to build up, you lose some degree of control over your behavior. The result: You may snap at your secretary, mull over easy decisions, smoke one cigarette after another, take it out on your family when you get home, and then put in a restless night trying to sleep.

The stress of modern life is not the price we must pay for our material comforts. You can learn to defuse your tensions before they are anything more than a clenched jaw or a quickened pulse. You can be envied as an executive who can make your opinions known during a heated discussion without raising your voice or pulling rank. You can be that strangely tranquil person whose honesty and self-acceptance draw people to you.

INDIVIDUAL REACTION

For some, stress is no more than anxiety or physical nervousness, but for others, stress can lead to despair and mental illness. The reaction occurs in both the mind and the body when you are forced to adapt or to readjust to an event, whether it be the death of a spouse or the sudden prospect of missing the evening bus home. Why some people become ill and others don't under the same stressful conditions is a question now being asked in several research projects. The hardy executives, say the researchers, seem to have more of a sense of control over their own lives, a commitment to themselves that involves their whole life rather than just work. They also view change as a challenge.

Being promoted can be as stressful for some people as being overlooked for a promotion. Fear of the unknown and an aversion to change, even a change for the better, may cause some people to withdraw, get depressed and angry, and reduce their activities. Others can accept being overlooked for a promotion because they have a general sense of vigorousness toward all aspects of life, not only their work. Because they can balance all their priorities, no event becomes an overwhelming threat.

IDENTIFYING STRESS SIGNALS

It is important to learn to recognize the symptoms of a mild tension state. You will have to make a conscious effort to be aware of the physical signs that mean your body is anticipating "fight or flight": stepped-up breathing, sweaty palms, butterflies in the stomach, racing heart, perspiration, muscular tension, feelings of unhappiness and/or depression, and an overabundance of nervous energy, any or all of which prime you for a physical or emotional surge—or a hasty retreat.

Become aware of your particular reaction to stress. Do you clench your fists, grind your teeth, smoke, or make frequent trips to the coffee machine? The answer is not as simple as it may appear. The best way to spot muscular tension is to study its opposite. Once you know what really relaxed muscles feel like, you will find it easier to recognize a state of muscular tension. When left unchecked, muscular tension and mental anxiety feed on each other in an ever widening vicious circle.

UNDERSTANDING YOUR STRESS

Going back to very early times, Western culture has pointed up that self-knowledge is basic to personal growth. Your stress reduction program will work only if you act on this knowledge. You must know why you become tense. In order to manage and control your own stress, make that knowledge work for you. Most executives are confronted with some kind of stress, simply because they are human and have to live and work in the real world.

THE PRESSURE OF BEING ALIVE

Abraham Maslow pointed out that certain needs are common to us all. When these needs are threatened, we feel stress. All human beings develop stress when life or well-being is threatened or when they suffer from such discomforts as too much heat, cold, pain, or fatigue. The loss of a job or of extensive material comforts, and certainly the loss of a family member, has the same effect. Unfair control and unjustifiable behavior on the part of those for whom we work creates distress, as does a sense of rejection or ridicule. Frequently the deprivation of a sexual relationship is highly stressful. For that matter, restriction of movement and sustained idleness become distressing.

Nonetheless, no two people ever react in completely the same way, nor does a single person necessarily react the same way twice to the same stress. The extent of anyone's ability to deal with stress is a product of that persons total life experience and the coping behavior he or she has cultivated over the years.

HOW WE DEVELOP

In the process of growing up we had the better part of our lives fashioned by our relationship with our parents. We were obliged to conform to their direction and were pleased when we satisfied their wishes. On occasion their acknowledgment of our responses gave us a sense of satisfaction. Our behavior and performance were rewarded in one way or another. The reverse was true if we failed to respond in an expected or demanded manner. As adults we substantially extended the behavior patterns of our childhood and adolescence into our growing adult years.

Alan A. McLean and Graham C. Taylor point out:

> Even as adults, by not working well on the job, we are attempting to unconsciously get back at our parents who set strict standards for us as children. By working in an inaccurate, sloppy fashion, we could also be really saying, "I'll show you I can do things my own way even though your way is right. I'll show you I can be independent even though I know I'm wrong."

The reverse, of course, can happen as a response to a continuous admonition by parents to their children to succeed. The children come to believe that failure of any kind is unacceptable and is attended by grave consequences and rejection by society at large.

CONSCIOUS AWARENESS

It is obvious that you cannot do anything about your past and your early values, but it becomes important to be able to reflect constructively on the nature of your growing years. By doing so you learn to recognize the impact of your early experiences, fears, concerns, and doubts on the development of your adult stresses and tensions.

It was well stated some years ago in a report of the Research Institute of America that

. . . you can gain a better understanding of your own needs and fears by considering the following questions carefully:

1. Is it easy for you to take orders from someone else, or do you tend to resent his or her authority?
2. Thinking back over various people you have worked for, did you get along best with:
   (a) someone who expected you to make most of your decisions with little guidance?
   (b) the person who established a clear policy and gave you considerable latitude to work within it?
                            or
   (c) the boss who gave you firm and close direction?
3. How much authority do you need in order to be happy in your work?
4. Do you think you are more anxious than others for recognition from your superior or from the group?
5. Do you always have to be first with your superior, or in the general esteem?
6. When you find out that somebody doesn't like you, does it upset you more if that person is your superior in the organization than if he or she is on your level or below?
7. Realistically, do you find that you tend to demand more affection than most of the people with whom you work?

You may not be able to understand all the reasons you need status or affection, or why one kind of person brings out the best in you while another forces you to show your worst side. However, a little self-knowledge may help you avoid those situations that exacerbate your emotional Achilles heel.

In the following chapters, we will apply this general knowledge of stress to the social forces that affect your life. You can better understand the nature of stress by seeing how it connects with how you live—the kinds of pressures you face at work and at home, how you interact with others and with your environment, and your reaction to life-change events. Here are some of the factors—internal and external—that contribute to stress:

External stressors	*Internal stressors*
Natural events	Living habits
People and animals	Attitudes and perceptions
Institutions	Emotions
Regulations	Instincts and drives
Circumstances	Anxieties

BALANCE

The key principle of a low-stress lifestyle is balance, arranging your life in such a way that your needs are fulfilled in healthy proportion and you don't become overloaded with any of the experiences or events that produce intolerable stress. Care should also be taken to avoid being deprived of significant challenge and stimulation. A delicate balance includes the following elements in a variety of settings:

Work and play
Challenge and ease
Stress and relaxation
Striving and taking it easy
Companionship and solitude
Exercise and rest
Discipline and self-indulgence

We will now turn our attention to stress in the work environment. The effects of job stress can add tremendously to your total stress score, and they will have a direct impact on your health. Job stress will also have an effect on the health of the organization of which you are a part.

CHAPTER 2
Stress in the Work Environment

UPDATING ATTITUDES
TOWARD JOB-RELATED STRESS

There was a time, not many years ago, when businessmen associated stress only with hard-driven top executives. They equated stress with stomach ulcers, the status symbol of high-pressure living, and by and large ignored the whole subject and its underlying dynamics. Today, those early attitudes are changing as updated medical and psychological knowledge about stress has spread throughout the business world.

Many leading corporations have accepted the fact that human resources constitute the most expensive form of capital for any organization and are becoming increasingly concerned about the costs of health breakdown. It is widely recognized that the chemical stress reaction within a person's body is a causative factor in most contemporary health breakdowns and that it is closely linked to many other disorders. It is now clear that many employee problems that cost money, hamper performance, and adversely affect employee overall health and well-being originate in physiological stress.

The hazards of occupational stress have been widely publicized. They detract from the quality of working life for a very large number of American workers. (The effects of stress in the work environment are shown in Figure 1.)

Nevertheless, most employers are keenly aware that some people do their best and most satisfying work under stress. Stress can be positive and useful in the workplace. In many fields, stress is an inherent part of the job and is stimulating and productive. It can enhance rather than diminsh productivity and job satisfaction.

[18]

Most executives are conscious of the excitement and challenges that make their jobs among the most rewarding our modern society has to offer. But there is an optimal stress level for every person in every job. If that level is not exceeded, and if constructive approaches are taken, stress can be used to provide an opportunity for increasing your effectiveness and that of the organization.

THE HUMAN DIMENSION

Executive management is increasingly aware of both the monetary costs and the disruption of effective operation related to stressful conditions. Management is starting to recognize that a serious loss of motivation may reflect a person's attempt to protect himself from stress by refusing tough challenges. Some employees welcome and thrive on heavy stress and pressure at work. Others recognize when they have had enough and refuse an advancement or a relocation. Most people want promotions, but some cannot tolerate the added headaches, stresses, and responsibilities.

HUMAN	SOCIAL	ECONOMIC
Alcoholism	Defensive behavior	Reduced productivity
Drug abuse	Violence	Increased errors
Emotional instability	Rage	High turnover
Lack of self-control	Irresponsibility	Absenteeism
Apathy	Role conflict	Accidents
Fatigue	Resentment	Disability payments
Loss of objectivity	Negativism	Sabotage
Depression	Marital problems	Thefts
Insomnia	Suspiciousness	Replacement costs
Insecurity	Inflexibility	Inflated Health-care
Frustration	Cynicism	costs
Anxiety	Scapegoating	Unpreparedness
Reduced motor	Antagonistic group action	Lack of creativity
performance	Expression of job	Indecisiveness
Psychosomatic diseases	dissatisfaction	Increased sick leave
Loneliness	Irritability	Poor judgment
Hopelessness	Pettiness	Loss of perspective
Helplessness	Distrust	Diminished memory
Boredom	Disloyalty	Poor recall
Mental illness	Detachment	Premature retirement
Suicide	Alienation	Organizational
Health breakdowns		breakdown
(cardiovascular, and so on)		

FIGURE 1. *The threefold effect of stress in the work environment.*

In addition to this backlash against job stress, a new body of law is being written in the courts as employees sue and frequently win compensation for serious stress-related conditions. Large judgments have been won against corporations in connection with suicides, alcoholism, and a variety of other medical conditions asserted to have been the result of work-related stress.

Aside from the threat of legal action, the threat of personal and subsequent organizational breakdown is motivating organizations to deal directly with stress. The widespread feeling by industry is that concern with stress management can no longer be viewed solely as a humanitarian activity.

Certainly there are humanitarian benefits, but the primary rationale is organization effectiveness and profitable operation. It is just good business for organizations to reappraise their methods of management, communication, and development of employee skills and potential. Paying more attention to the human dimension is absolutely vital to the continuing success of the economic dimension. Corporate recognition of the stress problem is simply a businesslike reaction to the threat of serious alternatives.

THE COSTS OF STRESS

The obvious costs of stress to business include huge losses in productivity, excessive absenteeism, swollen health insurance premiums, and the premature retirement or death of key people.

* Premature employee death costs American industry $19.4 billion annually—more than the combined 1976 profits of Fortune's top five corporations.
* Every year $26 billion is spent in disability payments and medical bills.
* The cost of recruiting replacements for executives felled by heart disease is about $700 million a year.

On executives alone, American industry loses more than $10 billion annually through lost workdays, hospitalization, and early death caused by stress.

Heart disease accounts for more than half the deaths in the United States. It also is responsible for an annual loss of 132 million workdays.

For every employee who dies from industrial hazards or accidents, 50 employees die from cardiovascular diseases, which are often caused by stress-related disorders.

At least 85 percent of all work accidents are caused by the inability to cope with emotional distress.

An estimated 12 million Americans are alcoholics, not including "closet alcoholics" who hide their problem. One out of ten employees has an alcohol problem. This problem alone costs American industry almost $16 billion a year in absenteeism and medical programs. Employees with this problem generally waste at least one fourth of their production time on the job. They cost at least twice as much as other employees because of wasted time on the job, absenteeism, and high health and accident problems.

Nearly one quarter of the American population is affected by headaches, which are the leading cause of lost time in business and industry.

An estimated 10 percent of Americans will suffer from ulcers at some time.

Psychosomatic diseases induced by stress create high rates of absenteeism and turnover. Replacement costs for employees may be as high as six weeks salary when lost production is averaged with double salaries. Intangible losses include the values of relationships built up and contacts cultivated outside the firm, and forfeiture of whatever working hours it took for training and the accumulated production lost to the company.

Of employee emotional problems, 80 percent are stress-related. More than half a million Americans use tranquilizers like Valium and Librium to obtain temporary relief from stress; their use results in job errors, accidents, and reduced motor performance. Worse, it prevents people from learning the coping skills necessary for dealing with stress.

UNDERSTANDING STRESS ON THE JOB

In view of these facts, the purpose of this chapter is to help you face up to the particular stresses of your responsibility in the work environment. Without attempting to minimize the demands on your intelligence, energy, and character, we hope you will achieve a deeper understanding of the sources of stress in your job:

1. The nature of your responsibilities
2. Your working relationships
3. Your personality structure

A practical knowledge of how much stress you can tolerate without breaking down will help you keep an even emotional keel as you learn how much stress you must undergo to meet the challenges of your responsibilities and perform at your best. In addition, we hope that these insights will enable you to get more enjoyment out of your daily round of activity and help to create a more productive and calmer atmosphere for you and your team within which to work.

DENYING STRESS

Oddly enough, although everybody wants to talk about stress, few executives or companies are willing to admit they are victims of it—or cause it! Thus, despite their awareness of the overwhelming medical, sociological, and psychological interest in the subject, many companies and/or individuals think the problem is someone else's.

The explanation for this seeming paradox probably lies in the widespread misconception of what stress really is. In popular usage, it is usually equated with anxiety, insecurity, feelings of obvious great pressure—even incipient mental illness. The average executive isn't likely to think seriously of himself as verging on emotional or mental disorder, nor is a company ready to admit its contribution to an employee's stress level.

Failure to recognize and accept the stresses suffered on the job is fully as dangerous to corporate welfare as it is to physical and emotional health.

LACK OF IMMUNITY

Executives especially have been bombarded with advice from all sources about the dangers of stress produced by their jobs. They are warned that it makes them more susceptible than the ordinary mortal to ulcers, coronary attacks, high blood pressure, and other serious physical and mental consequences. Migraine headaches, alcoholism, arthritis, psychoses, depression, insomnia, drug abuse, and strokes are other medical ills that can be traced back in part to the pressures people encounter and cannot manage at work.

We know that stress-related disorders occur frequently at all levels of management and supervision and are as serious among many groups of rank-and-file employees as they are among executives. Stress is an "equal opportunity" condition; it does not discriminate. It can be a positive challenge and draw someone to a job, or it can be dis-stressing and drive him away or down.

ABSENTEEISM AND TURNOVER

Some organizations experience absentee rates as high as 15 to 20 percent and some have turnover rates in the neighborhood of 30 percent. Some jobs in particular have especially high rates of absenteeism and turnover.

Personnel analysts have long recognized the direct connection between an employee's regularity of attendance on the job and his general level of health and well-being. A person who never uses sick leave at all can be assumed to enjoy good health and to approach the job with a reasonably positive attitude.

On the other hand, an employee who uses every day of the allocated sick leave during the year is either experiencing a breakdown in his health or trying to get away from the job. Both possibilities are worth considering when examining the bottom-line impact of stress on business organizations. Although we don't know exactly how directly stress relates to absenteeism and turnover, we do know that it has a lot to do with it.

Similarly, overall turnover rates can come from natural or stress-related causes. Retirement, people quitting because of voluntary changes in their lives or careers, and the occasional dismissal of an employee for cause can be regarded as a matter of course in normal business operations. Stress can also lead to early retirement or resignation or dismissal, causing the loss not only of some marginal employees but also of highly competent ones.

Furthermore, it is not uncommon for an executive or manager to "drop out" of what he perceives as a "rat race" and move to a rural community in Idaho or Maine. The slower pace of life and more limited demands on his time and energy are attractive to the once-harried organization man.

If you find that a large portion of your workforce takes a lot of time off, it is worth exploring whether some factors in the organization's environment are making the day's work psychologically threatening or otherwise unpleasant. Naturally, part of the absentee rate is due to unavoidable illness or injury.

However, the degree to which absenteeism results from personal distress or aversion toward the job is noteworthy. Almost everyone who has ever worked for an organization has at some time called in sick when he felt only half-sick but didn't feel motivated enough to make the effort to come in. Likewise, a number of people have, at one time or another, had a negative and deteriorating relationship with a boss or co-worker that has made him want to avoid going to work.

Intolerable physical working conditions, unfair or bullying treatment by supervisors, and a lack of perceived purposefulness or importance in the job can interfere with a person's ability or inclination to remain on the job.

THE COMFORT ZONE

To probe deeper into the underlying dynamics of job-related stress, let us look at the problems of pressure, job satisfaction, productivity, and quality of working life, first from the viewpoint of a single person in the organization.

An individual believes he is working productively when he is working at high capacity, at tasks worth doing, and with acceptable competence at a reasonable level of compensation while staying within his own personally defined comfort zone. (The term "comfort zone" refers to that level of stress and challenge that will optimize a person's performance without producing undesirable side effects.)

Just as the organization's needs must be served or the employee will not have a job, so personal needs must be served or the organization will not have people to do the work. These two sets of needs modulate each other in the daily flow of activities in the productive organization. To have an appropriate match between the person and the organization, the individual must interact with the job and the job environment in such a way as to satisfy both himself and the organization.

Your comfort zone must be within certain tolerance limits if you are to function effectively and find satisfaction in your work. Many factors come into play for each individual, but eight basic ones indicate the level of loading experienced by an employee:

Workload	Assignment diversity
Physical conditions	Interpersonal relations
Job importance	Physical demands
Accountability	Mental stimulation

Most attempts to deal with stress-created difficulties that avoid or deny the existence of stress complicate the problem in the end and create even more stress. Stress is natural and must be dealt with directly and frankly.

Workload

When a job is too easy or is not challenging enough for a person's abilities, a condition known as stress underload develops. Over the years we have become increasingly aware of the debilitating effects of too much stress, but few of us recognize that too little stress is a definite type of stress in itself. An employee without adequate work to do usually begins to feel frustrated and anxious about his worth and position in the organizational hierarchy.

Without enough stimulation, the body and brain simply do not function normally. Sensory deprivation leads to impaired judgment and reasoning ability. Depression, indigestion, alcoholism, overeating, tension, irritability, fatigue, and insomnia have often been traced directly to stress underload. These conditions are attributable to jobs characterized by monotony and lack of challenge and responsibility. Job performance may be reduced and lead to the need to hire additional people to get the work done. Overstaffing can be a hidden cost related to stress in the workplace.

Whereas stress underload is a problem for a significant number of workers, paradoxically, the symptoms of stress overload or sensory overstimulation produce similar results. An overload means that the employee has been assigned an unreasonable number of tasks or an unreasonable level of production in a given period.

Unrealistic deadline demands and rigid behavior on the part of an employer who is unperceptive or tyrannical can push an employee beyond his stress capacity. When this happens, the employee may exhibit reduced performance, lowered confidence, loss of objectivity, defensiveness, irritability, and poor judgment. Mental confusion, strained interpersonal relations, fatigue, and insomnia are other possibilities. Consequently, production drops off, mistakes accelerate, and on-the-job injuries increase.

It may be to the advantage of corporations to take a closer look at the pressure placed on employees to help determine whether current management practices are increasing or decreasing productivity and job performance. The key to superior productivity is the determination of the optimal stress level for each individual. Techniques for decreasing or increasing stress to improve job performance are outlined in Part III.

Physical Conditions

Physical conditions in the work environment play a part in the employee's overall reaction to the job situation. Temperature, humidity, lighting, weather, and air pollution are but a few areas influencing a person's comfort zone. Others include chemicals or processes harmful to the skin, vibration, and fatiguing bodily positions for working. Though some people enjoy prerecorded music piped into their offices, it annoys others and is a constant irritation to them. Also, large office spaces without walls may produce more interaction among employees but also reduce privacy. "It's like working in a fishbowl," some employees complain; they find it difficult even to make a phone call in a room full of other people. For most of these physical variables, some middle range defines the individual's general level of optimal functioning, where he can work in the environment rather than fight against it.

Job Importance

In our society, where work is such a big part of our lives, it is to be expected that job status can produce a lot of stress. Work contributes a large proportion of a person's self-concept: The kind of job classification a person has communicates a good deal about him or her. In the American culture, job title is perhaps the best indicator of social status. Within the organization it denotes power, importance, earning capacity, influence, and value in the hierarchical structure. A person's official rank tends to influence his or her general social behavior—manners, outlook, opportunities, and power. It also affects communication, incentive, and control.

Status underload causes some psychological discomfort in those who perform low- or negative-status jobs. It may manifest itself in absenteeism, work slowdown, defensive behavior, alcohol or drug abuse, or suicide. Perceiving himself as unimportant or not worth very much makes an employee particularly vulnerable to stress disorders.

Accountability

High cumulative stress scores can result from too much or too little responsibility for the outcome of something within a person's control. The degree and amount of control over the results and the risk in task performance directly affect stress level. For instance, first-line supervisors and middle managers are often caught in the pressure of implementing a plan they did not design but for which they will be held accountable. They may be told to increase business on the one hand and cut inventory on the other. Or they may be told to increase output and cut the workforce at the same time.

Some jobs, such as those of industrial psychologists and air traffic controllers, have such a high risk element in performance and such a limited degree of control that the people holding them operate under accountability overload much of the time. The opposite, accountability underload, occurs when an employee does not believe that his work makes any difference. The assignment of busy work and lack of useful feedback about task effectiveness can cost an employee respect for himself, his supervisor, and the job. Without frequent variety in accountability tasks—mixing high and low demands—the employee may feel frustrated, alienated, and anxious about the quality of his contribution.

Assignment Diversity

Task diversity ranges all the way from monotonous, repetitive, predetermined job tasks to confused, unpredictable, completely unprogrammed job situations in which the employee has very little idea about what will happen or what to do next. Jobs that deny a person control and meaning and lack responsibility are experienced by the worker as deprivation. Natural tendencies toward loyalty, incentive, and identification are undermined.

Most human beings have a basic neurological need for a moderate level of variety in physical experience to meet the needs of the brain and nervous system for stimulation. Denied variety in his or her job, an employee may exhibit signs of fatigue, anxiety, tension, or extreme irritability. In an effort to cope with the situation, a person may become apathetic and emotionally withdrawn. These responses to the distress experienced on the job detract from effectiveness in the work environment and impact on the quality of a person's life as well.

Interpersonal Relations

Contact with other people is one of the most fundamental human needs. In order for a person to stay within his comfort zone, he needs to be enriched by occasional contact with other people. Human contact varies with the situation: staff meetings, planning sessions, co-workers, general public, business contacts. The degree of pressure and stress experienced in these encounters is relative to the load factor. Interacting with too many people on a regular basis can be as distressful as interacting with too few.

The desire to relate to others on an impersonal and/or intimate level is an integral part of human nature. The strength of a person's relationship, whether to the organization or to co-workers, depends on whether it serves or frustrates that person. The way people behave is largely determined by their reactions to each other and by their membership in groups.

Social relations are at the foundation of both motivation and control. Social isolation weakens social control and is distressful. If a person is uninvolved with others, there are fewer occasions to assess the consequences of his actions, either for himself or for others dependent on him. The need for "strokes," affirmation of our existence, is one of the most fundamental human needs.

Lack of positive reinforcement and encouragement from a viable support group frequently causes anxiety and ambiguity to accumulate at dangerous levels. Both prolonged isolation and too much interpersonal contact dramatically increase stress. The lonely night watchman and busy personnel interviewer alike frequently have feelings of restlessness and anxiety. Once again, underload and overload cry for balance in a person's life to prevent mental or physical illness.

Physical Demands

Sedentary living and working are other potential sources of health breakdown from understimulation. Many jobs require little more than the ability to talk and operate a ball-point pen. For a physically energetic person, sitting at a desk all day may produce anxiety and frustration. For a less active person, the lack of exercise or physical stimulation may not produce emotional stress, but it can produce health problems.

Sedentary living predisposes a person to low vitality, overweight, susceptibility to colds, flu, digestive upsets, heart attacks, high blood pressure, and stroke. It seems that the sedentary person does not handle stress as well as the active, physically fit person does.

Conversely, too much physical challenge can also lead to injury or illness if the demands of the task are beyond the capabilities of the person assigned to perform it. Some jobs induce considerable stress by the element of personal danger and risk of life that is ever present. Such occupations include those of explosive experts, police officers, and construction workers.

Repetitive demands requiring dexterity, physical skill or strength, stamina, or physical mobility affect day-to-day performance on the job. Lack of demand can be equally detrimental.

Mental Stimulation

People perform more effectively and gain greater job satisfaction when they are mentally challenged and psychologically involved with their work. Some of the processes that stimulate brain activity are observing, recognizing, memorizing, monitoring, comparing, evaluating, deciding, and reasoning.

Feelings of exasperation, frustration, or detachment and a desire to escape to something more stimulating may come when a job does not provide enough mental challenge. On the other hand, when an employee's job demands mental activity beyond his level of competence and training, feelings of inadequacy and frustration may detract from job satisfaction and performance.

The eight processes that stimulate mental activity focus almost entirely on the employee as a person rather than on organizational factors. Inasmuch as high productivity requires high involvement, high commitment, and overall job satisfaction, it is important to understand what workers get from their jobs. Job satisfaction is directly related to the level of stress and subsequently to the quality of working life.

ANTISOCIAL ACTS

The cost of antisocial acts on the part of employees can be linked to negative stress. Theft, sabotage, deliberate waste or breakage, and "invisible" slowdowns are expensive. Of course, we have no way of knowing which of these costs are directly stress related and which are simply isolated events. However, we recognize that overstressed employees are more likely to engage in damaging behavior either against fellow employees or against the company in retaliation for or defiance of some perceived wrongdoing.

ORGANIZATIONAL STRAINS

Factors such as stress loading, lack of job satisfaction, unrealistic expectations, and the "Peter principle" have significant implications for organizational policies. They direct our attention to the amount of stress experienced by employees in everyday organizational life. Conditions in the workplace can actually foster mental illness—or at a minimum aggravate physical illness.

People generally perceive their jobs as their greatest source of stress, because occupational stress is more common than other kinds of stress. Executives cite pressure, while other employees cite poor working conditions and boredom. The causes of a large proportion of work-related stress fall into four categories:

Taboos against negative emotions
External controls
Ambiguity
Employee corporate identification

Taboos Against Negative Emotions

Work conditions in a corporate office usually demand that an employee contain his or her emotional reactions. Overt expressions of anger, frustration, and hostility are frowned upon in American business life.

Although these feelings are completely normal and are experienced by most people from time to time, there is a fear of dealing directly with emotions in the office. Fear of appearing immature or inadequate in the skills of living and working causes people to repress their anger and other so-called negative emotions.

So many people live in conscious or unconscious fear of direct conflict with colleagues, subordinates, or superiors that they resort to manipulation and maneuvering as a means of survival. These defense mechanisms may mask anger and give the outward appearance of a compliant, calm individual, but the buried emotions will surface in various ways.

The outwardly pliable and cooperative individual may subtly undermine the work effort by a "misrouted" memo or "oversight" in excluding someone from a planning meeting as a means of achieving occasional one-upmanship. The smiling, anxious-to-please co-worker may wait for opportunities to attack from behind because he is unable to face people with strongly felt differences. Such sugar-coated manipulation or two-faced, hypocritical styles of dealing with conflict are an enormous waste of human energy. Attacks and counterattacks detract from the business at hand. They lead to distrust, adversary behavior, and factionalism in the psychological warfare acted out in boardrooms and offices.

Inability to take things in stride or to avoid becoming upset at small provocations can kill productivity as well as cause people to suffer from the internal turmoil between natural emotions and what is considered reasonable overt behavior. Often the emotional restrictions a person imposes on himself are difficult for him to maintain over a period of time, and the pressure builds up.

Suppressed feelings typically cause a person to withdraw from and avoid whoever annoyed him, or he may overcompensate for his hostility by being jovial in the hope that the problem will be forgotten or dissipate. But it rarely goes away, and the distressed individual takes out his frustration on his secretary or quibbles over minute details. Eventually the pent-up feelings can explode in a fit of rage or violence, further contaminating the atmosphere and stressing other people.

Whether or not a person vents his anger against others, the anger surely attacks him as the flood of fight-or-flight hormones hit, affecting health and well-being. Psychological and physiological symptoms may appear, such as fatigue, headaches, depression, generalized anxiety, insomnia, overeating, overworking, loss of sexual interest, drug abuse, excessive alcohol consumption, muscle spasms, or loss of appetite. These symptoms may cause other problems at work and at home, further intensifying the stress levels experienced and widening the circle of those affected by antisocial behavior. Emotions, whether expressed or repressed, can impair judgment and lead to costly mistakes. Dealing effectively with one's own anger and that of others is essential to healthy people and healthy organizations.

Awareness of some of the common sources of irritation can also help you recognize the early warning signs of anger. Perhaps tardiness, insubordination, or carelessness makes you tense in the back of your neck or makes you lose your appetite. When you identify the stressor or feel your body reacting, figuring out exactly what triggered your response will help you deal constructively with the situation and with your emotions before they get out of hand.

The stream of upsets, delays, conflicts, and frantic rushing that characterize so many days contributes to activating the fight-or-flight response that was a lifesaver for our Stone Age ancestors. The same physiological reaction enabled prehistoric man to produce extra reservoirs of energy for fending off predators. However, the surge of adrenaline, increased heartbeat, and muscle readiness are no longer useful in today's jungle, where physical confrontation and flight are equally inappropriate and ineffective in combating the mental or emotional threats challenging modern man.

Mental health days off, aggressive exercise rooms, counseling, assertiveness training, and team-building programs are a few of the activities major companies are offering to improve their overall social climate. It is important, as we have seen, that bottled-up feelings be released, lest people become prey to their own physiological needs.

External Controls

Certain rules and policies are required and enforced in the workplace, thereby substituting external controls for the employee's instructive freedom of choice. The control factor, whether it is control by other people or by the workplace, is especially stress producing. Both the kind and amount of control built into the formal structure of an organization will determine the stress level an employee generates within himself and passes on to others and the response the employee makes to this stress.

The chief executive creates a great deal of stress if members of his organization feel that only he can make decisions. Exclusion from the decision-making process within a manager's area of responsibility is a degenerating disease. Powerless, managers operate under fear of losing their jobs, lose initiative, and become apathetic and useless liabilities to the company. Lacking the freedom to try innovative methods and weighted down by red tape, an employee's creativity is stifled as he perceives his opportunities for recognition and advancement limited by the regulations of an inflexible structure or a rigid supervisor.

Pressure from constraints that demand behavior or actions in harmony with predetermined role expectations is a subtle source of emotional distress. Typecasting of behavior patterns restricts personal expression and style, which can be emotionally draining. For example, expecting, if not demanding, that a manager entertain clients, take on extra projects at work, or be involved in civic organizations or community projects may elicit enthusiasm or passive acceptance as the only way to get ahead in the organization. Stereotyped requirements may lead to personal conflict as the individual feels weakened by the pressure to conform to the mold.

Ironclad procedures are another potential source of stress. The "we've always done it this way" rationalization for adherence to perhaps outmoded procedures discourages a fresh approach or an effectiveness study of established procedures. Blocked from input into the organization, an employee may seek employment elsewhere, with a company he feels may listen to his suggestions.

A frequently overlooked factor in structural practice is the push for movement up the ladder. But a person may be promoted unwillingly, although such unwillingness seems odd in our achievement-oriented society. Whether employee reluctance to move up is due to the lack of confidence or preparedness or satisfaction with present circumstances, the push to move on in a direction he does not wish to go can produce a lot of stress.

Ambiguity

In addition to the stress caused by unreleased emotions and external controls, stress may also be caused by ambiguity. The responsibilities of each employee can be defined by the organization chart, job description/classification, on-the-spot instructions, general hints, and/or unverbalized assumptions. When these clues are not clearly understood by the employee, his effectiveness and security are threatened. The task he performs and the methods of their performance should correspond fairly closely with the task he is supposed to perform. Consequently, when there are discrepancies between actual work patterns and nominal responsibility patterns, stress results.

An ever greater number of employees must learn to adapt more often and more quickly to shifting organizational environments and demands. Therefore it becomes increasingly important to eliminate the possibility of having job parameters changed without an employee's knowledge. A clear, unambiguous statement of duties, responsibilities, reporting relationships, and scope of authority will help minimize the number of occasions on which an employee may be stressed by not being sure about what to do. Communication processes as examined in Part III are possibly the most essential component of stress-reduction techniques.

Employee Corporate Identification

The last major category of company-induced stressors is the merging of personal identification with that of the corporation. The corporation, for its own survival, encourages its employees to define their identity in terms of the organization and to depend on it. (In this way, any work-related problem becomes a more central and engrossing dilemma.)

Dependency on the corporation not only for employment and financial return but also for educational, medical, and social benefits can generate hostility if the employee's expectations are not met. Since he has built his life around the company, rather than integrated other support systems and resources into his life, if his relationship with the company is threatened, not only his livelihood but also his very well-being is on the line.

None of these circumstances can be avoided entirely, and each may develop into a conflict situation to which a corporate employee must adapt.

Many other factors contribute to job stress: Job fit, role conflict, political alliances, time pressures, budget constraints, production quotas, communication problems, and peer pressures are typical negative stressors on the job.

The 1977 Quality of Employment Survey by the Institute for

Social Research revealed that Americans are less satisfied with their jobs than they were in 1973. Fewer employees felt their jobs are useful and relevant to future productivity. The number of people who believe their job skills will be useful and valuable five years from now declined significantly from 68 percent in 1973 to 63 percent in 1977. Also, employees reported underutilization of their skills and a feeling of lack of control over their job.

Change has a lot to do with job stress. The constant influx of new technology, methods, management styles, and bottom-line authority bombards employees before they have had an opportunity to assimilate the new knowledge, apply the new methodology, or get used to the organizational structure and before it is changed—again. Only about 25 percent of the workforce was doing the same job a year ago. As businessmen move up through the ranks and are transferred from city to city, experts say that too little preparation is given to assessing the advantages and disadvantages of the change, and that lack of preparation adds to the feelings of loss and uncertainty accompanying any new post.

The sense of value in work is threatened by increasing specialization and fragmentation. This alienation from the end results not only lowers morale; frequently it also affects the quality of the product adversely because an employee feels that his job doesn't matter. He no longer sees himself as part of the whole or part of a team.

Lack of communication on the job is equally stressful. Too few supervisors say "job well done"—or even "job acceptable." Therefore the successful technique for problem solving is not reinforced and may not be repeated when the next problem comes up.

Troublesome stress may also appear when things go well—for example, when goals are achieved or employees receive promotions or special recognition from superiors. And these are but a few of the stress-provoking aspects of the work environment.

VOCATIONAL STRESS RANKINGS

The National Institute for Occupational Safety and Health (NIOSH) is also looking at occupational stress. By examining death rates and admission records to hospitals and mental health facilities in Tennessee, NIOSH was able to rank dozens of occupations by their degree of stress. From a ranking of 130 occupations by

NIOSH, among the jobs with the highest incidences of reported stress disorders are:

Laborer	Guard/Watchman
Secretary	Machinist
Inspector	Mechanic
Clinical lab technician	Public relations person
Foreman	Registered nurse
Manager/Administrator	Sales manager
Office machine operator	Sales representative
Computer programmer	Telephone operator
Electrician	Warehouse worker

In particular, machine-paced workers, people who deal with distressed clients, and shift workers show a greater incidence of minor health problems, more time lost from work, and less overall satisfaction with the quality of their lives.

Among the 12 lowest-stress jobs (in order of increasing stress) are:

Checker	Heavy-equipment operator
Stock handler	Freight handler
Craft worker	Personnel worker

SPECIAL EXECUTIVE PRESSURES

At the bottom of a person's emotional makeup are some emotional scars or unresolved problems derived from earlier experiences. On top of these sensitive areas are the immediate pressures of the daily tasks at hand. For example, the public speaker is under pressure every time he appears before an audience; the trial lawyer, whenever he goes into court, and the surgeon, during every operation. There are opposing viewpoints as to where the greatest pressure is felt in the executive suite, where decision making frequently causes great stress, whether only one or two decisions or hundreds are made in the course of everyday routine.

Despite this commonality the following are some stress-producing problems peculiar to executives.

The Stress in Success

There is an elusive quality to success that is realized only by those people who have arrived at a high point of achievement. Many executives discover that once they receive the promotion for which they fought so ardently, they do not experience the satisfaction they expected. Psychological research has demonstrated that often the faster and further an executive moves up the ladder of success, the greater the possibility that somewhere along the way emotional difficulties will be encountered.

With each new success, the possibility of failure may become more frightening. Great responsibility often creates a sense of loneliness and strain because the decisions are one person's, but the consequences affect many; responsibility for people causes more stress than responsibility for things. Also, having compressed his climb to success into a few years, the executive may feel that he has paid too heavy a price for the executive suite; that his advancement was achieved at the expense of other personal values. On getting to the top a person may even resent the fact that he or she has reached the end of the road.

Mental health specialists point out that often success does not make friends. Each success increases the risk of other people feeling distrust and resentment toward the person on the move. That person, in turn, feels the strain of possible failure in social relationships. To compensate for these uncomfortable feelings, the executive may bury his or her unresolved fears and problems in even more activity.

Fear of Failure

Many an executive falls victim to the popular myth that he or she is superhuman—or should be. This is true not only at the top, but also at middle management levels. These people may suffer immeasurably as they strive to live up to the high—and often inhuman—image those in the company and in the community have of the successful businessperson. Consequently, executives stretch themselves beyond their limits and/or develop an unnatural fear of admitting weakness or deficiency in any area.

Selye contrasts turtles and racehorses to illustrate the point of individual differences, capacities, and role fit. Laurence J. Peter somewhat humorously wrote about people rising to their level of incompetence. Both authors address a very real problem in the business world—trying to live up to an unrealistic standard of behavior that often taxes people beyond their capacity to survive.

These people are afraid of being labeled unambitious or accused of holding back. Many of them are promoted out of satisfying jobs into positions that they are ill equipped to handle in one way or another. The costs are bidirectional—both the company and the individual pay a high price.

Those who try too hard to live up to all of the following expectations are heading for trouble:

Submission to authority without resentment
Strong drive toward material rewards
Ability to bring order out of chaos
Decisive nature
Knowledge of what you are and what you want
Feeling that you must keep moving
Need to be active
Fear of failure
Concentration on the practical, immediate, and direct
Self-identification with superiors who constitute the symbol of
  your goals
Isolation and severed emotional ties from home

Self-Doubt in Middle Age

Studies have shown that the development of an acute consciousness of age and generalized feelings of anxiety are particularly marked among people in their forties. Once men and women reach their fifties their outlook frequently improves. Apparently people in their forties are particularly conscious that they are not really young any more, while those in the next age bracket have accepted the fact that this is a new stage of life, discovered some of its advantages, and adjusted to its limitations and opportunities.

This "late forties" anxiety is particularly common among executives on the upswing. At this stage in their careers they often face the critical job tests that determine whether they have reached their maximum achievement and usefulness or will be promoted even further. They are also highly conscious of the promising go-getters who have their eyes on their positions.

It is well to remember that there is very little relationship between age and productivity. Dr. Leonard Himler, member of the Committee on Industrial Psychiatry, has pointed out that personality problems are not so much a result of age as of defeatist attitudes that may exist at any age.

Fear of Retirement

As people approach the time when retirement may be mandatory, necessary, or desired, some executives begin to fear the loss of power, importance, and control. An active, efficient, driving executive may resent the fact that he is expected to hand over the reins. There are numerable examples of the stress involved in transferring control and responsibility from one party to the next.

Many people have trouble letting go of the power, decision making, scheduling, and relationships associated with their positions. The retiree may find excuses to postpone the selection and/or training of a successor. There are many maneuvers through which a person feels he is buying time. At the same moment he is distressingly aware that time is running out in more than this one area of his life.

Retirement will be much less of a problem if it does not mean the end of all productive activity. Many executives have found a genuine challenge to their abilities and rewarding relationships in charitable teaching or civic responsibilities that can be continued well beyond the usual business retirement age. During a person's working life, such public service has the added advantages of contributing to company public relations and of exposing the executive to full-time opportunities in other areas.

EXTRAORGANIZATIONAL STRESSORS

In addition to these job-related stressors, many causes of stress originate off the job and are disruptive. At home there is constant stress, both positive and negative, in relationships with spouse and children, financial planning and control, home maintenance, and some social events. These problems are frequently taken to the office—just as office problems are taken home—and impede the effectiveness of the employee in both spheres of life.

The impact of extraorganizational stressors should never be underestimated. Psychiatrists and other physicians who have worked in business and industry report that as much as 80 percent of an employee's emotional problems are of this nature. The best any manager can do about these stressors is to be aware of their potential significance, to be alert to their presence, and to show compassion, interest, and understanding. Attempting to intrude on such stress-filled situations as marital problems or child-rearing practices is definitely not recommended. Well-meaning managers who attempt to play amateur psychiatrist may find that the only thing they have accomplished is to elevate their own stress levels.

Other stressors more difficult to control are evident throughout our environment, including crowding, noise, traffic jams, crime, and pollution. These are examined in later chapters. The list could go on and on. Stresses result in lower and poorer production, difficult relationships with other employees, inadequate attention and concentration, memory lapses, tardiness, absenteeism, and poor reasoning. How functional or dysfunctional tensions are depends on their magnitude, the person's understanding of them, and his or her predisposition and preparation for dealing with them appropriately.

PROFESSIONAL BURNOUT

When people and corporations do not practice managerial/organizational techniques they know are effective, "burnout" may result. The behavioral symptoms of burnout include (1) poor adaptability of mood, (2) ineffectuality, (3) increased irritability, (4) low frustration tolerance, (5) anxiety, (6) hostility, (7) unreasonable suspiciousness, (8) feelings of helplessness, and (9) increased levels of risk taking.

In an attempt to mediate these symptoms people frequently turn to tranquilizers, barbiturates, narcotics, and alcohol—all of which may lead to addiction. In addition to these symptoms, increasing rigidity is a major manifestion of the syndrome. People become closed in their thinking and inflexible in their attitude. There is also a pronounced degree of negativism, further complicating the problem. The employees become cynical about their work or role in an organization.

Characteristically, as the syndrome progresses, these employees question not only their own ability to perform but the abilities of their co-workers, and of the organization as a whole, to accomplish stated tasks. They spend increasing amounts of time to complete a fixed amount of work, but the quality of the time spent and productivity decline dramatically. When off the job, those at this stage of burnout are unable to relax. Among the repercussions they report are the abandonment or reduction of recreational activities and social contacts, feelings of isolation, and marital discord.

ORGANIZATIONAL BURNOUT

The other side of the problem is "organizational burnout." The organizations in which burnout has occurred appear to have several structural similarities:

- Excessive performance demands placed on personnel.
- Employees with a heightened sense of personal responsibility and involvement with the public.
- Ambiguous lines of actual authority; that is, the authority to implement and make decisions differs from that defined by the organization.
- Managers with the assigned responsibility for decision making but without the appropriate authority.
- Work priorities with low-yield personal satisfaction greater than those producing job satisfaction.

The symptoms of organizational burnout include (1) high personnel turnover, (2) increased absenteeism, (3) frequent scapegoating, (4) antagonistic group actions and pairing, (5) a dependency mode of operation manifested by anger at superiors and expressions of helplessness and hopelessness, (6) the maintenance of critical attitudes toward co-workers, (7) a lack of cooperation among personnel, (8) a progressive lack of initiative, (9) increasing expression of job dissatisfaction, and (10) expressions of negativism concerning the role or function of the department.

EMPLOYER PROGRAMS

Once a corporate employee has suffered enough distress to require medical or psychological assistance, corporations generally support the employee through established health insurance programs. Some large corporations have created special in-house facilities for counseling and therapy to provide better help for distressed executives so that they will learn how to handle their problems before they are overwhelmed. For example, some companies have a psychiatrist visit with employees to discuss the stresses and strains under which they work.

Health care and educational facilities often allow an employee to take a "mental health day" to get back on an even keel. And in some banks executives and managers are being trained to watch for signs of stress in themselves and in others.

Each of these instances illustrates that steps are being taken to alleviate occupational stress at its source, before job performance suffers too much and before stress-produced medical ailments appear.

STRESS MANAGEMENT TRAINING

It appears that corporations cannot help being a major source of stressors for their employees. However, they can protect themselves and their employees from the all-pervasive influence of unchecked stress overloads by underwriting the costs of stress management training for employees.

Both the corporation and the employee appear to profit from such an exchange. As we have seen, the costs to the corporation of hard-working, dedicated employees with chronic stress-related disorders are of considerable magnitude. The major costs are to be found in ineffective work time due to the interference of symptoms with the cognition and behavior of the afflicted employee and in the effect of the stress carrier on other employees.

Subjects who undergo stress management training show positive and often dramatic objective and self-reported changes in muscular tension, symptom elimination, and behavior, with probable corresponding positive economic consequences during and after treatment. When the posttreatment savings afforded the corporation in regained employee efficiency and lowered health center medical costs are compared with the costs of treatment, it is clear that a profit is returned on the investment. With respect to the common causative and sustaining features of such stress-related disorders as generalized anxiety and vascular or muscular headache, it appears that stress management training may be a valid treatment procedure, significantly better than conventional medical care.

LEARNING TO LIVE WITH STRESS

It is crucial to recognize that people cannot deal with stress by vainly attempting to remove all stressors. Stress is an integral part of life. Some stress is needed within the work environment to act as an energizer or promoter of action. To hope to eliminate stress from life is neither realistic nor desirable. Therefore, we must accept stress and learn to live with it. In this regard, Dr. Selye makes this statement:

> It is our ability to cope with the demands made by the events in our lives, not the quality or intensity of the events that counts. . . . [What] matters is not so much what happens to us, but the way we take it.

Fortunately, effective techniques are available to cope with stress on the job. Properly managed, stress can become a positive factor, a motivator, a stimulant rather than a threat. The fact that people can learn to cope with and manage their stress offers employers a major opportunity to reduce the cost of stress-related organization deterioration and to learn how to utilize the positive aspects of stress as a managerial asset.

CHAPTER 3
Time and Stress

The urgency of time drives modern man in his race to keep pace with the world around him. The tyranny of the urgent is oppressive as demands exceed the time available. Overloading means that stress response is dangerously aroused. Irritability, impaired judgment, hypertension, chronic headaches, and indigestion are frequent early signs of distress and potential illness.

Time stress comes under the category of emotionally induced stress. It is a form of self-induced stress triggered by situations to which normal human beings respond without strain or stress. The preceding chapters assert that the everyday stresses of life are always there. Most people are able to adapt successfully to—or even thrive on—minor difficulties, challenges, and frustrations. This chapter discusses situations, processes, and perceived possibilities that present significant levels of stress in life and that undermine health and peace of mind.

THE AMERICAN OBSESSION WITH TIME

The ingredients for time stress are built right into our culture and language. The fact that almost every American home, schoolroom, shop, business office, restaurant, automobile, and church has at least one clock is indicative of our preoccupation with time as a commodity. Radio and television stations broadcast the time; wristwatches have alarms and dual dials for different time zones; telephone recordings tell us the time; and billboards, banks, public places, and freeway signs remind us that life is ticking away.

Americans speak of "taking," "losing," "wasting," "stealing," "gaining," and "killing" time. We regard time as a substance—something to be bought, sold, measured, manipulated, and structured. Consequently, our behavior is largely governed by our mental abstractions of time. This psychological stressor can trigger an

[44]

anxiety response that varies with each individual's characteristic pattern of reactivity; that is, his or her typical patterns of perceiving and responding to pressure.

SENSE OF URGENCY

The stress from demands made upon their time is a daily source of frustration and apprehension for most people. It stems from feelings of too much to do, guilt for not having accomplished more, boredom from lack of challenge, and anger from interminable delay or duration. Being on a waiting line in traffic, at the bank, or in a store can agitate many people.

Each person has a fairly well-defined sense of time urgency within which he or she works effectively and gains a sense of accomplishment. Beyond this comfort zone of reasonable time pressure, deadlines threaten, time seems to run out, there is not enough recovery time for a change of pace, and the person begins to feel overstressed.

Time stress, although physically it creates the same effects as all other stressors, has its own special mental aspects. One feels desperate, trapped, miserable, and often helpless. Depression, psychosomatic diseases, anxiety, and heart attacks are so prevalent among management personnel today that they are accepted and endured as the price to be paid for high-pressure jobs.

Alternatively, these problems are compounded by solutions unrelated to the real abuses. Drugs and alcohol may offer relief from a demanding lifestyle by deadening the senses and seeming to slow time down. However, these temporary solutions frequently become problems themselves. In Part II we will examine the effects of alcohol and drugs as antistress devices.

You can understand your own stress better by seeing how it connects with how you live—your daily pace, the kinds of pressures you face, your perception of time. In other words, you must see stress as connected with the way you use time on an everyday basis.

TIME—THE RAW MATERIAL OF LIFE

The proverb that time is money understates the case. Time is the inexplicable raw material of everything. Each week has 168 hours, each day 1,440 minutes. No one has enough time, yet everyone has all there is to have. Regardless of wealth, fame, or position, everyone receives a new 24-hour supply every day. Despite this democratic allocation of resources, many people look enviously at co-workers, friends, or family as having "more time" or protest that they "have no time" for rest, exercise, or companionship.

TIME PERSONALITIES

The "workaholic" never has enough time; he is constantly "racing against time." He sees time as the enemy, something to be conquered; he fights the clock. The workaholic differs from the work addict—someone who is addicted to his job with enthusiasm and who finds pleasure in it—in two major respects. One is his inability to get on top of the job because of ineffective use of time. He is guilty of procrastination, lack of priorities, and wheel spinning. The other is his subconscious desire to be snowed under by his work. Being overloaded is synonymous with being successful and important in his eyes. It is also a means of escape from facing his martyr complex, from an unpleasant home or social life, or from an inability to enjoy leisure activities.

To the *mañana* personality, "Time will take care of it." Time is regarded in a fatherly way, and effort is abdicated in favor of letting time rectify the situation. This person lumbers through the eight-hour workday, shuffling papers, getting done whatever gets done, and leaving for tomorrow whatever is left over. Time is neither friend nor foe, but is regarded passively. This person succumbs to routine, takes little initiative, thinks planning ahead is a waste of time, and thinks goals are for hockey players.

"Time flies!" exclaims "the doer" who is trying to attain given results within a certain time. This achiever is more involved in working toward goals than counting the minutes. Acknowledging the steady passing of time, he can adjust his schedule to the realities of time and pace his workload to the time available with an eye to achievement rather than to activity.

The system of time is an important and demanding parameter of daily life that serves to regulate human activity.. However, many people have not learned how to cope with the stress of having to meet deadlines, pace activities, say "no," and deal with other stress-producing time problems.

CHRONIC OVERLOAD

The continuous battle with the clock in order to succeed is characterized by the feeling of being constantly behind schedule, with never enough time to get everything done. Because other people represent demands on one's already short time, those suffering from chronic overload are in too much of a hurry to allow for warmth or emotional sensitivity in their interpersonal dealings. In fact, free-floating hostility usually accompanies the struggle against time. This hostility is a major stressor not only for the person who isolates himself, but also for those he alienates.

The following self-assessment questions are suggested. Do you:

Rush your speech?

Hurry or complete other people's speech?

Hurry when you eat?

Hate to wait in line?

Never seem to catch up?

Schedule more activities than you have time available?

Detest "wasting" time?

Drive too fast most of the time?

Often try to do several things at once?

Become impatient if others are too slow?

Have little time for relaxation, intimacy, or enjoying your environment?

Most of us go back and forth between such hurried behavior and a more relaxed schedule, but if you answered yes to most of the above, you may be suffering from chronic overload.

An incessantly fast-paced, harried life is a stressful life, and stress is correlated with heart attacks, high blood pressure, and abnormally high blood cholesterol. Avoiding chronic overload in the first place is vital for health and personal effectiveness. Slowing down and using skills and strategies to get power and control over time are imperative if you are afflicted with this common ailment. Only then can you reach selected, high-payoff goals.

PACE OF LIFE

Obviously, people live a faster pace of life in a rapidly changing society like ours than in a simpler one. In fact, many of the organizations in which we work or live actually require us to succumb to "hurry" sickness. If your lifestyle is fast paced, you probably will experience:

A greater number of stressors

A greater variety of stressors

A higher proportion of new, unfamiliar stressors

A greater number of intense stressors

Faster movement from one stressor to the next, with frequent overlap

More demands for adaptation or adjustment

A greater intensity of stress

Higher chances of distress because of the number of stressors and intensity of stress

Greater distress is not inevitable. Some people can and do live faster, because their bodies and minds can handle a faster pace. Others learn to adjust to a faster pace. You can learn ways to remain healthy while living faster. But the chances of distress are greater, especially for people who are not aware of the dangers or do little or nothing about them.

LEADTIME

Associated with any activity are two necessary time periods—leadtime and afterburn. Consider, for example, an employee facing a work evaluation, an especially important one on which his promotion and accompanying raise depend. Leadtime is the period of emotional and intellectual preparation he needs the day before and on the morning of the review. If he feels he hasn't had enough time to prepare for the review, as he anticipates either being passed over or being promoted and the ramifications of each, the employee will feel slightly off balance, a bit tense. This anticipatory stress, or leadtime stress, is his response to expected stressors. Mind and body prepare in advance for change, crisis, or challenge.

Anticipatory stress is often useful in modest amounts, because it prepares your body and mind for events that are about to happen. Such stress increases sharpness and motivation. But it can also interfere with aspects of life in the present. This sometimes accompanies chronic overload. A person pays more attention to what may happen than to what is happening. It also affects people who lack confidence or who are seeking an escape from involvement in the present.

AFTERBURN

Afterburn is the time an employee needs after the evaluation by his superiors to think about how he fared, feel it, talk to his friends, implement awareness gained, and set the experience to rest. If the employee feels he has not had enough time to "come down"—to relieve tensions built up during the anticipatory stage and the pressures of the review—then the energy that surged during the experience will not be released, and the body and mind will remain stressed.

Residual stress occurs after the experience has apparently passed. though the body remains in a state of alarm for some time. The stress is unrelieved because the problem is unresolved. Athletes may have difficulty sleeping the night after a victory. If normal balance is not regained relatively quickly a person is likely to experience some type of distress.

A significant challenge in managing stress is to develop ways of returning the body and mind to normal levels of stress quickly after challenges, crises, or changes. "Afterburn" time must follow intense experiences if a person is to return to normal. How much time is needed depends on both the event and the person.

No single instance is significant, but ignoring the need for adequate lead-in and afterburn time thousands of times during a lifetime can create an enormous buildup of many small tensions and stresses.

PACE

A fast pace, especially if it is led by someone who needs quite a bit of lead-in and afterburn time, can be a significant source of tension, stress, and disease. Various ailments—colds, asthma, chest pains, high blood pressure, sore back, stiff neck—are often the result of too many activities crammed into too short a span of time.

Pace of life and comfort zone are closely related. If you have a broad comfort zone, you can be comfortable and healthy at either a fast or slow pace of life. You can live with a little or a lot of stimulation. But if your comfort zone is near the lower end of the tolerance scale, you need and are comfortable with a relatively slow pace.

Many people live at a pace that is either too fast or too slow for them. There is never enough time—or time weighs heavily on their hands. Sometimes the situation you find yourself in requires a pace that is neither comfortable nor healthy for you. For example, you may accept a job in a setting that requires more activity than you either need or want.

UNFINISHED BUSINESS

Some experts believe that many people suffer from stress-related ailments because of unfinished business, manifested in unexpressed feelings and in uncompleted tasks.

The more "civilized" we are, the more limitations we place on how we may express our feelings.

Unexpressed feelings clearly are related to the pace of life. If you move too fast and leave too little time for expressing how you feel about the things you are doing, the people you know or meet, the personal reactions you have along the way, you will experience distress. Then, too, if you are on the go much of the time you may fail to cultivate close friends with whom you can share your feelings. This tends to be especially true of men; for some, being masculine means producing, keeping busy, being "strong"—and not venting feelings, either in words or in physical acts.

The second kind of unfinished business is the uncompleted task. When you carry with you many incomplete tasks, assignments, or projects, you multiply the stressors—and the stress. Each unfinished task adds another ounce or two of strain. Each seems insignificant in itself. Combined, they create wear and tear. For many Americans, living with too many unfinished tasks is a way of life. Learning to avoid accumulating incomplete tasks and taking the time to express your feelings regularly will help you to control stress and prevent disease.

LIFESTYLE TRAP

Some people get trapped into too many obligations and duties. The working life of many people is a rat race of deadlines and time commitments with few identifiable rewards. When this happens in too many aspects of life, people find themselves in a lifestyle trap. For example, busy executives, mothers, agency directors, and volunteers may have real difficulty in slowing down because they have taken on too many commitments in too many areas of their lives. As the activities and responsibilities increase beyond normal limits, they note a decrease in time, energy, and satisfaction.

Finding a pace of life that matches your comfort zone is vital to good health and productivity. Managing the pace of life—that is, controlling the number, variety, and intensity of stressors to which you expose yourself—is at the root of successful time management. You must be aware of your time problems and how they affect you and must choose the pace of life that is best for you so that you can deal with the inexorable demands of late-twentieth-century living.

Is your day controlled by time pressures like these?
Does it seem everything you do is high priority?
Do too many things come up that have to be handled right now?
Do you end up having to do other people's work for them?
Do you have two or more jobs to do at the same time?
Do you have difficulty getting long-winded people off the phone?
Do your project deadlines coincide?
Do your customers and boss demand attention at the same time?
Do constant interruptions break your concentration?
Do unorganized people always ask you to solve their problems?
Do unproductive meetings consume too much of your time?

All these time pressures have one thing in common; they are caused by others and are seemingly out of control. But they really don't have to be.

TIME CONTROL

Consider who and what really controls your time. Time gives you incredible power over your life. It is your responsibility to establish the parameters of your involvements. Few people can impose on you without your consent. Just as others have the right to ask for your time, you have the right to say yes or no or defer. Each second of time you have will be displaced by someone or something. Who or what is ultimately your choice. But you don't always exercise the power you have to make this decision, although the power remains in your hands.

Your reservoir of time is often used in living, working, personal enrichment, growth, and development. However, it can be depleted by inappropriate use—something you could do but don't, or time wasters like interruptions, unnecessary paperwork, and unnecessary meetings.

CLAIMS ON YOUR TIME

Much of our time seems to belong to everybody else. Chief executive officers, especially, are captives of their corporations and often of their communities as well. In today's "tyranny of urgency" it is the recurring crisis rather than the creative side of business that swallows up time. The business at hand is not necessarily the business planned. That is, the matter being dealt with—for example, answering the telephone—is not on your priority list. You had scheduled the time for preparing your speech for the afternoon's meeting.

A conflict in priorities reduces the payoffs of your actions and produces distress. When your activities are not contributing to your goals, frustration, hostility, anger, apprehension, and anxiety threaten your well-being and impede your effectiveness. Time becomes the enemy and a volatile stress-producing agent.

THE DEMANDS OF TIME MANAGEMENT

In setting out on the immense enterprise of living fully within the limits of 24 hours a day, we realize the extreme difficulty of the task, the sacrifices and endless effort time management demands. People do not manage time per se: They manage their own behavior to accommodate that inexorable movement and flow of time—the pace of life.

Since no one has more than 24 hours a day, you must pay attention to how well you regulate the flow of activity in your personal environment and in the environments of those with whom you interract. Coping with the clock can make the difference between straining to get things done and stretching your opportunities for accomplishment.

Although time management isn't a new idea to most people, it is a badly neglected art. Chances are the reason you haven't been able to make better use of your time is that you don't fully understand where you're not using it effectively. Saving time means organizing time to make every minute move you toward your goals instead of ticking away from them. No matter how organized you may think you are, if you don't know where every minute goes, you're just not getting enough out of life.

By learning how to perceive the basic patterns of your activity, to outline your goals specifically, and to apply the rules of valuing time, you can implement the simple skills of time management to eliminate time wasters and earn dividends on your time investments. As Alan Lakein puts it: "To waste your time is to waste your life; but to master your time is to master your life and make the most of it."

The skill of time management holds great potential for reducing stress while accomplishing more. We will be examining the broad range of information available about time, and then specifically examine and practice the "know-how" techniques for using time to the fullest to reduce the stress associated with poor time management.

Your degree of awareness of your time personality, pace of life, and loading level is indicative of the way you relate to time and its use. This information now needs to be followed by a plan to reach your objectives.

VALUES AND GOALS

Stress is closely linked to the achievement of goals. One of the key ways of reducing time stress is to pay more attention to accomplishment than to the time involved. To work comfortably and effectively, you must establish a workload that you or your subordinates can accomplish reasonably well within the time available.

For the individual, this means examining what is important to you and where you want to be six months, five years, and ten years from today in your career or in life. Take a moment to write down your immediate response to what your goals are for these three points of time in your life.

For the manager, this means defining the specific results you want from the job under consideration. If the job is part of an interlocked group of jobs, you should also define the overall objective of the team assigned to the task. The job objectives can be defined on two levels: (1) activity objectives (such as supervising the accounts receivable section) and (2) creative objectives (such as matching products with customers' needs). Without a clear definition of the job objectives, there is no way to measure performance, decide what the job is worth, decide who is qualified to perform it, or determine what is a reasonable amount of time within which to accomplish the objective.

Writing down goals and objectives brings the future into the present by giving you a clearer view of and perspective on what the desired achievements look like. There is a mystique about the written word, something committal about the tangible quality of a written list. Keep these goals readily visible so that you ask yourself daily, "Is what I am doing now moving me closer to one of my goals? Are my methods appropriate for achieving my objectives? Or am I creating stress by fighting the clock and the calendar instead of making them work for me?"

Setting Priorities

By setting priorities, you start managing your time by objectives rather than simply handling things as they come up. Tasks that work toward your goals take priority over those that do not.

Priorities are items for which you make time and upon which you act to work toward the accomplishment of stated goals. Having set your goals provides a measuring stick against which to gauge alternate activities as they come along. They help you feel in control of your time and your destiny. It is important to set goals in every area of your life, to stimulate well-rounded growth, and to avoid a distortion in your various activities (avoid, for example, developing tunnel vision or becoming a ne'er-do-well). We will deal with your job-related goals, but the methodology can be applied just as well in the other areas of your life: personal, family, social, community, financial, and spiritual.

Stating Your Goals

A well-stated goal contains the following five elements:

1. The desired goal must be expressed in specific terms. What is to be achieved?

2. It must have a single, measurable result that is realistic and attainable but still represents a significant challenge and strengthens your overall effectiveness. How does it benefit the company and your place in it?

3. It must set a target date that takes into consideration the priority of the task and what you can do. That date must also be one that will be willingly agreed to by those who will be making a significant contribution to the attainment of the goal.

4. The cost in terms of effort, money, and manpower needs to be stated in the goal. For example, the goal might be to gain five new accounts in the Financial Plaza during the month of July, exceeding the district quota, with the aid of three of the top life insurance salesmen in the company.

5. It must give clearly defined and feasible methods by which to achieve the goal.

Now review the list of goals you formulated a few minutes ago and revise it as necessary according to this formula. Specifics make difficulties surmountable and goals personal, real, and possible. Vagaries make them distant, impersonal, unreachable, abstract, frustrating, and "distress" producing. Often the reason things aren't going as planned is because there is no plan. Increase your areas of self-worth and increase your value on the job by working toward measurable goals.

By setting your goals you can maintain more control over your time. The next step is to make others aware of the direction in which you are working.

Communicating your goals to your subordinates or to workers sets a standard for achievement, clarifies your expectations, and enlists team effort. Your organizing helps them manage their time by providing a reference point for achievement and can eliminate wheel spinning and misdirected energy down the line.

Specific goals are easier to plan for because the groundwork necessary is often obvious. For instance, to exceed the district quota you will have to identify your three top salesmen, establish contacts in the Financial Plaza, research the needs of those companies, and tailor your presentation to meeting customers' needs in the most responsive and persuasive manner.

Failing to Achieve Your Goals

The six major causes of failure to achieve goals are:
1. No plan
2. Vague goals
3. Lack of awareness of job requirements, company values, and objectives
4. Lack of specific steps needed to reach the goals
5. Gap between verbal and written statements, leading to misunderstanding of the goals to be achieved and costing precious time and energy
6. Competing influences that detract from the task at hand and create goal conflicts

To be effective, each person must not only establish measurable goals but also set specific criterion levels for those goals. Progress must be reviewed regularly (a minimum of once a month) so that the intermediate goals mesh with the goals of the organization.

Competition for your attention can stimulate you to increase the quality of the time you spend on each goal and the creativity with which you seek to achieve it. It is a matter of priorities when it comes to goals of equal value or worthiness.

However, if you don't share the sense of urgency someone else places on the item demanding your attention, frustration and stress result. Time is not yours alone but is shared with your associates at work five days a week. Your right to be the ultimate judge of how you use your time in the work environment is altered and mediated by the invisible agreements you made when you accepted the job.

If you are in the "work game," you are accountable to others for how you use your time. There are certain parameters within which you must operate. This might mean working in the office from eight to five, attending a weekly department meeting, or handing in a report the first of the month. Your priorities must align themselves with company policy as long as you value your job.

The ultimate decision to comply or not rests with you, but you must consider your boss as a significant factor in your decision in terms of your overall values and long-term goals. It would be wise to have him or her clarify the company's objectives. Perhaps your job description is perceived differently by you. If your responsibilities are not clearly understood and agreed upon, your goals and efforts may go unacknowledged and unappreciated. Because time is a commodity shared with others and in the working world you are paid by others for your time, you must have a clear understanding of the framework within which you work (including what the goals are) in order to set appropriate objectives and use your time well.

One of the most important realizations you can make is the fact that, to a high degree, you are the cause of your own effects. We are responsible for our current levels of effectiveness and, to a very high degree, the cause of the things that happen to us. Our perceptions have produced our comfort ranges, and our opinions of and responses to people have a great effect on their responses to us.

The frantic, overworked person is in reality overworked by his own choice. He has learned to concentrate on working per se—instead of on getting results. He has lost touch with the priorities of his job. He is, above all, a time waster, with an above-normal distress level.

One of the basic illusions in managing time is the lack of distinction between efficiency and effectiveness. Efficiency is doing the job right, regardless of its importance, while effectiveness means doing the right priority job correctly. Just because you're doing the job right doesn't mean that you're doing the right job. For instance, your report may conform to company outline and be perfectly typed, but ask yourself the following key questions: What am I doing that doesn't need to be done? Doesn't need to be done frequently? As well? For so much time? It's not being busy that counts, but rather what you are busy doing.

TIME TRAPS
The Illusion of Busyness

The illusion of busyness (not business) is a common time trap. It is frequently an escape mechanism generated by a fear of failure or fear of success. Keeping busy provides a comfort zone of activities that are manageable, low risk, pleasant, and relatively easy. By keeping busy at less challenging tasks, you don't risk failing, nor do you have to expend all the effort success requires.

If large projects overwhelm you, break them down into component parts and start chipping away at that mountain of work step by step. You may very well discover many tasks that are incidental to achieving your goal and can be eliminated and other tasks that can be delegated. Many people have a tendency to put off the top-priority item because it requires more perfection. All your busy work—low-priority items, in terms of overall importance and pay-offs—prevents the high-payoff items from being done. What you do illustrates what your priorities are. The most important things will only get done when you set a priority commitment of time and action for them.

Juggling Time

A frequent stressor is time juggling, attempting to cram several activities into a time span that is generally appropriate for just one. In time sharing a computer can perform several discrete computations simultaneously by fitting one computation into the brief pauses that occur between other computations. The human brain, however, seems to lack this capacity to perform many simultaneous conscious operations efficiently. It's difficult to prevent one task from interfering with another. Too many pressures can lead to wear and tear on the body. Too much stimulation or too many demands can lead to distress—a heart attack, high blood pressure, skin ailments, headaches, poor sleep, hostility, or violence. Overloading can kill you.

Overcommitment

A very natural behavior for many people is their inability to say "no" to almost any request. The consequence of this is frequently a great deal of stress generated by the subsequent awareness on the part of the person obligated to perform that the commitment cannot be met at all or in the time allowed. Overcommitment also occurs when overzealous people obligate themselves when they know at the time that the likelihood of completing the task is remote or even impossible.

On other occasions, the "I can do it" attitude often fails to take account of all the circumstances and ingredients involved in making any commitment. To avoid these stress-producing consequences of failure because of overcommitment, one needs to carefully assess in advance all factors involved in commiting oneself.

Procrastination

Busyness, time juggling, and overcommitment not only demonstrate a lack of judgment in discriminating between the important and unimportant and a lack of planning; but they are also forms of procrastination. Procrastination is really fear. Fear is false evidence accepted as reality. Consider that the worst that could happen to you if you don't start is that you can't finish; if you don't try, you can't succeed.

Self-Imposed Obligations

The multiplicity of demands that modern life imposes on our limited store of time exerts powerful pressures on us to behave as though we were capable of doing several things at once. Much of our life stress comes from self-imposed obligations. Do you undertake crash projects, accept deadlines, and agree to do challenging tasks without taking a realistic view of your capabilities and the time available?

If you take on tasks without comment, others will assume you have the time and energy to meet the demand. Frequently, people will obligate themselves out of fear of saying no, as if turning someone down were admitting to being incompetent or lazy. In an effort to please, people can get in over their heads. In the end they may disappoint those they attempted to please by taking too long to get the job done or turning in a sloppy job.

Also, the person who overcommits himself becomes his own slave driver and frequently becomes anxious at the thought of not performing as well as he wants to. He pushes himself at all costs, suffering great personal stress and often passing the stress on to his co-workers and friends.

Other people may exert pressure, try persuasion, and even make occasional veiled threats. But only you can obligate yourself. Therefore, you need to maintain a flexible attitude toward your commitments, agreeing to those that you can reasonably keep, renegotiating those that are no longer feasible, and declining to make those that are more than you can handle and that would bring your stress level to an unhealthy high.

DECISION MAKING

Decision making—consciously choosing how you do your job and lead your life—is essential to stress control. Therefore, understanding the process is important to developing more constructive behavior patterns.

Decisions are made for six basic reasons:

1. Habit. Deciding to do something automatically, routinely.
2. Demands by others who are key influences on what you do.
3. Daydreaming about doing something, rather than doing it.
4. Escapism. As Henry David Thoreau said, "Not to decide, is to decide." Many decisions are the result of default on your part—waiting for others to make the decision for you.
5. Spur-of-the-moment decisions, which are frequently those we regret most and categorize as wasted, nondirected time.
6. Obviously, the best basis for decision making is a conscious decision, made by planning ahead.

It has been said, "Men's natures are alike; it is their habits that carry them far apart." Self-management is the key to time management—directing your activities toward desired goals by conscious decision making. One of the key tools in making a habit of productive choice is what Alan Lakein calls the "Action Required." It is the basic tool for planning. Effectiveness means selecting the best task to do from all the possibilities available and then doing it in the best way.

Making the right choices about how you use your time is more important than doing an efficient job on whatever happens to be around. Making the right decision is fortified by a visual reminder of your daily priorities, which serves as a guide to action. It helps you manage a proper balance in your activities. You end up with enough challenges to stimulate productivity, but not so many that you are overwhelmed. Managing the stress of time wisely means knowing what your stress tolerance is and keeping control of the pace of your life so you neither stagnate nor are immobilized by too much to do.

Concentrate intently on what has to be done. Do not accept responsibility for more than can be given your effective attention. Time will be wasted because problems that are not disposed of decisively bounce back again and again.

Putting your plan of action in writing by detailing the steps necessary to achieve your objective(s) enables you to look objectively at the task ahead. It provides a guideline for streamlining the work. You do only those things that are important to reaching your goals because unnecessary activities are pointed up and can be eliminated. It also helps you schedule your time by enabling you to estimate how much time each step will take and to total the investment of time and effort involved. Once you have done this, you can not only schedule blocks of time but also make the most effective use of odd moments to achieve your main goals.

A benefit of breaking the project down into manageable parts is that it brings to light areas in which others can help you realize your goals. Proper delegation or sharing of tasks can get the job done more quickly and more efficiently by utilizing the skills of others.

A "Things to Do" list should be kept daily, with items arranged by priority. There are different formats available commercially, or you can draw up your own, according to your unique needs.

Your appointment calendar identifies where you must be at a certain time on a given day. In the same way your list is a guide of things to do, a visual reminder of knowing that nothing is missing. It affirms all your important activities. It is a resource bank from which items can be drawn as needed. Crossing off items you have finished or don't need to do gives you a sense of satisfaction and control over your time.

Items can be listed according to activity required: to see, to telephone, to follow up, to think about, to decide. They can be organized according to functional similarity of the work content (everything about the budget due by a certain date); or geographically (errands, sales contracts). Whatever format works for you is the appropriate one; try several. Getting too bogged down in procedure is one of the biggest time wasters.

Once you have your list of things to do, put them in order of priority—and then schedule them according to the prime time considerations discussed earlier. In other words, match the activity to the time and resources available.

Flexibility is important—indeed, essential. Scheduling is more than just fitting all the things you must do into the hours available; it also means making time for what you want to do. Rigidly adhering to a time schedule does not allow for pleasure, let alone the unexpected interruptions, distractions, and crises that arise if we let them.

PLANNING YOUR TIME

Time for planning is essential: The less time you feel you have to spare, the more important it is to plan your time carefully. Planning ahead helps prevent stressful conditions and situations. Failing to plan will free up very little, if any, time. By failing to plan, you will almost certainly fail to set proper priorities.

ABC ratings should be set up. In general, *ABC* ratings are based on priority. That is, the *A*s are the tasks that must be done, the *B*s should be done, and the *C*s represent things you would like to do. The ratings take into account the importance of reaching your goals and the possible repercussions if tasks are not completed on a timely basis.

"Out of sight, out of mind" weighs heavily on your inability to accomplish the important things. Don't do *C* work while you let more important activities go because you want to avoid the feeling of doing *A*s inefficiently or because you have lost sight of the important things. You settle for the temporary satisfaction of doing routine things because they give you the feeling of having accomplished something, but that feeling doesn't last long and generally you have very little to show for your time.

"Getting set up" or "cleaning things up" before deciding which *A* to do is a common time trap. Although preparedness and organization are virtues, don't delude yourself into being satisfied with a polished desk at the end of the day instead of the weekly market report you should have written. Because you spend all your time doing the nonessential things, you don't have enough time to do the really important work that needs to be done. Remember Parkinson's Law: Work expands to fill the time available. We frequently stretch a *C* task, because it's easy and pleasant, into the only time available to work on the important things. Every minute counts, so count every minute.

The Pareto Principle

The 80/20 Pareto principle says that "if all items are arranged in order of value, 80 percent of the value comes from only 20 percent of the items, while the remaining 20 percent of the value comes from 80 percent of the items." Therefore, be discriminating in your selection of the productive 20 percent.

We are more apt to recognize our physical limitations than we are willing to accept a 24-hour day. If we are to order our environment according to our own needs, we must learn to pace ourselves in the quest to get those things done that we must do, should do, and would like to do.

Communication of Time

Communication or the lack of it creates anxiety or fatigue in a time-frame orientation. "I'll get it to you in just a second" "Be with you in a minute" "It will take me only a few minutes" "He left just a little while ago; he should be there soon." Often these are verbal contracts we can't keep because they are unrealistic.

It is imperative to set realistic deadlines based on personal experience because you know yourself and what has happened under similar circumstances. There are many variables to consider when communicating time, and wishful thinking will not hold the clock back or push it forward. You can deal more effectively with time if you are honest with yourself. Instead of fighting a frustrating battle of trying to manage Father Time, manage what is within your control; namely, doing what you have to do in the time you have.

Control Factor

Your goals and objectives must be looked at realistically and faced head-on. Why "must" you do something? Why "should" you be doing something else? There are two categories for this type of decision making: goals within your immediate control and those within the power of someone else.

For instance, you must get the price quotation in on a job by a certain day or jeopardize your job because the bid is too late for the company to act on it. The controlling factor in this situation is whether or not you value your job. If you do, you must act within the parameters of the job requirements to do or not do something.

Assertion Skills

These decisions involve being able to say yes or no with conviction. You can't manage effectively if you are afraid to say no, if you shy away from conflict situations, or if your major concern is being well liked. Yet many people approach their lives this way. People are encouraged to be friendly, obliging team players. They are rewarded for becoming adept at sidestepping conflicts and for cultivating the art of "not ruffling anyone's feathers," of being a peacemaker.

You should develop assertiveness skills so that you may confront with confidence situations that typically produce anxiety, frustration, guilt, and other unpleasant emotions and cause stress. Learn how to say no without feeling guilty; how to combat the fear of rejection or of making mistakes; how to gain the confidence necessary for making difficult decisions and for implementing controversial (or even unpopular) procedures. In short, assertiveness is a blueprint for confident, effective management with honest, open communications, a receptive climate for innovation, and a healthy tolerance for the normal conflicts of everyday life.

Test your own assertiveness:

- Do you feel guilty when you have to turn down a request even if your decision is entirely justified?
- Do you agonize over the prospect of turning in a poor evaluation review/report for a committee member or co-worker?
- Do you sometimes feel that others are taking advantage of your "good nature"?
- Do you feel extremely uncomfortable when called on to take sides in a dispute?
- When an unpleasant assignment comes along, is your first impulse to handle it yourself rather than delegate it up or down the decision-making ladder?

Saying yes to something is a time commitment. Look upon your time as something valuable and guard against others' infringement on your life by depleting your most valuable resource—time. They cannot repay you for the time they have taken up; once the time is spent, it is gone forever.

TIME SLOTS

Once you have decided to commit your time, slotting the appropriate task into the right time segment is true time consciousness. Time takes on different values under different circumstances, although each hour is always 60 minutes long.

Consider prime time advertising on television. During the showing of a top-rated spectacular, advertising sells for $250,000 a minute. Cost is reduced for "off hours"—early in the morning and late at night—when the viewing audience changes composition and numbers. Keep this concept in mind to get the most effective use of your time. Do things when they are most needed and appreciated. Not everything deserves or requires the same attention. Timing is crucial to your decision-making process. Consider which activities are most important to you at any one time, and decide on the basis of your time consciousness.

The inherent value of the activity may depreciate with time from actual changes in the situation. Also, it is possible that unknown changes have occurred and your evaluation of the situation needs changing. The usefulness of the activity may also depreciate with time: you may have lost someone's attention or be unable to attract attention or appreciation for your efforts. Loss of interest because a specific activity is no longer necessary or of any great value changes its impact.

You should dole out your time carefully. The greatest return on its use can be obtained by dividing your time correctly among things to do and by doing them in the proper sequence. Prime time for you is the best time to do the tasks at hand.

There are two kinds of prime time: internal and external.

Internal Prime Time

Internal prime time is the time during which you work and concentrate best. Your mood, your mental alertness, and your physical energy are all components of your internal prime time. An important consideration in allocating your time is to match your physical and creative tasks to variations in your cycle. Many people call the early hours the golden hours, the time in which they feel their best and can accomplish the most. Other people don't function effectively until mid-morning. Find and use your best hours.

You can plot your cycle on a graph, dividing your waking hours into three segments, labeled high, medium, and low. Using three different-color pens (or chalk) to represent your emotional, mental, and physical level, you can plot your ups and downs. Where all three intersect shows you the best and worst times of day for you. You can also plot demand times—that is, the energy demands made by work or family. When are meeting, interview, report, mail, and telephone demands the heaviest? Once you are aware of how you really operate and what the pressure times of day are in your work/home environment, you will also gain some awareness of why you succeed or fail in some activities and why some times of day are particularly stressful.

External Prime Time

The second type of prime time is external prime time—when it is best to attend to other people and when external resources are most readily available for decisions, inquiries, information, or responses. Sensitivity to co-workers' prime time enables you to maximize the resources available to you to get the job done. Scheduling meetings, deadlines, and appointments with an eye to when other people can best handle them helps to get the job done. Achievement is not a matter of luck but of timing.

Chances are, most of your work gets done in only a portion of your day—the Pareto principle outlined earlier. Many people ignore their prime time and spend those hours doing routine tasks that don't require the energy, concentration, and creativity available at that time. The best time of your day should be spent on the things that matter most. So, schedule your one or two highest-priority tasks for the day in your prime time, and work at the low-priority items when you can. An awareness of your peaks and valleys and of the ebb and flow of the work schedule can help you plan and achieve accordingly.

Situations constantly change around you, and as they do your mind and body attempt to adjust. When stimuli are familiar and not very intense, your responses are uncomplicated. Less familiar, less routine, or more demanding stressors elicit more intense and complex responses. Therefore, matching demands with resources can reduce the negative effects of time pressures. Working against yourself produces stress.

Many people might have to get up an hour earlier and plan the day before the family gets up. They might have to get to the office a little early, before the phone starts ringing and the demands of others begin intruding. Some employees prefer having lunch at their desks once or twice a week to sort out their schedules.

Tempo is a reflection of the attitude of the person in charge. If that person is goal oriented, knows exactly what the objective is, and is ready to begin, the pace is brisk and productive. If that person is also procedure oriented, focusing on a particular way of accomplishing something, consciously taking appropriate risks, success is likely. On the other hand, if the person dawdles, drifts, and works at the periphery of a task instead of doing it, the pace is sluggish.

Ask yourself the following questions:

Exactly why am I trying to do this task?
Is it really worthwhile?
Have I set a deadline for myself?
Have I resolved to meet the deadline?
If my life depended on doing the task in half the time I have allocated, what shortcuts would I take?
Is there really any reason not to take the shortcuts?

As Charles Ford put it:

The key is controlled urgency, treating every matter as something urgent to get done and out of the way. It means less time spent on useless conversation, less waiting patiently for someone else to move before you do, more action rather than putting things aside for later (whenever that is).

Time becomes "the enemy" when:

You feel rushed. There's not enough time to get done what you have to do.
There isn't any time left for what you want to do.
Other people make demands on your time.

You or someone else is late, putting you behind schedule.

Your anxiety builds because of procrastination, an inability to decide and act.

Poor timing and constant interruptions lead to anger.

The drain of time wasters—phone calls, meetings, paperwork, drop-in visitors—becomes enervating.

Too much time is available for the task at hand or extra, unplanned-for time is available.

Time is distressful when used poorly. By the same token, time can evoke eustress when managed right. As Peter Drucker says when businessmen complain that there are only 24 hours in a day, "No, there are at most one or two." He's referring to the important hours over which we have a choice.

Examine the situations in which you feel rushed, when there is not enough time to get those things done that you must do. Ask yourself, "Why must I do this at this particular time?" Sounds simple enough, but actually most of us move at such a hurried pace that we never sit back and ask ourselves if what we are doing is necessary.

Most of us live with strain. We move about under pressure and don't have to have the word "stress" defined. It's headaches, insomnia, overeating, overdrinking, panic, losing some control over behavior. If there were more time, we complain, we would find a way out of the pressures of everyday life. But we accept the stress of modern life as the price we must pay for material comforts. However, studies have shown that we can no longer afford, as a society or as individuals, to accept the "rat race" side effects as "coming with the territory."

Time pressures—deadlines, punctuality, procrastination—rank high on the list of tension triggers. Life never seems to allow us to set our own pace and to do things in an order of our own choosing. We become slaves to the clock, required to be here or there and to do this and that at set moments, and with a hurry that leads to confusion, fatigue, sometimes hostility, and often ineffectiveness.

The truth is that most of the time it isn't practical to rush as we do; but it is still less practical to refuse to adapt to circumstances that of necessity require us to rush. Therefore, it becomes essential constantly to evaluate time-demanding commitments.

Stress is the physiological and psychological response to a demanding, challenging, or threatening situation or to pressure. It is not the pressure itself. It is not the fact that it is 2 P.M.; but a result of the reaction to the pressure of knowing you have to be somewhere else at 2 P.M.

You can be sure of four things in life: death, taxes, time, and stress. Stress is a fact of modern life both in business situations and in private life. Like time, it is inescapable, but the two can be allies rather than enemies, positive rather than negative influences. People must learn to cast off the effects of pressure and maintain a calm sense of composure in pressure situations.

HABITS

A successful and effective life is the result of productive habits made second nature. Rushing to meet priorities and goals is not unfamiliar to you, but it is important to practice good habits. Here are seven steps you can take to replace an unproductive habit with a productive one:

1. Be aware of your bad habit, such as spending too much time on the phone.
2. Develop a desire to change—that is, *want* to spend less time on the phone.
3. Decide what you can do about it. For example, vow to cut telephone calls to three minutes and limit the people you call and to whom you will speak.
4. Enlist help. Ask your secretary or your family to time you; set an egg timer; warn the other party. Have your secretary screen calls. Have your family get names and numbers for you to call back (at a more convenient time) after finding out what the caller wants. (Perhaps it can be handled by someone else.) Set your timer or watch for three minutes. When appropriate, have your calls referred to someone else or handled directly by your secretary or your answering service.
5. Plan of action:
   • Have a purpose for calling.
   • Identify yourself, your company, and your purpose for calling at once to cut down on amenities and establish the call as a business one.

- Know what you are going to say, the points you wish to make, requests for information, and so on. Have all the information you need in front of you.
- Practice ways to get off the telephone when the other person wants to continue talking without offending that person. Be polite but frank, saying:

    You are in a rush to complete something.

    You have a visitor and must go.

    You have another call waiting.

    You must leave for an appointment or meeting.

    Your secretary will take the information.

    He or she would be better off talking to another, more knowledgeable person.

6. Evaluate the plan—the ways you expect to cut down on the time you spend on the phone.
7. Practice the new habit until it becomes second nature both to you and to those on whom you rely to help you reduce the time you waste on the phone.

Mastering the skill necessary to use time effectively must be self-generated. Life is what happens while you are making plans. Begin now with the patience and perseverance life control requires. Establish priorities for your clearly defined goals in terms of importance, payoffs, and the potential penalties not doing them would incur. Accept the fact that the universe is not going to change and follow through on making those changes in your own world that will put you in charge of your life.

If you grow more aware of yourself and what you want out of life and learn more about the nature of stress and how to handle time demands, you are more likely to make stress work for you. By choosing your actions wisely, you increase your chances of becoming a winner rather than a loser. You need not be at the mercy of the clock; to a large extent, you can create your own future by learning how to deal with time.

The great value of time management is that at the end of a hard day's work you have feelings of achievement from having done your high-priority tasks and the distress in your life is significantly reduced.

CHAPTER 4
Stress in Our Daily Lives

The difficulties of adjusting to the stresses and strains of daily living in our modern society sometimes seem too much to bear. In an alarming number of people, the adjustment exacts a heavy price psychologically and physically.

Contemporary America is characterized by urbanization, technological innovations, an accelerated pace of life, mass communication, mobility, intergroup tensions, and multinational corporations. These realities are mixed blessings, for they bring with them a whole new set of stresses.

Today's stresses are not as direct and immediate as the physical threats and deprivations of previous centuries. The new stresses are subtler and more constant and cumulative. They comprise a whole catalog of psychological irritants and subliminal physical effects. Daily exposure to noise, air and water pollution, crowding, and socioeconomic pressures is wearing. Variables of group dynamics such as personal space, competition, values, and differing backgrounds and behaviors are daily stress-producing factors.

Yet it is a fact that many things one person finds stressful someone else enjoys. Therefore, the amount of stress in the immediate environment cannot be determined by examining the sources of stress alone. The context in which the stresses occur and the attitudes and previous experiences of the people affected are also important.

Today's world is a stress-filled environment, and it is doubtful that tomorrow will ever be different. The accelerated pace of change today makes life even more stressful (see Figure 2). It is therefore essential to develop the capacity to cope more effectively with extensive social change. This can be accomplished by a deepened understanding of the psychobiological repercussions of the multiplying demands that characterize our time. However, learning more about what environmental factors cause stress and where to look for its effects can also help develop survival skills. With these skills you can modify your behavior and attitudes to make even a stressful world pleasanter and more livable.

Most stressors in the environment occur at levels below that which would cause immediate damage. Noisy streets, smoggy air, and crowded freeways, even when uncomfortable, usually do not cause obvious physical maladies like a broken bone or immediate blindness. The discomfort may be felt immediately—a throbbing headache or painful breathing—but it is the total physical impact of these stressors that is cumulative and far-reaching.

Unfortunately, the human organism tends to accommodate to these kinds of stressors to a degree. It gets used to them and tends to block out their existence. But internal damage to the system continues, and deleterious results become evident in the form of disease. The source of the cumulative discomfort must be found at levels other than that of gross physical damage.

STRESS FACTORS
Change

Given the rapidly accelerating pace of life today—with one international or national crisis after another; unpredictable job and stock markets; social, political, and economic instability—one thing that touches us all is the inexorable effect of change. Conditions are changing faster than many people—and organizations—can adapt to and assimilate.

Novelty

The environment is filled with change and novelty. Just as the body cracks under the strain of environmental overstimulation, the "mind" and its decision processes behave erratically when overloaded. The response is marked by confusions, anxiety, irritability, or withdrawal into apathy.

Population Growth

One reason for the increase in the pace of social change is rapid population growth around the world. Currently, mankind numbers about 4.321 billion people. At the present rate of growth this will

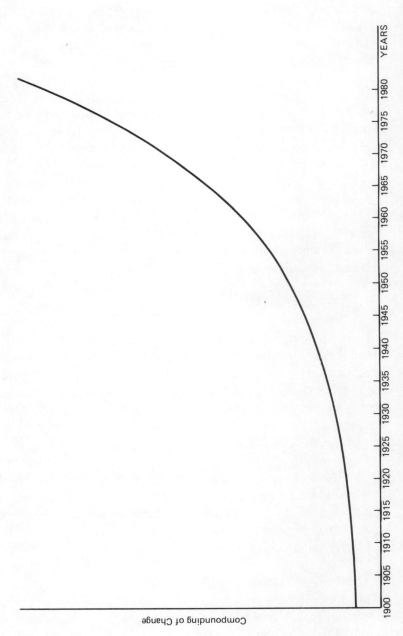

FIGURE 2. *The accelerated pace of change in a single lifetime.*

EVENTS

- Aircraft
- Electric lighting

- Synthetic fabrics

- Radio broadcasting

- Mass-production techniques

- Aircraft carrier
- Antibiotics
- Electrification of homes
- Plastics

- LP record
- Motion pictures
- Rocket

- Chemical fertilizers
- Food preservatives
- Jet engine

- Radar
- Television
- Xerox process

- Atom bomb
- Mass transit
- Audio tape recorder

- Ballpoint pen
- Computer
- Phototypesetting
- Polaroid camera
- Transistor

- Frozen foods
- Injection Molding
- Laser
- Nuclear Power
- Supermarket
- Video Recorder

- Telemobility
- Credit card
- Electron microscope
- ICBM
- Life support machines
- Mass-cargo ship
- Metal extrusion
- Skyscraper
- Birth control pill

- Rising divorce rates
- Microcircuit
- Bureaucracy

- Communication satellite
- Jumbo jet
- Moon landing
- Organ transplants
- Space travel
- Diversity of lifestyles

- Environmental pollution
- Consumer awareness
- Women's liberation
- Holistic medicine
- Interpersonal crowding

- Audio cassette
- Pocket calculator
- Miniature computer
- SST
- Word processing
- Energy depletion

- Genetic manipulation

double in about 35 years. More people means more mouths to feed, bodies to clothe, houses to build, goods and services to be produced —more crowding, more change, more stressors.

Overcrowding

Researchers have discovered that overcrowding is a major psychosocial factor contributing to frustration, insecurity, exhibitionism, and depersonalization for many people. Social scientists continue to investigate the essence of these and other effects of increasing human density upon the overall quality of life.

Crowding for the human population is not only a function of space allotted per person, but also the sensation or perception of being crowded. A variety of experiments with animals have concluded that crowded conditions impose a stress that can lead to abnormal behavior, reproductive failure, sickness, and death. However, the impact of crowding on the health and happiness of people is more complex because it includes complex sensory and thought processes that may be different for different types of people.

Your perception of being crowded—when the presence of other people inhibits your natural or desired behavior or keeps you from attaining your goal—is highly relative. Three could be a crowd in certain circumstances and 53 would not be a crowd in a different situation. If a person perceives himself or herself as being inhibited by the presence of others (crowded), overcrowding exists and the stress response results.

Whether the crowding of urban life acts as a stressor depends in part on a person's sense of control or lack of it. Commuting is one of the most common stressors exemplifying this problem. Getting caught in rush-hour traffic, dodging cars, and competing for position are familiar stressful experiences driving to and from work. Traffic is potentially distressing because of the delays it imposes and the hostility it often provokes.

Recent research on the behavioral "aftereffects" of this environmental stressor suggests that the emotional demands of driving may result not only in impaired road performance but also in emotional and behavioral deficits upon arrival at home or at work. The potential impact of commuting demands on the behavior, personality, and health of travelers is suggested by elevated heart rate, increased frustration and impatience, a heightened sense of time urgency, and a sense of lack of control.

The degree of congruity between commuters' expectancies and their experiences of travel constraints is significant in the cumulative stress experienced. Furthermore, highway driving may expose commuters to a higher rate and number of environmental risks—noise, vibration, increased risk of injury from traffic accidents—than they experience at slower speeds on city or town streets.

Noise Pollution

A by-product of crowding is noise pollution. This is another disturbing aspect of modern lifestyle—the relentless and discordant sounds of screeching tires, the clamor of machines, honking horns, and ringing telephones, and the din of people.

Almost every situation is surrounded by sounds. Our overall stress level is partially dependent on the kinds and frequencies of the sounds that enter our near zone. They become a part of us and affect our overall level of adaptation to our environment.

Each sound is assimilated by the nervous system through the auditory sensory system. Sounds of various sorts affect your interactions with others—how you feel and behave. To improve your personal life and the lives of those within your work environment, it is useful to be aware of the connections among sounds in the environment, how you deal with them, and how you feel throughout the day.

Although human reactions to noise generally resemble those to crowding, there is an important difference. The destructive effects of noise are specific: Noise erodes hearing and blocks desired behavior in subtle ways. As with other stressors, noise is more noticeable to some people than to others. Restful music for one listener may be noise for another.

Research subjects exposed to noise, whether the sounds were loud or soft, predictable or unpredictable, exhibited higher frustration and lower performance levels than subjects working in quiet. Noise, especially loud, meaningless, irregular, and unpredictable noise, can have damaging effects at levels above 70 decibels—the noise level of a relatively quiet city street. The autonomic nervous system is aroused, often without the person's even becoming aware of it. Hormonal changes probably occur that could lead to physical and mental difficulties.

Research indicates that the annoyance threshold is 50 to 90 decibels, and that the threshold of actual pain is 120 decibels. Noise compounds the effects of crowding by multiplying the demands on the human organism. The stress of working in a busy office with closely placed desks is compounded by the noise of typewriters, telephones, and adding machines and of the movement of people, chairs, and papers. Even the subtler sounds of air conditioning and music arouse the autonomic nervous system.

The cumulative detrimental aftereffects of noise correlate with loss of hearing, difficulty discriminating between words, and impaired reading skill. In addition, the case against noise as an insidious source of distress is evidenced in stress-induced disease. Studies around the world have shown that employees exposed to high noise levels—particularly when the noise is intermittent, unexpected, or uncontrollable—have higher than normal:

Percentages of heart, circulatory, and equilibrium disturbance problems
Incidences of digestive and circulatory troubles
Deterioration of the digestive tract
Accident rates and absenteeism

The evidence is serious and incontrovertible. The World Health Organization has estimated that the cost to the world's industries from the detrimental effects of noise on job performance and health may be $4 billion a year. The overall cost of noise in our daily lives in terms of frayed nerves, insomnia, and the physical and emotional problems that stem from such causes is incalculably greater.

People's subjective evaluation of noise—like their evaluation of crowding—depends largely on context. For instance, the sound of typing outside a busy executive's office when he is trying to concentrate on getting a report out can be perceived as positive if his secretary is typing the report or as irritating if someone else's secretary is making the noise.

Sounds are most disruptive when they are unwanted, unpredictable, and inappropriate. If you are trying to sleep, most sounds will annoy you. When you are giving a speech in a restaurant, intermittent noises from the kitchen interfere with your train of thought and the tempo of your talk. Laughter in the hushed rooms of a library is an illustration of a context in which people perceive otherwise tolerable sounds as intolerable.

Noise and crowding are but two of the most easily categorized stresses in the world in which we live.

The bumper sticker that says "Living Is Dangerous to Your Health" provides an ironic commentary on the almost daily discoveries of toxic factors in our environment. Red dye No. 4, defective automobiles, bone chips in hamburger meat, polluted water, the side effects of medical cures are indicative of the multiplying sources of stress in the environment. Lack of control over the quality of goods and decreasing confidence in government and consumer regulation are frustrating at best and unhealthy in the long run.

VARIABLES
Personality

Personality differences provide a set of variables that affect the amount of distress experienced. Again, perception of the situation and habits of dealing with a recognized problem are significant. For example, a lack of control over road and traffic conditions is a major source of stress. To the degree that the time you travel and the route you take can be altered, distress can be relieved. However, this flexibility is not always possible.

Some personal solutions to mediating the impact of traffic conditions include moving closer to the job, changing routes or timing, riding in car pools, purchasing a more comfortable car, or commuting by train or bus. Some corporations promote ride-sharing programs or provide busing.

These solutions can reduce but do not necessarily eliminate the stress of commuting. For instance, although sharing the driving in a car pool or riding trains or buses may provide you with time to read or relax, you are also subject to the stress reaction response discussed later in this chapter. In this instance, the response is triggered by greater interpersonal contact with fellow riders.

Research has shown that commuters who board the train or bus at the beginning of a ride experience less stress than those who board later. The key to this contrast in subjective feelings is largely a question of freedom and control. That is, the first passengers have the greatest selection of seating and storage space for coats and briefcases. By contrast, later arrivals have a limited choice or no choice in selecting where they sit, next to whom, and where they put their belongings.

From the crowded highway or busy street, a typical city worker tries to find a space to park, goes into a densely populated office building, rides up a crowded elevator, and works all day surrounded by people or in contact with them by phone. He or she may eat lunch in a crowded restaurant or lunchroom, caught between congestion in the parking lot, in reservation lines, and on the busy street.

City dwellers or workers usually spend a large portion of their waking hours in fairly close proximity to other people, especially if they work for large organizations. People feel crowded when this situation interferes with what they intend to do or requires more social interaction than they care for. Waiting in lines at the bank, at the gas station, in traffic, at the movie theater, and at the sales counter is stressful.

Many people experience a vague sensation of imprisonment when surrounded by cars, shopping carts, or other people. But there is little means of retreat and relaxation from close contact with other people. Modern society and working conditions make solitude practically a thing of the past.

Some people seem to thrive on the stimulation that comes from rubbing elbows with a variety of people and find pleasure in the hustle and bustle of the city. Others find even short-term crowding beyond their comfort zone. People vary in their tolerance of and appetite for contact with other human beings.

The same person who enjoys the crush of other football fans rooting for the Rams might well lose his temper when he learns he will be sharing his office with another employee. Removing physical barriers in modern space planning frequently causes behavioral barriers to spring up as employees seek out ways to maintain their privacy and personal space.

The Comfort Zone

The human animal is instinctively territorial, and lack of personal space produces stress. Vast apartment complexes, open office space, crowded sidewalks, and busy airline terminals all bring anxiety.

Each person has his own comfort zone within which he can maintain a healthy arousal level. This "near zone" surrounding the body is roughly three to five feet. Uninvited penetration of this area causes discomfort and prolonged close contact can be extremely stressful for some people. Typically, concentration is disrupted, nerves are on edge, and productivity is diminished in relation to the length and intensity of exposure. Modern man seems to have learned to live and work in crowded environments; some people even prefer them. Nevertheless, they take their gradual toll on health and well-being by overstimulating our natural response mechanism.

THE STRESS RESPONSE

This reaction is characterized by elevated blood pressure, excessive stress hormone secretion, inordinate adrenaline secretion, atrophy of the thymus gland, which involves the immunity system, and atrophy of secondary sexual characteristics. Mere contact with other people almost automatically stimulates the individual's whole endocrine system.

Such changeful circumstances as operating within close proximity to other people mean a constant high level of interpersonal interaction and compel a person to make frequent adaptive reactions. This repeated activation of what is known as the "orientation response" and the "adaptive reaction" is linked to physical problems caused by overloading of the neural and endocrine systems.

The Orientation Response

The orientation response is a complex bodily operation. Basically, we use our muscles involuntarily to direct our sense organs toward the incoming stimuli. For instance, the pupils of the eyes dilate, photochemical changes occur in the retina, hearing is momentarily more acute, and our general muscle tone rises. There are changes in our brain waves, our veins and arteries constrict, blood rushes to the head, and our breathing and heart rate alter. This reaction takes place literally thousands of times each day as various changes—from novel sights or sounds to novel ideas or information—occur in our physical and social environment. Any perceptible novelty activates certain bodily responses.

The Adaptive Reaction

The orientation response is the initial phase of the more encompassing adaptive reaction. The adaptive reaction provides a much more potent and sustained flush of energy. The orientation response is based primarily on the nervous system, the adaptive reaction depends heavily on the endocrine glands and the hormones they shoot into the bloodstream. Chapter 10 will explore the chain of biological events triggering changes in the body chemistry and the physiological results.

For our purposes here, we can see the potential wear and tear on the body as a constantly high level of interaction which makes a person attempt, both consciously and unconsciously, to adjust.

DEALING WITH STRESS

On a day-to-day basis, people are attempting to adjust to their overload of concerns in the only ways they know how: by ignoring them, by not getting involved, or by adapting to them.

Ignoring Problems

Many people ignore the problems and strains of contemporary living. They pretend that nuclear war, devaluation of the dollar, unemployment, and excessive taxation do not exist. At least they do not worry about things over which they feel they have no control.

Adaptation by Avoidance

By not getting involved, keeping their distance, and avoiding entangling alliances with strangers and causes, people seek to reduce overloading their finite supply of energy. By minimizing their personal investments, they feel they are also reducing the risk of failure. Yet adaptation by avoidance has its limits, too. This outer aloofness frequently disguises inner feelings of helplessness and hopelessness. Such people become restless, irritable, withdrawn, insecure, and lonely.

This defensive reaction to the stress of constant demands for our attention not only blocks negative stresses but also prevents us from enjoying the positive ones. Removing oneself from the mainstream of life can put one out of touch with realities and lead to a distorted view of life, which in itself can be the source of distress. This can happen when actions or expectations are out of synchronization with the true situation.

Ignorance of the laws of nature and society is no excuse for inappropriate behavior. Only with an increased conscious awareness of what is going on around you can you deal with life's problems effectively. Additionally, by keeping people at a protective distance, you are indiscriminately cutting yourself off from a viable source of stress relief—a personal support network.

Adaptation at a Price

The effects of the environment on health are further complicated by man's adaptive ability. That is, he seems capable of adjusting to environmental pollution, intense crowding, and monotonous, ugly, and stressful surroundings. However, these adjustments are bought at a high price. The increase in chronic and degenerative diseases is due largely to the environmental and behavioral changes associated with urbanization and industrialization.

Unfortunately, man cannot overcome the diseases of civilization by adapting biologically to environmental insults. Many changes in the human organism that appear adaptive at first sight are destructive in the long run. For example, smoke and fumes in the air around us elicit from the lung an overproduction of mucus. At first this mucus protects delicate lung tissues from pollutants. Eventually, however, the protective response gives way to such chronic pulmonary diseases as emphysema and tuberculosis.

People living near an airport or freeway frequently learn to block out their perception of the loud noises—but impairment of the hearing apparatus also limits the ability to hear musical tones and the finer qualities of the human voice. By accommodating to persistent exposure to loud noises, we lose some quality in our ability to hear and distinguish among sounds. Yet the sounds are there, causing stress without being consciously heard.

In an effort to adjust to life in extremely crowded environments, many people develop psychological attitudes and defenses that block out excessive environmental stimuli at the cost of impoverished human relationships, which may be blocked off to reduce stress.

Such mutilations of the physical and mental being should not be regarded as adaptation but rather as undesirable side-effect mechanisms of tolerance. The human organism may not display the usual unfavorable effects of environmental insults outwardly, but healthy or normal functioning is physiologically affected.

Adaptation through genetic changes proceeds slowly and does not dramatically impair health during the first decades of life. Even if man could adapt to automobile fumes, the noise of jackhammers, and the traumatic experience of rush-hour traffic, many generations would be required for the process of natural selection to work against a susceptibility to environmentally induced diseases. For instance, certain air pollutants cause cancer. Yet, chances are great that people sensitive to the carcinogen will have children before the disease becomes incapacitating. As a consequence, the children may be as susceptible to the cancer-producing agent as their parents were.

In practice, biological adjustments are a form of tolerance achieved at the cost of reduced or impaired functioning. The situation is not as hopeless as it may seem, however. Since people adapt to a stressful environment and this adaptation may have unfortunate consequences, it is instructive to look at the specialized techniques by which control can reduce these effects. Seemingly greater amounts of physical stress may be much easier to cope with if they are accompanied by greater feelings of control and greater actual control.

Five ways personal and public social engineering can provide necessary modifications in the environment to reduce aftereffects include:

Relaxing rather than getting worked up
Placing stress in a favorable context as useful or necessary
Regularizing the environment to make the occurrences of stress
  more predictable
Arranging situations to control or reduce stress
Being sensitive to long-term consequences of everyone's behavior

These and other coping mechanisms will be covered in detail in Part III. They are mentioned here as a comment on the nature of the relationship between external (environmentally induced) and internal (emotionally/physiologically induced) stress.

THE INTERNAL ENVIRONMENT

Survival and health depend upon the ability of a person to maintain his or her *milieu intérieur* (internal environment) in an approximately constant state, despite large variations in the external environment. Insights into physiology and biochemistry enable us to identify some of the mechanisms that the body employs to correct departures from the ideal state and to maintain itself in a state of dynamic equilibrium.

As Harvard physiologist Walter B. Cannon showed by physiological experimentation, the phrase "homeostatic processes" describes the multiple physiological and metabolic reactions that continuously adjust the vital mechanisms of the body within safe limits in order to maintain the integrity of the conditions for life. The limits are precisely defined for each organism and delicately stabilize the internal environment.

Homeostatic mechanisms are the outcome of evolutionary adaptations, but because they emerged in response to the environmental challenges of the Paleolithic period some 750,000 years ago, they are better suited to the conditions of the past than to those of the present. For example, the immune response protected the primitive hunter from wounds and infections but works against the modern surgeon's boldness in transplanting vital organs. Chapter 12 explores adaptation and contemporary life in greater depth.

Purely homeostatic processes are largely unconscious. Similarly, a large percentage of responses to environmental forces are determined by instincts that operate outside consciousness and choice. Instincts intrinsically enable man to deal decisively and often successfully with life situations similar to those experienced by his forefathers during his evolutionary past.

But precisely because instincts are so specific and mechanical, they may be of little use in new circumstances. We have no instinct to warn us of the dangers inherent in odorless chemical fumes, invisible radiation beams, or subliminal forms of noise or brainwashing. Instincts do not enable us to deal successfully with the unforeseeable complexities of contemporary human life. Therefore, we need to consider seriously bringing our autonomic nervous system into play.

Whereas instincts stand for biological security in a static world, awareness, knowledge, and motivation account for the adventurous liberty and creativity necessary to the human spirit for future security in a dynamic world.

In the final analysis, we can make choices concerning our behavior and surroundings, choices that will prevent or minimize undesirable changes in the milieu intérieur. Manipulation of the external environment inevitably affects mental characteristics and the constituents of some body tissues, as well as the quality of social relationships. Thought processes also play an important role in shaping the internal environment. Part II describes how they can profoundly alter hormonal secretions and consequently physiological mechanisms.

Obviously, following one's instincts passively is easier than directing one's creative responses. The contrast between the unfaltering behavior of most animals in the wilderness and the worried expression on human faces at a time of decision illustrates this point. But to be human means being creative and making choices that often require painful effort—mental even more than physical.

Human health transcends purely biological health because it depends primarily on those conscious and deliberate daily choices by which we select our way of life and adapt to its experiences. Many have affirmed the human ability to create our own personhood and shape our own lives. The overall state of health of human beings reflects man's success in adapting to the many environmental challenges this and other chapters explore.

CHAPTER 5
Challenging Life Changes

Why are the major transitions inherent in the life cycle devastating for some people and growth-promoting for others? At characteristic times of life, typical events happen. Adolescents have identity crises. Young adults face stress and uncertainty about what marriage partners and careers to choose. Adults have children to raise, mortgage payments to make, and older parents to look after. Older adults have retirement to face, grief to overcome, illness and death to accept. Change and stress both seem to pile up in later life. These developmental events are the "life crises" of the stressful life experiences that require change in wisdom and growth in maturity.

We alternate between periods of equilibrium and disequilibrium and need to learn to accept them as essential steps to growth and personal effectiveness. That is, each new circumstance challenges earlier patterns of adjustment and provides opportunities for developing positive coping behaviors.

Though a turning point is a crucial period of increased vulnerability, it is also one of heightened potential. Psychosocial development proceeds by conscious or unconscious decisions for progress or regression. At these points, achievements are won or failures occur—leaving your future better or worse to some degree, but in any case, restructured.

PREDICTABLE MARKER EVENTS

Everything that happens to you—marriage, divorce, remarriage, parenthood, the start of a career, the death of a spouse—affects you. These marker events are the concrete happenings of your lives.

Marriage

For most adults, marriage is a normal, expected, yet stressful development. Although this change may be precipitated by a

[85]

conscious decision on the part of two individuals, it remains a novel experience, requiring the development of new roles and new self-images. As a transition event, marriage presents a series of adjustments—a shift from self-orientation toward achieving a balance between mutual interdependence and individual autonomy.

For both men and women, marital stressors bear a closer relationship to depression and an accompanying behavioral and physical malfunctioning than other social stressors, such as job, finances, or parenting.

Marriage brings many new tasks to be handled in the development of new roles and new self-images. These are part of working out the details of everyday living. The establishment and maintenance of a home, with the attendant problems of handling finances, maintenance, communication, seeking shared interests, planning for the future education or career of both husband and wife, and thinking about the possibility of becoming parents are a few of the stressors that follow marriage.

Satisfaction in marriage impacts on job performance—attention to work, attitude toward co-workers, and perception of one's abilities. When an employee comes to work after arguing with his wife at breakfast, his resources are diminished unless he has mastered some coping abilities to enable him to shift gears and attend to the work at hand. Chapter 6 focuses on specific marital stressors, for which Part III identifies constructive coping behaviors.

Parenthood

Becoming parents and having to reorganize their lives accordingly is another stressful event in the adult life cycle that many employees experience. The development of a parental sense of competence, the added responsibility of another person's life and future, increased financial pressure, reorganization of the marital relationship, assumption of the parenting role, and time and emotional demands all require adaptation.

Career

Another change experienced by most adults is that of starting a career. How you plan for and deal with early career decisions has a great bearing on other aspects of your adult life. Work and a commitment to a vocation or a career are important factors in a person's well-being. A large part of your time during the week is spent at work. The type of work done and the office location are influential in deciding where to live as well the kinds of social and leisure activities you pursue.

Work can be health-enhancing by meeting interests, fulfilling personal needs, supplying a sense of achievement and well-being, and developing personality and growth. A good fit between your needs and the demands of your occupation can produce personal satisfaction. This satisfaction, in turn, can make you a more effective employee.

Unfortunately, many people make their occupational choices at a time in life when self-insight and data about opportunities are not adequate to make an informed choice. Young adults usually need to seek more information about careers, and they need to develop more self-awareness about how they want to spend their time for the quality of life they desire.

Many people discover too late that living with a job is far different from choosing one. The circumstances that produce lasting satisfaction may prove to be quite different from those that made the occupation or position seem attractive in the first place. Screening and interviewing techniques that accurately describe the work, chain of command, and company goals can help reduce the possibility of poor job fit and thereby reduce employee turnover—a major source of stress to the company.

Issues such as pay and job security have an important bearing on satisfaction with the job. At different stages in a person's life, they take on more weighty considerations. A young adult without a family to support may feel the experience and education of being associated with a prestigious large firm are most important. A family man may choose employment with a small firm that offers greater chances for advancement through independent achievement during his middle years, when he is pushing to establish himself in his chosen career field.

Likewise, retirement can be viewed as a normal rite of passage. Many people look forward to giving up a full-time active work role, with all its financial, social, and psychological implications, and others dread it. Retirement requires adjustment to a new use of time, new ways of relating to neighbors, or, if you move to a new community or a smaller home, different surroundings and a loss of familiar things and people.

At the same time, the retiree has new demands, new expectations, a new self-image, a new daily routine. For many people, this combination of new and interrelated stressors at retirement creates intense distress. The anticipatory stress of forced retirement can interfere with life in the present and interfere with a person's effectiveness. Fear of retirement may prolong stressful employment at a grave risk to health.

Fear of retirement particularly affects people who lack confidence or are seeking an escape from involvement in the present. For some people, preoccupation with approaching retirement impairs concentration and effectiveness on the job. They don't perform as well or complete assignments because of a feeling of hopelessness. "It doesn't matter anyway. I won't be here much longer." The sense of loss of investment in the future and in the outcome of the work can lead to nonproductive, even counterproductive, behavior by an employee facing retirement. A person may experience withdrawal, bitterness, low morale, and low self-esteem if he or she does not plan ahead constructively.

However, most people are able to cope with giving up full-time work by developing new interests, pursuing hobbies, getting involved in community activities, and doing things they never found time to do before. Utilizing these positive means of coping with retirement, a person can maintain his or her self-esteem and a feeling of usefulness as well as derive personal and social satisfactions. He or she is able to contain a potentially stressful situation within manageable limits.

Death

The death of one's spouse is the last major life change for many people and rates the highest on the scale of stressful impact. Although we know death is inevitable, having to "say good-bye" and adjust to life without the lost spouse is a wrenching transition and almost always traumatic. People pass through remarkably similar patterns of grief. Individuals experience this sequence in different ways, but all five stages are common in reacting to loss:

Shock
Denial
Intrusion
Working through
Completion

The shock of the spouse's death elicits an almost automatic response. Weeping, anger, screaming, resentment, panic, and fainting are varied forms of anguished outcry.

Denial refers to a numbing or avoidance of the reality of the loss. For example, the surviving spouse will appear to be "doing very well," return to work and other activities, and give the general appearance of strength. But while he is outwardly "holding up well," his body remains in a state of alarm for some time after the trauma. In the six months after the death of their spouse, widows and widowers are 40 percent more likely than the average person of their age to have high rates of illness and depression and die (especially from heart attacks).

Weeks or even months after the loss, the intrusion or preoccupation phase takes place. Generally, the steady visits and notes from friends and relatives have been reduced to the normal occasional call. The person feels the emptiness and futilely tries to combat the loneliness through dreams, recurrent reminders of past events, and perhaps visual images of the deceased. During this adaptive stage he or she might fluctuate between periods of denial or outrage and avoidance of the reality.

Usually, learning to cope with life without the spouse takes at least six months to a year. Working through this period of adjustment is stressful, with all the changes required. This time is one of sorting out one's life and feelings. Working through the anger that such a thing should happen, dealing with guilt feelings about things that were left undone or unsaid while the spouse was still alive, and depression are but three of the potentially damaging emotions with which the widow or widower is forced to cope.

Facing the many emotions evoked in the normal process of grieving can be particularly distressful in a society that looks more favorably on stoic containment, out of some misplaced sense of dignity and strength. Bottling up his or her feelings may reduce the stress in those around the grief-stricken individual. However, that persons suffers inwardly by not being able to share with an understanding friend.

Compounding the problems of this painful and often bewildering period are the many practical decisions and plans that need to be made. Frequently, the bereaved individual will make too many changes in too short a period of time, complicating his or her life with more stress. Changing residences, jobs, patterns of recreation, and daily routines may be the right decisions in the long run. However, giving up too soon those familiar things, places, and people that once provided security can overwhelm a person.

The completion stage is reached with the person slowly returning to a more normal emotional state. The widow or widower is able to go on to a new stage of life with a new understanding of self and plan for the future.

Knowing the predictable pattern of grief may not make mourning less intense, but it can help give hope and encouragement that the crisis can be worked through and stress minimized.

UNEXPECTED LIFE EVENTS

Marriage, parenthood, career, retirement, and death are more or less predictable changes in the adult life cycle requiring intense personal adjustment. People have always had to cope with the expected and the unexpected. But the rapid social changes and the faster pace of the twentieth century bring a number of additional life changes. Among the most important of these are divorce, remarriage, and geographic mobility.

Divorce

Next to the death of a spouse, divorce is the second most stressful life event. About 33 percent of new marriages ends in divorce and 40 percent of those divorced marry a second time. The rising divorce rate is largely a result of the eroding effects of accelerating social change on the marriage partnership. Whether divorce is considered necessary for survival, initiated unnecessarily because couples cannot cope with the effort involved, or forced upon a spouse involuntarily, it exacts a considerable toll in terms of stress for both petitioner and respondent.

People adjust to the demands of coping with this disruption in their lives in a variety of ways and over different periods of time.

Sometimes the period of intense stress is brief, and sometimes it lasts for several years. The end of a marriage affects people in many ways. Basically, each person has to deal with the following issues:

Loss of companionship and emotional bond, aloneness
Change of habits
Adjustment to new routines
Accumulated feelings of hurt, uncertainty, resentment, anger, jealousy, failure, humiliation, rejection, fear, and guilt
Loss of self-esteem and self-confidence
Impact of children and visitations
Alimony/financial obligations
Development of autonomy
Residual attachments to past life
Change in social life and friendships
Character of contact with former spouse

Whatever the particulars surrounding the separation, divorce is generally accompanied by higher rates of emotional stress, illness, and even death than occur among married people.

Remarriage

Like divorce, remarriage solves some problems and creates others. A successful second marriage sometimes reduces stress levels. Nonetheless, there is a period of adjustment to the new life and the stressors it brings with it:

Combining families, finances
Assuming the role of a stepparent—attempting to accept and be accepted
Dealing with new and former in-laws
Seeing things in a new way
Compromising with new partner on money, time, children, and so on—running a joint household

Geographic Mobility

The average American moves about 14 times in his lifetime. Twenty percent of Americans move one or more times a year. A geographic move is a major life change and therefore produces stress.

People move for a variety of reasons, ranging from job opportunities to improving health to seeking a new physical environment. The reasons are as individual as the people themselves, and so are the repercussions. The newness of surroundings, activities, climate, and employment when people move requires a number of adjustments.

The demands of moving impact on the entire family as it makes the transition. Each break with familiar places, things, people, habits, and organizations requires adaptive energy. The uprooting may also cause sadness and a sense of loss.

The move itself is demanding on body, mind, and spirit. Sleeping, eating, and relating patterns are stressed, whether the move is across town or across the state. Physical discomforts, fear, fatigue, and resistance may cause tempers to flare, boredom to set in, and a host of minor ailments, like colds, diarrhea, headaches, and stomach upsets, to appear.

Relocation in a new country is particularly stressful as the vast collection of micro-changes increases with the changes in culture, language, diet, and time zone. A complex process of perceptual and emotional orientation is set in motion during the settling-in period. Apprehension, insecurity, and loneliness are frequently experienced by the newcomer. He or she feels drained by the pressure to set up house, make new friends, locate services, and take care of all the other necessities of establishing ties and a new equilibrium.

Some people are accustomed to a nomadic lifestyle and adjust rapidly. For instance, many service families have developed successful coping routines over the years that enable them to minimize the distressful effects of frequent moving. However, some people are not accustomed to change and add to their stress by resisting the inevitable.

The number of symptoms of distress related to moving are likely to be greater when the move is involuntary or considered undesirable. For instance, job transfers in the middle of the year for a family man can be particularly stressful when a teenager must transfer high schools in the senior year or a wife is in charge of a community endeavor.

A corporate wife often suffers from depression and hostility when expected to move. Her transition is not always as easy as her husband's. Frequently she has to start from scratch in integrating herself in the new community, without the transferable credentials and ready social unit the husband experiences at work. Most of the burden of setting up the home, enrolling the children in schools, and locating doctors, babysitters, and recreational facilities falls on her shoulders. If she is also trying to find a job or pursue her education, that can add significantly to her stress level. Stress on the marriage and on the family unit as a whole may reach unhealthy proportions.

Studies of the lifestyles of engineers, scientists, and technicians in American aerospace centers and in other, more normal, communities revealed marked emotional and physical signs of distress:

Depression
Deterioration of health (increased chances of heart attack)
Very little community involvement
Few close friends
Strong dependence on marital relationship for emotional satisfaction
Conspicuous number of alcoholics
Pervasive feeling of social anonymity
Diffusion of individual responsibility for social acts, resulting in lack of involvement
Destructive aggression
Cold impersonality
Marital discord
High divorce rate

OTHER MAJOR LIFE CHANGES

In addition to the marker events (major transitions) built into the adult life cycle and the particularly common changes examined in this chapter, a variety of other stressful changes may occur:

Engagement or broken engagement
Beginning or ending of living with someone
Acquiring or breaking the habit of illegal drugs
Quitting smoking or drinking
Changing jobs or careers
New work responsibilities or promotion
Death of a close friend

A crippling injury
Legal trouble
Changing sexual relationships

The changes may be voluntary or forced, expected or unexpected, pleasant or unpleasant. All require adjustments in order to minimize their potentially adverse effects.

AGE AND THE LIFE CYCLE

We have been looking at the more typical events that take place in the adult life cycle. These are external aspects. In addition to these social changes, there are internal aspects of the cycle that relate to how great the total impact of the life events will be on the individual.

The fact that most people now live into old age has led to a changing configuration of the life cycle as a whole, with an increasing number of socially definable life periods. People who were formerly regarded as old at 40 are now divided into groups of over-30, middle-aged, mature, and elderly. Each of these life periods has its distinctive psychological and social behaviors, its distinctive preoccupations, incentives, and personal goals, and its distinctive patterns of adaptation.

In addition to the frustrations and problems, there are significant shifts in motivation throughout the adult life cycle. Needs that are important in one phase of life become relatively fulfilled, change in importance, and give way to other needs. A company that is in tune with these developments can cope better with the realities of its employees' problems and can maximize the human resources available to it.

For example, when a career-oriented man reaches middle age and has achieved economic security and occupational success to a satisfying degree, his need to get ahead may be much less impelling than the need of someone who has never felt job fulfillment. Affiliation or service needs—family or community activities—may become the focal point for sources of gratification.

Those men and women who adapt to life successfully in the middle years—roughly speaking, those between 45 and 60—have a wide range of both emotional and mental flexibility. This capacity to shift feelings of involvement from one person to another and from one activity to another is necessary throughout life, but it is especially crucial in middle age. During this time, many people experience important personal losses, as parents die, children grow up, friends move away, and some of the effects of aging begin to set in.

Open-mindedness is a particularly valuable quality at this stage of development and can make all the difference in coping competently. Stagnation may set in from a sense of loss of meaning in life or from a general feeling of having worked out a set of answers to life. The plateau phenomenon—men and women feeling they have gone as far as they are likely to go in their jobs—is distressful as people feel a sense of coming to a dead end.

As people reach a plateau on the job, they feel a loss of upward mobility in their career and may find less fulfillment in it. This is a period of personal reevaluation that may result in a loss of self-esteem.

For some middle-aged businessmen, the appearance of young executives raises doubts of self-worth, fear, and a sense of resentment at the thought of spending the rest of their lives working for 30-year-olds. They are fatalistic in thinking they will probably be passed over in promotion considerations. Some older executives give up; others try to compete with the younger staff; but the healthiest attitude is to realize that their knowledge is of great value and to continue to provide it. An awareness of one's own competence and the company's on-the-job reinforcement help an employee cope with this plateau phenomenon.

For women, middle age may mean making the transition from being a mother to a new role in life. It is a time of pursuing new directions and finding new meaning in life. Sometimes this period will be approached enthusiastically, with a new sense of freedom and opportunity. Alternatively, a woman may feel perplexed and depressed about her future.

For people whose children have already left home, this is often a time of severe stress and one that places a great strain on the individual adult and on the husband–wife relationship. Problems arise when the gap left by departing children is not filled. It can be a time when the marital relationship is reinforced with renewed interest and devotion. It can also be a stressful period during which the man and woman must get reacquainted as individuals instead of dealing with one another in the parental role.

Additionally, if the wife was working to supplement the family income in order to help get the children through braces and college, her reason for working is gone. She may not have looked at her job as a career or found much satisfaction in it. A job change or retirement can be stressful on the marriage relationship. Return to school or entry into the job market can also be stressful as both husband and wife try to adjust to a new schedule, new interests, and a new circle of acquaintances. The husband may resist his wife's new independence—financial and social—and resent her attention being focused outside the home.

The cultural emphasis on youth tends to increase middle-age concerns about status and self-worth. Also concern about the loss of youthfulness—balding, wrinkles, weight gain, or loss of sexual attractiveness—may be personally threatening.

True, definite physiological changes are taking place. There is a lessening of physical energy and some decline in activities. The likelihood of serious illness is greater at this time of life than it has been before. Concomitantly, there are major endocrine changes taking place in women (the menopause) and lesser hormonal changes taking place in men. But the exact relation of these changes to behavior remains for future research to determine.

Here, as elsewhere, a person's established coping abilities are significant in mediating biological changes. In general, they need not be a traumatic experience. Acceptance of the inevitability of menopause and the natural progression of aging can buffer the distressful aspects of growing older.

CONCLUSION

The psychological meanings of time arise from the complex interplay of biological, cultural, historical, and social time. The individual's ever changing identity throughout his or her lifetime expands on this purely psychological view of time.

In learning what age-appropriate behavior is, men and women learn the socially prescribed timetables for the ordering of major life events. They develop a mental map of the life cycle, anticipating that given events will occur at given periods in life. They become aware of the social clocks that operate in various areas of their lives, and being on time or off time shapes self-concepts for them.

It is usually the timing of the life event, rather than its occurrence per se, that is significant in creating a sense of psychological well-being or in precipitating an adaptation crisis.

People can learn to recognize the risk they are under in the amount of life change to which they are exposed or to which they expose themselves. What happens to a person in life is intertwined with his health, as we have seen in relation to the job and the environment. The amount of life stress on a person's thoughts, moods, and emotions can influence the onset, course, and outcome of disease (see Figure 3). Recent life-change events signify transitions in a person's psychosocial life adjustment and reflect the current environmental demands to which he or she must try to adjust. Psychological and physiological efforts necessary for such adjustment, if severe and/or protracted in time, appear to predispose people to illness.

Clearly, life events occur at different times for each person and, accordingly, they have a different impact. For instance, the adult lives of a couple who married and had children when they were in their early twenties differ from the lives of a couple just marrying when they are 30.

As we have seen, certain situations and personality changes are common to each stage of your life. At specific points along the life cycle you feel stirrings, sometimes momentous changes of perspec-

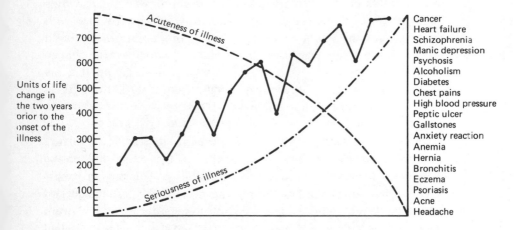

FIGURE 3. *Correlation between the quantity of life change and the seriousness of illness.*

tive, often mysterious dissatisfactions with the course you had enthusiastically been pursuing only a few years before. Both these internal and external turning points come up with relentless regularity and similarity in all our lives. These periods of disruption can be baffling. And if a momentous event coincides with a critical point in your life cycle, you may be overwhelmed.

A coherent vision of the transitions we must all experience can help us manage our own stress and understand that of others, to achieve what is potentially the best of life. By becoming familiar with the life events and the amount of change they require, we can plan for some of them well in advance and alter the course of physical and emotional distress.

Pacing work as well as personal commitments may prevent stress overload when too many demands are made on someone in too short a period of time, before that person has a chance to adjust or to cope. An investigation of the relationship between magnitude of life change and seriousness of illness has revealed increased probabilities of chronic disease with a bigger life change. The probability of getting diabetes, schizophrenia, a heart attack, or cancer is much greater for those people experiencing a lot of change in their lives than for those with a more stable lifestyle.

In other words, if a person goes through a divorce, has a major change in his or her financial situation, is getting less sleep, varies food intake, reduces recreational activities, or has troubles with his employer, he has a 50 percent higher probability of getting a major disease in the near future than someone with lower life change scores. Someone who is having in-law troubles, remodeling his home, or planning the wedding of a son or daughter is more likely to get a headache, mononucleosis, asthma, or an anxiety reaction rather than one of the more serious diseases.

Once you are aware of your cumulative life situation, internal and external, you can make use of some of the many preventive techniques available to reduce the probability of damaging stress. Awareness, pacing, and accepting the inevitability of change and aging are helpful. The weight a person assigns the impact of each turning point reflects his own preception and is a significant determinant in any maladaptation or disease. Therefore, introspection into activities, abilities, needs, personality, and behaviors can provide some degree of insight into the more unpredictable life changes, such as losing a job or a serious argument with a spouse. For some people, how they habitually respond to circumstances that arouse them is a determining factor in the incidence of disease. Chapter 14 focuses on the role perception plays.

As explored in Chapter 2, work constitutes a major portion of life. As such, it is a controlling environmental and psychosocial factor in the number of demands most people try to meet. A number of forward-thinking firms have recognized their role in employee health and have responded constructively. They maintain good ties with community resources such as family-counseling services to help employees, offer insurance plans that cover psychiatric and psychological services, and hold in-house stress reduction programs.

Research continues to show that disease is a by-product of human striving and of the techniques people use to achieve their goals and aspirations. These techniques are apparent both in the work environment and on the corporation's bottom line.

CHAPTER 6
Stress at Home

PERSONAL PROBLEMS AND THE CORPORATION

Americans spend more than $1.2 billion annually on health insurance alone. This expense is directly reflected on the corporate bottom line. To say that an employee's personal life should not concern the employer is foolhardy. We are not suggesting that the personnel departments become Dear Abby franchises, but it is sound business to develop a more conscious awareness of human situations that are potential health hazards when the people involved are unable to cope with the inherent stress.

Many companies have an unstated rule: "Don't bring your personal problems to the job." However, as long as you expect an employee on the job, you can expect the entire person to punch in, bringing his problems as well as his skills. The employee comes to work with his training, experience, and personality; but also with his problems, frustrations, and perhaps his bad temper or self-consciousness (see Figure 4).

An employee whose mind is free of personal troubles is more likely to deal well with work-related demands. Consequently, perhaps the most significant transition in the adult life cycle—marriage—needs to be examined closely as a common stress-producing agent that impacts on the job.

The kind of marital relationship a person has profoundly affects his or her physical and mental health. We know from considerable research that people engaged in a mutually supportive relationship cope better with the stresses and the problems of life. A poor relationship between a husband and wife sets the stage not only for neurotic problems or worse but also for a host of psychosomatic illnesses such as migraine headaches, high blood pressure, and gastric ulcers. A conflict-riddled marriage can also produce enough

[100]

FIGURE 4. *Personal factors affect an individual's ability to function at work.*

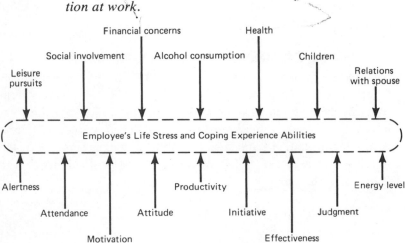

stress to aggravate coronary heart disease and may even lead to sudden and unexpected death.

A MULTIDIMENSIONAL APPROACH TO POTENTIAL DISTRESS

When you recognize the natural, successive stages that occur in marriage, you will be able to take appropriate steps to prevent some of the potentially distressing situations. Realistic expectations of what lies ahead can reduce the risk of dealing with each separate stressor in a haphazard and ultimately unsuccessful way.

Knowing that you are not alone in experiencing a particular problem can reduce the feeling of helplessness in trying to overcome it. When you realize others have resolved this problem, you feel you can too. Also, being aware of what signs to look for so that you can ward off a problem before it grows can help you to develop positive coping behaviors. A social network of friends, relatives, and professionals can be supportive and constructive in their interactions with a troubled person and build confidence in him or her that a solution can be found.

This awareness of common marital problems, what signs of stress to look for, and how necessary it is to maintain a social support system and balanced lifestyles is a component of a multidimensional approach to problem solving. Feelings of loneliness, a tendency to ignore clues to problems, isolation from others, and personality type may cause personal distress that will spill over into the work environment.

THE IMPORTANCE OF MARITAL STRESSORS

Stressors connected with marriage are the most common causes of depression. Of the 43 life events on the Social Readjustment Rating Scale of Thomas Holmes and Richard Rahe, one-third are marriage or family situations. The death of a spouse, divorce, marital separation, marriage, and marital reconciliation are in the top ten life-change events listed bearing the closest relationship to the onset of illness.

THE MARRIAGE CYCLE

As outlined in the last chapter, crises through which people go at various phases in the adult life cycle can be predicted. So too can major points of transition through which marriages go. There are basically three major stages in the evolution pattern of a marriage: coupling, family orientation, and partnership.

The Coupling Stage

The coupling stage starts the moment you marry and continues until you have children. Committing yourself to another person and a different way of life immediately sets off a series of psychological vibrations. As developed in the overview of stress (Chapter 1), each person's response to stressful events is unique to him or her. Some people have a difficult time adjusting to the new world of activities and tasks with which they have to deal in marriage.

If this change in lifestyle is eagerly awaited and regarded as the beginning of a new life with a future and growth, the change may not produce an overwhelming amount of stress. However, if marriage is seen as a threat or even a calamity because of impending uncertainty, responsibilities, and possible failure, the experience may be highly distressful.

For most people, marriage is a normal, expected part of adult life. However, role transitions from "me" to "we" require new behaviors and adjustments. These transitions cause stress—and sometimes distress. When a person's new role requires behavior that is not comfortable, healthy, and productive for personal growth, the chances of distress are heightened. The "we," "our," and "Mr. and Mrs." of being identified as a couple mark a new kind of life, requiring the development of new roles and new self-images. Foremost among these is a shift from a self-orientation to one of mutuality.

There is a certain sense of loss related to things valued in single life. The loneliness is gone, but so is some of the independence. You are no longer as free as you were. Now you have to account to someone else for your presence, time, attention, and love.

Adjustments to each others' habits, lifestyle, and tasks can be stressful. There may be impatience, conflicts of interest, and hurt feelings. The degree of anxiety and depression that may occur during these periods of adjustment can be attributable to the troubles or discord of a normal response to the stresses encountered. By becoming aware of the potential stress in these new marital events, the individual can help transform a sense of unmanageable crisis into a positive feeling of potentially useful challenge.

The Family-Orientation Stage

The next stage in the usual course of a marriage is family oriented and begins with the birth of the first child. The addition of a new life into the marital relationship brings about many changes in the spouses and in the relationship itself.

A child can bring a blend of joy, anxiety about financial consequences, and worries about the child's health and safety. Freedom, mobility, and the ability to react spontaneously may disappear for a while in the marital relationship. The world now includes colic, babysitters, and other demands on attention and care. Becoming parents is a stressful event that may initiate more concerns about money, a decrease in sexual ardor, boredom, irritability, and fatigue.

Unconsciously, each person has an image of what it is to be a "mother" or a "father." This image is based on an identification, either conscious or unconscious, with one's own parents. Certain traits of our parents slip into our own mannerisms and attitudes, not only in how we relate to children, but also in how we deal with a spouse. The shadows of the past and the present realities mix to produce stress for a while, as each person's expectations of parenthood and family life are adjusted to the couple's particular situation.

A further shift—though still part of the child-oriented family stage—occurs when the last small child enters school and continues as the youngsters grow up and enter their teenage years. Even though you may welcome your new liberty, you cannot avoid experiencing a sense of loss. The mother has more time available to do the things she wants to do—go to school, work, follow hobbies— and this too can be stressful as she seeks to identify what she does want. She may want to work or seek activities and friends she and her husband had not previously enjoyed together. The father and the family in general may have to adjust to the wife and mother being away from home. Schedules, her availability, and routines may be disrupted.

If there is additional income, how it is to be spent and what kind of contribution it makes can be disruptive to the equanimity of the family. This is a critical juncture in a marriage. At this point marital partners rediscover each other, and sometimes they don't like what they find. Each may have changed so much over the years that the original relationship no longer holds. If a couple avoids recognizing this situation or cannot deal with it realistically, it may be headed for emotional separation. Thus, the marriage relationship is subjected to the strains of personal evolution.

During the adolescent pull toward adulthood, the changing parental relationship with the growing child can be stressful. Adolescence can be a difficult and anxiety-provoking age with which to deal. There are bound to be arguments and scenes as youngsters begin pulling away and experimenting. You may not be sure how to discuss sex with them, or what to expect of their behavior. You lie awake at night wondering if they will get home all right. You worry about their driving while you are at work. You wonder what they are doing.

Partnership

Then, suddenly, it is over. The next major stage in marriage begins. By now you are probably in your mid-forties, the children are gone, and you and your partner are left to deal with each other—alone for the first time in years. The time has come for you to start designing the sort of life you want for yourselves in the unpredictable years to come. This may mean a smaller home or apartment, going back to school, planning for retirement, the advent of grandchildren, caring for elderly parents. There are many unforeseeable opportunities and challenges.

These three stages may be the normal course of the marriage cycle, but it does not always run its full course. About one in three new marriages now ends in divorce. Studies consistently show that divorce exacts a considerable toll in terms of stress. For some, the period of intense stress is brief as the partners cope with an initial loss of companionship, a change in habits, and adjustment to new routines. For others, the intense stress of divorce lasts several years. Divorced people also suffer from higher rates of emotional stress, illness, and death than married people.

CHANGING STANDARDS

Rapid change, as discussed in the previous chapter, accounts for some of the cultural stress impacting on marriage. At the same time, our culture has become more tolerant of different lifestyles. It is now generally acceptable to be single, divorced, religious, an agnostic—or even married. This flexibility offers alternatives that highlight the heterogeneous character of society. The forces that once inherently held many marriages and families together are weakened as society becomes so diversified.

Perhaps the most significant pressure placed on contemporary marriage is a fundamental shift in the standards against which the success of marriage is measured. The once central considerations of economic stability, similarity in social backgrounds, building of a way of life together, shared friends, and children have given way to a new scale, one that focuses hard and almost exclusively on the quality of the interpersonal relationship between the husband and wife. The influence of traditional social and religious codes that once provided strong support for the permanence of marriage has diminished. The promise of happiness in some other life, if we do not find it here, is no longer enough to sustain us.

PLANNED OBSOLESCENCE

Marriage, then, has been the special victim of the trend toward individual freedom and self-fulfillment, whatever the cost. The urgency for immediate solutions evolves from the conviction that time is running out and does not allow for the development of positive coping behaviors.

Coupled with this instant gratification syndrome is the "disposable" mentality paralleling our attitude toward throwaway products. Many marriages end unnecessarily because couples cannot cope with the demands for restatement of commitment necessary for the relationship to endure. Bound up with the accelerated change in our society, relationships are viewed in almost the same light as product obsolescence. When the needs of the consumer (spouse) change and the functions to be performed by the product (marriage) are altered in the course of life cycles, obsolescence occurs—and the old mate is exchanged for a new model.

Instead of being with a mate over a relatively long span of time, people are linked for brief periods in successive relationships. Primarily preoccupied with themselves, some people view their marriages almost exclusively in terms of whether they help or hinder their own chances for personal happiness. This myopic view fails to take the total relationship into consideration.

We have been conditioned to be good consumers, building products—including our lives—so that they wear out. In other words, we are no longer culturally oriented toward renewal and repair. Therefore, we have trouble maintaining a commitment. This orientation brings about a self-fulfilling prophecy—marriages viewed as temporary become temporary. Rather than develop the creativity and insight necessary to absorb the impact of the stresses that transitional periods produce, we let the relationship fall apart, usually producing even more stress.

To compound these distressful events, many people rush into another marriage before identifying the stressors contributing to the dissolution of the previous marriage.

INDIVIDUAL EVOLUTION

There is a delicate balance between developing oneself and caring for others. Some people have been able to change their outlooks and embark on new lives without having to break commitments they made to their marriages. They do not experience personal growth and attachment to another as mutually exclusive.

The pattern of individual evolution is never a straight line forward. If you marry in your mid-twenties or early thirties and you expect to stay in this marriage for the rest of your life, you are talking about a probable lifespan of 40 years or more for your relationship. This is an incredibly long time. It is the distance between World War I and the space probe to Mars.

As mentioned before, the world is constantly changing. There are enormous social and environmental changes taking place besides those that will occur within yourself and in your relationship with your partner. Marriage is subject to the stresses that stem from many changes. Times change. People change. Yet, ordinarily, we hold on to obsolete images of ourselves, of other people, and of situations. After years of marriage, many couples react to each other as they once were, not as they now are. When the images we hold on to no longer apply, our actions are often obsolete, and stress may be the result.

In some instances, the marital relationship has indeed been a barrier to personal development. However, too often it is perceived that way without sufficient reason. As long as two people remain obsessed with the confinement marriage represents, they seem unable to consider appropriate options. The partner then becomes the enemy, a person to struggle against and ultimately defeat.

The couple may, for example, begin to look at the marriage bond as a labor–management contract, imposing written rules and agreements more suited to the automobile workers union and General Motors than to an intimate and complex human relationship. Sometimes spouses are left floundering, unsure about who they are and what they are expected to do. Their expectations do not match those of their partner, and they have no common point of communication.

Tied to this current emphasis on self-fulfillment is another major source of stress in marriage—sex.

THE IMPORTANCE OF SEX

The national preoccupation with sex is apparent in movies, newspapers, and magazines and on billboards. Sexual pleasure rates high on the scale of gratification experiences people seek. "How-to" books, sex therapy clinics, and open discussion of sexual encounters are indicative of the importance people place on their sex lives. Sex seems to have acquired the status of an inalienable right to be defended at any price—even the price of marriage.

When sex is available as a resource in a marriage, it operates at conscious and unconscious levels to give pleasure. It can promote and renew the bond between a couple and offer reassurance in times of stress. Because sex is so important as a constructive and integrative force, when it is unsuccessful or disappointing, it has enormous disruptive potential. It can signal failure in interdependency, failure to fulfill needs, or an inability to respond to personal developmental changes.

Sexual difficulty is rated thirteenth on Holmes and Rahe's Readjustment Scale predicting stress-related illness with a life-change value of 39 points (the same as gaining a new family member or business adjustment).

Changes in social values and the increasingly stressful pace of our lives play a significant part in the sensitive area of sex in marital life and in the difficulty of relations with the opposite sex among single people.

Given few clues as to what kind of behavior is rational under the new mores, men and women are disoriented and anxious about sex. The fragmentation and impermanence of relationships today sometimes lead to a frantic sexual encounter that is a desperate effort to make contact with someone. However, the superficial intimacy shortcuts any sense of involvement with or responsibility to the whole person.

Additionally, new birth technologies splinter our traditional notions of sexuality, motherhood, child rearing, and love. The pill, surrogate mothers, vitro babies, genetic manipulation, and artificial insemination are but a few of the moral and emotional choices that confront men and women in the coming decades.

In addition to these concerns, a person who concentrates on his career to the extent of neglecting his marriage can cause severe marital disharmony and an attendant sexual disturbance. Impotence, loss of interest, frigidity, and extramarital affairs are symptoms of maladaptive coping.

Most often, sexual behavior stems from a complex set of motivations rooted in a person's physical, mental, and emotional condition, maturity level, and personal value system. Such a mixture of determinants is bound to defy any easy analysis. Yet, for our purposes here, exploration of some of these causal factors is essential if we are to understand what produces some of the stress that detracts from a person's general well-being and subsequent effectiveness.

The history of a person's general state of health and life stresses can reveal causes of sexual dysfunction and accompanying distress. Diabetes, hypertension, arteriosclerotic vascular disease, a small stroke, a traumatic episode, and sexual failures may be diagnosed as causal factors. If these or other physical causes are not present, there may be emotional factors to consider.

THE NEED FOR BALANCE

A balanced arrangement of profession, friendships, interests, marriage partner, and children is the outflowing of healthy ambition in the mature individual. Specifically, a well-integrated individual with a low-stress, high-satisfaction lifestyle is one who maintains a realistic assessment of his own needs and accomplishments rather than a grandiose one.

THE ACHIEVER

The traditional ideal of masculine success in American society is that of the "achiever," pursuing ever higher business or professional positions. This value is nurtured from the crib, reinforced in our educational system, and encouraged by the communications media, and it becomes an internalized part of one's ego ideal.

When work, because of time, energy, or interest, preempts the option or capacity to perform as a sexual and loving adult over an extended period of time, it becomes very stressful for both parties in the relationship. The ambitious husband suffers from the conflict between how much time he needs for his work and how much time for his wife and family. His dilemma is distressful, and the inner conflict eats away at him and at the marital relationship.

The wife often fights her own conflicting battle. She feels angry and jealous of the time and intimacy that have been taken from her. She also may feel guilty for wanting her spouse to meet her needs, when doing so might compromise his career. She is told he is working for the family, yet she is bitter and struggles with the feeling that his career is destroying the family. He feels unappreciated; she feels ignored. They both have problems in coping with these stressful feelings.

A husband's single-minded pursuit of achievement does exact a toll on his and the family's life. The long hours, heavy emotional investment in work-related matters, and relocations often necessary for advancement can be disruptive to the quality of his personal and family life.

Ongoing research on the overlap and interaction between work roles and family roles presents compelling evidence that excessive involvement of men in demanding work roles can result in the alienation of the men from their wives and children. The result is greater stress on the entire family unit. Now that more and more women are seeking high-level careers, they may find themselves trapped in the same syndrome.

When people are wrapped up in work or in any one preoccupation to the exclusion of anything else, they have a tendency to push other things aside—sleep, interest in food, recreation, family, and leisure activities—and their sex lives may not get the attention necessary to maintain a healthy balance in life.

The characteristic work addict has an exaggerated sense of the success ethic. He works long and hard hours, constantly under deadline pressures and conditions of overload. In addition to competing with others, he drives himself to maintain his own high standards of productivity. He often carries work home evenings and weekends and shows an inability to relax, even cutting vacations short to get back to work. Increasing numbers of working wives are developing the same patterns.

The hard-driving and productive people who are often held up in our society as models of success have a propensity for creating stressful environments for themselves and for those whose day-to-day lives are intimately connected with theirs.

The spouse's preoccupation with career may not only be creating the prospect of a shorter life but may also increase psychological strain on the marriage partner. Certain negative feelings, such as depression, worthlessness, anxiety, tension, guilt, and isolation, are most pervasive and prevalent in people with workaholic spouses. The abandoned one may seek relief in alcohol, drugs, affairs, or profligate spending.

TWO-CAREER MARRIAGES

The strain resulting from the spouse's compulsive work orientation is magnified when both husband and wife pursue careers. Such employment has had a great impact on the quality of marriage and parenting. Forty-eight percent of women over 16 are now in the labor market, including half of all mothers with school-age children. That represents 40.5 million women and is predicted to rise 50 percent in the next ten years. Like any change, this rise in the number of working women will cause strains on the women and on their interpersonal relations. The greatest confusion might be expected as new roles are developing. When these roles become more established, adaptations and coping behaviors will relieve some of the accompanying stress.

For many years newly married women have commonly retained their jobs or careers, particularly prior to having children. What recently has become more distinctive is that many women, especially those with careers, are continuing to work outside the home even as they rear children. Also, many women have resumed their educations and pursued careers after they have been married a few years or even after child rearing.

Whatever the stage of marriage, however, changes that take place in two-career marriages are frequently accompanied by transitory, intermittent, or chronic conflicts. Some conflicts are merely exaggerations of problems encountered in conventional marriages during similar periods; others seem to be peculiar to the two-career family.

The most stressful conflicts are related to changes in the balance of power within the marriage. Arguments concerning the spending of money, child rearing, the delegation of responsibilities within the home, and decreased interest in sex are the most common stressors.

The distinctive feature in these two-career marriages is the wife's growing capacity to influence decisions because of her increased purchasing power, assertiveness, and feelings of independence based on her outside career success and expanded social contacts.

Equality

For many couples, inflation is creating a condition of equality in the marriage. The need for more money comes along just at a time when women and men are rethinking their roles. For many women, necessity is the final push over the line into partnership. At the same time, inflation is strangling the idea of choice. Lack of choice produces distress as people feel a sense of loss of control over their lives.

In the last decade, women's lives have been transformed by the new options that enable them to choose work and career either by themselves or in combination with marriage and motherhood. However, financial pressures have frequently closed off the options to go back to school, to work as an unpaid volunteer, or to stay at home to devote all their time to raising a family. The wife's salary is needed for a couple's continued membership in the middle class.

Consequently, increasing numbers of couples are limiting or deferring having children. New mothers are returning to work shortly after having children because the family can't manage on one income. The result may be frustration, anger, or resentment. Those feelings are not always directed at the husband, but they affect the marriage and are distressful to both the husband and wife.

Money Management

Often money is used as a weapon or source of power and control over a spouse. When there is additional income it frequently becomes a matter of contention if the distribution and expenditure of that joint income fails to take account of the opinions and views of both parties who contribute to it. The resulting stress for either party must be considered. It can be disruptive and substantially hurt the balance of the family.

Basically, couples deal with the wife's paycheck in five different ways.

1. The more traditional couples regard the husband as the sole financial provider and frequently regard the wife's income as "pin money" for her to spend as she pleases. Her work is secondary to her household responsibilities and her husband has ultimate veto power over what the wife purchases. He may disapprove of her salary being used for such things as a separate vacation or a piece of furniture he regards as extravagant. Otherwise, the wife's earnings are often ignored. Fewer than 10 percent of couples now think it's right for a wife to keep a private hoard.

2. A large proportion of working couples—perhaps 40 percent—include the wife's money in the family budget but often segregate it for a special purpose or special bank account. Wives like having a visible intended purpose for their income as visible evidence, though it is generally considerably less than their husbands', that they have contributed to the budget.

3. Close to half of all working couples prefer pooling their

earnings and budgeting the total together. For most couples, however, pooling means careful planning and strong communication in
setting priorities. Some families find it difficult to give the partner
with smaller earnings, generally the wife, as big a voice in family
decisions as the partner who contributes the lion's share.

4. Another way of handling money is bargaining, carefully planning who is responsible for what and dividing household expenses.
The partners have separate accounts and own as little as possible
jointly. These couples are in the minority, but they recognize money
is important and feel this is the most viable solution to keep it from
spoiling the relationship.

5. In some cases, the wife's money is regarded as hers alone,
when, for example, it is a dowry, or when it is not needed to support
the family.

Factors such as both partners' attitudes toward money, work, and
roles influence the amount of stress in the two-career family. If they
express their feelings, respect themselves and each other, and do
not have "hidden agendas" that corrode their mutuality, couples will
have reason to celebrate the wife's salary.

Wives with High Income

However, if the wife inherits or earns more money than her
husband, new tensions may result. Such cases include the wife who
is a performing artist, writer, physician, scientist, or able executive.

The wife's higher income may be perceived as a threat, and the
husband may feel emasculated. If they have grown up feeling that a
man's salary determines his self-worth, he may feel "put down" and
inferior in his wife's eyes. The wife may share this viewpoint or may
develop a sense of guilt about being more successful than her
husband. Social contacts may intensify these problems if the man is
referred to as Mrs. S's husband. All these factors might combine to
reduce the husband's self-esteem and his wife's respect for him. If
that is the case, there may be repercussions in their sex life, decision
making, and other areas of their married life.

Money is a volatile issue. It has unique associations and meanings
for different people. If the couple is not open with each other or is
locked into traditional sex-role stereotypes, the stress of money
decisions will affect their entire relationship. Marriage is, after all,
partly an economic arrangement—in all cultures.

In addition to conflicting shifts in power in the two-career marriage, there are increasing conflicts related to energy levels. Diminished sexual drive and/or lowered frequency of sexual intercourse are fairly common. Sheer exhaustion, lack of time, and lack of concentration after heavy work and family schedules can diminish the emotional and physical energy available for interpersonal relationships. This distancing is not only from the spouse, but also from children and the social network. All three ordinarily supply a positive support network and having no time or energy for them can lead to a breakdown in a person's well-being if he or she is estranged for long periods of time.

Covert hostility when the wife earns more than the husband or when her job competes with the time and attention she used to give him can result in overt jealousy or petty arguments, sulking, or sexual passivity. Many women lose some interest in sex after having children, and some still regard sex as merely the price to be exacted for their economic protection.

Some couples arrange their lives so that they are constantly busy, tired, or tense. One of the critical issues is whether being preoccupied is a defense against intimacy and sexuality, or whether it in fact represents a reality that is difficult to postpone or avoid. For instance, sexual fulfillment is one element in the wide range of expectations a husband and wife may have. There are marriages in which the delicate balance in a stressful relationship can be tipped in the direction of breakdown by sexual disappointment, frustration, or frigidity.

For some people who work very hard, sex enhances their productivity. It releases tension, provides pleasurable relaxation, and maintains intimate communication with the spouse. For others, sex interferes with the work project. They lack the time, energy, and physical desire to pursue an active sex life. Sex may then be a forced endeavor, an accommodation, a duty, or practically nonexistent.

Frequently, the overstressed spouse has lost touch with feelings—the medium of exchange in an intimate relationship. Such time-honored coping strategies as "Don't worry about it" or keeping busy can be maladaptive if used with lack of awareness of the emotional aspects of the situation.

Perhaps there is overt denial that there are emotional aspects and repercussions when a couple's life is so fully scheduled with work that there is no time for closeness. A "conspiracy of silence" frequently develops. Communication breaks down as feelings are buried alive to keep the peace. Unfortunately, the issues and feelings are only covered up, not deactivated. A person may become a walking mine field, touched off by the slightest provocation, exploding inwardly against himself or outwardly against family, friends, or work associates. One or both partners can easily be tempted into extramarital affairs, with divorce a possible result.

On the other hand, a general improvement in the climate of the marital relationship, the resolution of a stubborn conflict, a breakthrough to more genuine communication, the clarification of goals and values, can reactivate warmth and tenderness, enrich the sexual relationship, and generally enhance a person's well-being and outlook on life and work.

SUMMARY

A person must learn to distinguish between the transient "unbalancing" effects produced by occupational stress—including his or her interaction with life-cycle issues (Chapter 5)—and underlying personal, marital, or family pathology.

There are at least 10 significant areas in which excessive job demands may have an unbalancing effect and potentially negative impact on home and family life:

Geographic location and/or relocation
Personal relationship between husband and wife
Spouse's physical and mental state and habits at home
Couple's social life—singly and together
Both spouses' relationship with their children
Spouse's participation in home activities
Weekend and vacation time
Couple's involvement in common and separate leisure pursuits
Community role model
Spouse's health and safety

Increasingly, the work arena is becoming the context in which most people meet fundamental psychological needs. The marital contract closely resembles the psychological contract between person and organization, with implicit and unconscious expectations that change over time and that are binding upon the parties to them.

One must also appreciate sources of stress in the workaday world, as well as the fact that the influx of women into the workplace has produced marital and family stresses. The changing status of women and dependency relationships are prominent problems. Fear of abandonment and trepidation about the effects of employment or unemployment tend to increase marital stress.

Of course, we have not listed all the potential stressors in a marriage, but we have pointed out several of the most common. By developing your overall awareness of marital stressors as a means of improving your own stress tolerance, you can also develop a better understanding of this source of stress in your co-workers. This understanding will help you to reduce the potentially damaging effects by enabling you to face the accumulation of life stress as a business problem and to deal with it creatively.

CONCLUSION

What relevance does the employee's marital, sexual, and family life have to industrial stress? A great portion of any organization's effectiveness derives directly from the personal effectiveness of its employees. The physical health and mental well-being of these employees directly affects the quality of the overall operation. People invest not only their talents but the rest of themselves as well.

Everyone experiences job stress to some extent. If the stress level is within the tolerance zone of the employee or is motivational in character, he or she can function effectively and deal with the job as a constructive and satisfying part of life. However, if the stress level is outside the limits for a particular employee, or sufficiently distressful, it will inevitably create problems both in job performance and in personal health and well-being.

A person's well-being is affected by his or her own distinct combination of life stress, job stress, and stress relief skills. A manager must deal with the effects of the sum total of a person's stress experiences. For example, an office worker whose job tasks do not involve any unusual degree of pressure, who works with fairly congenial people, and who receives supportive supervision from the employer may suffer from a number of difficult problems in his private life. If so, he will be operating outside the comfort zone for much of the time, even though no specific feature of the work situation involves an unreasonable level of pressure. When an employee is suffering from chronic stress, he is generally not able to function at or achieve his full potential and effectiveness.

In general, chronic distress means a continuing deterioration in the quality of a person's life. As mentioned earlier, life stress is the sum total of unrelieved stress the person feels. Life stress depends greatly on the overall balance of activities and experiences in one's life. The organizational costs of unmanaged stress derive directly from the collective individual costs.

Some people escape from uncomfortable stress feelings by alcohol abuse, drug abuse, overeating, or isolation from others. A person with a drinking problem almost always reduces his job effectiveness, damages his interpersonal relationships, and jeopardizes his health.

Similarly, drug addiction, whether in the form of cocaine, tobacco, marijuana, heroin, morphine, or tranquilizers, interferes with the ability to carry on the normal business of living and often leaves the user foggy, detached, and dependent on the drug in a vicious cycle that tends to make reality all the more unrewarding and oblivion all the more attractive.

In addition to the fact that an overstressed person works well below par in his own job, as mentioned in Chapter 2, he becomes a stress carrier and disrupts the work of other employees and of the organization in general. An employee who insults or affronts customers or who snaps at fellow workers has a negative impact on the organization's effectiveness, although it may be rather difficult to isolate and quantify that impact. In addition, other employees may have to take over parts of the work or redo work improperly done by the problem person.

Some people escape from uncomfortable stress by overeating. An overweight appearance makes fat people less attractive to others, makes them less inclined to exercise and enjoy physical activities, and causes them to tire easily. However, overeating proves to be only a temporary solution to stress and creates more problems. These effects certainly represent a loss in the quality of life and productivity of these people.

Many people seem to have difficulties with their personal lives and many of these difficulties spill over into job performance and attitudes. Stress reduction training can enable these people to gain greater control over their lives in general and consequently to function more effectively on the job.

The organization can help its employees deal more successfully with their lives for their mutual benefit. This is not to suggest invading anyone's privacy. Rather, organizations should recognize the opportunities they can provide to improve human effectiveness on and off the job. The basic ability to control one's reaction level, de-escalate the internal arousal level, interact with others in low-stress styles, and reorganize one's activities can help the work team in many ways. When the members of the team learn how to cope effectively with emotional problems, difficulties with liquor or drugs, poor personal relationships, and living habits that endanger their health, the improved sense of well-being will ultimately be reflected positively on the bottom line.

CHAPTER 7
Social Stereotyping and Stress

Many people still hold stereotyped views of "others"—men and women, black and white, Protestant and Jew, handicapped, young and old, and those of different ethnic origins. Social stereotyping in the workplace, as in society at large, can ultimately be detrimental to the health of a corporation and to the people who perpetuate these attitudes. Stereotyping, discrimination, and prejudice can be distressing factors in dealing with other people and can produce unhealthy encounter stress.

OBSTACLES TO COHESIVE EFFORT

Racial and cultural diversity may be obstacles to cohesion within an organization and interpersonal relations may frequently be strained. People viewing others as members of a class, race, or sex, rather than as individuals, frustrate communication. The focus, instead of being on situation at hand, is on a generalization incorporating assumptions about predictable behavior and/or characteristics.

Even generalizations that may correctly apply to a group can be misleading when applied to any particular person in the group. That is, two things may be labeled alike (black, woman, manager) and yet act quite differently. No two people or events are identical. Attributing an automatic response to members of certain groups does not allow for individual expression, creative problem solving, or personal acknowledgment, much less one's own personal growth.

NEGATIVE FEEDBACK

In addition to setting up barriers to communication, creativity, and individualism, social stereotyping frequently gives negative feedback and undermines the situation. If a person is told enough times that he cannot handle something or that he has a certain problem, self-fulfilling prophecy can come into play. The stereotyped behavior may materialize and be reinforced as the person internalizes others' concept of him. A person's self-esteem and well-being are heavily influenced by the social network around him. A positive, encouraging milieu can motivate one to greater achievement, while alienation or a negative environment can produce toxic levels of distress.

SUSPICION

Alliances are shaky in a power structure that appears to require or at least permit an adversary relationship or a scapegoat. The pecking order eventually affects everyone. Hence, members of minority groups tend to be guarded in their relationships and associations on the job. The underlying suspicion of others as potential adversaries or threats to status or job keeps the body in a constant state of preparedness, ready to strike or defend. This preparedness is wearing on the body and mind and drains energy and attention that could otherwise be used more productively.

INHIBITING FACTOR

An organization with a governing philosophy that focuses on differences and comparisons factionalizes its workforce rather than mobilizing the available variety of a group's dynamic resources. By limiting participation, discrimination prevents people from achieving your corporate goals, for which they are equipped when you hire them or toward which they aspire. As a consequence, they tend to drop in performance and lose a sense of personal dignity and worth. Their lowered self-esteem results in increased anxiety, defensiveness, and aggression.

The woman or man learns to fear retaliation if aggression is expressed overtly and feels he or she must control the expression of some impulses "insiders" may express more freely. Therefore, that person compensates in one of a variety of ways. The result is that internal stress is increased and spontaneous expression is inhibited.

COMPENSATORY REACTIONS

One compensatory mechanism is underreaction—a general apathy and depression accompanied by feelings of isolation and passivity. Increased absenteeism, frequent visits to the health center, a work slowdown, or intentional mistakes may be the employee's way of asserting his power and venting his frustrations.

Another coping behavior is more overt and has the potential of distressing others in the work environment. Weak self-esteem is bolstered by overreaction—the attempt to raise aspirations evei higher and aggressively to emulate the standards of "insiders." Bu overreaction antagonizes others, and their response brings on more self-contempt and more desperate efforts to counter it.

As a last resort, physical violence, vandalism, industrial espionage, and even suicide can be the extremes to which some people will go to fight back at a system they feel keeps them down and frustrates their individual merits.

THE SEARCH FOR A COMMON GROUND

The personalities of all people are a product of adaptation to a specific environment. The environment of an oppressed minority imposes more stress upon the individual and offers less adequate opportunities for adaptation than are afforded to the majority. Outsiders trying to break into the system, with its rules and structure that may seem ambiguous to them, are under a great deal of stress.

Insiders understand and support each other, the structure, and the rules. These people share common aspirations and dreams, grow up with similar backgrounds, play together, learn together, and compete by the same rules. Their rules of behavior, style of communication, and modes of relationship grow out of their developmental experience.

But their knowledge of how others live may be limited. Increased awareness of how different peoples see the world challenges all people. They need to make an effort to find more common ground and a workable understanding in order to establish a productive working relationship and reduce stress.

Given the complexity of interaction with other people, stereotyping becomes a shortcut to pseudoadjustment. It has served as a way of abstracting a number of behavioral qualities, organizing them into a pattern of expectations, and responding to the person as though he automatically fit the pattern. Stereotypes can lead to accurate predictions only when they are based on rather well-structured roles and on accurate knowledge of the groups concerned.

Adapting to our changing times means constantly updating our information. Stereotypes are carryovers from the past and are based on generalizations of how certain types of people have been perceived rather than on individual evaluations of people as they are. The error in prejudging is greater when the person has less experience and has not unlearned the erroneous stereotype. This person is basing his attitudes and behavior on a source of information that is unreliable, inadequate, and misleading.

Distress would seem to be inherent in prejudiced behavior because that behavior is frequently based on misinformation, erecting barriers to the clear communication and understanding necessary to change prejudice. A great deal of stress in interrelations happens because they are based on inadequate and inaccurate data. This deficiency leads people to construct—or perpetuate—stereotypes that are invalid. Stereotypes cause people to make inaccurate predictions about behavior and potential. This misfit can lead to anxiety and bad feelings, anger, disappointment, and hostility on the part of both the prejudiced person and his victims.

New developments in social values, changes in family life, changing roles for men and women, and the restructuring of business invalidate some of the stereotyped responses in which people have found security in the past. The influx of women, diverse cultures, and racial minorities into the white male working environment has necessitated adaptive responses on the part of both the newcomers and the establishment.

Even when businessmen attempt to do something about the so-called social issues, they may unconsciously reinforce their own biased attitudes by treating most women and minorities as if they were a defined group with common or homogeneous ambitions and demands, instead of treating them as individuals. That members of a minority group are all alike is a particularly convenient assumption in corporate life, since the easiest way to deal with a group is to use rhetoric and make small concessions.

It is much easier to justify the way things are by giving in to women on small points, for example, than to deal with the individual problems. It is more comfortable to discuss "the national problem of housing for minority groups" than to deal comfortably with the real black family that has moved in next door. It is also easier to talk about the company policy toward women than to face the fact that it is difficult for some men to fit women into an existing hierarchy, with all its collective masculine assumptions.

It is just as true that men fall into the habit of treating women as members of a separate and rival group as that some women stereotype men on a similar basis. Until people free themselves from fixed attitudes toward one another, the misunderstandings will continue to produce stressful situations on the job, with a subsequent drain on productivity.

Seeing other people as stereotypes, whether from fear or habit, makes us into stereotypes ourselves. There is a growing general humanistic trend that says that each person should be able to fulfill himself, free of discrimination, stereotyping, and prejudice. There is a general culturewide protest against artificial barriers to meeting the demand of the ego ideal for anybody in any part of society.

When a person's goals are blocked by virtue of some artificial barrier—skin color, religion, or sex—without his even being given an opportunity to prove himself, frustration, anger, and hopelessness may result. Lack of control in determining your own fate because you are being held back on the basis of something you can't possibly control is particularly distressing.

THE LAW

Equal Employment Opportunity and Affirmative Action legislation mandates equal opportunity. However, that doesn't mean that people who have traditionally been discriminated against can automatically take advantage of whatever access to opportunity now exists. They may not have the ability, or they just may not be accepted. Beliefs, attitudes, and assumptions that people have about themselves and others, and their resulting willingness or unwillingness to accept each other, are almost untouched by law alone.

The random hiring by quota of females with black, Latin, Asian, or other ethnic characteristics more often than not sets them up for failure and frustration and confirms white stereotypes. It does little to change the basic social setting that limits the development of their potential. The laws mandating equal opportunity provided the impetus for change. The implementation of the spirit of the law is up to individuals on a day-to-day basis.

WOMEN IN THE WORKPLACE

As we have already noted throughout Part I, change is stressful. It often requires a readjustment in attitudes, beliefs, and behaviors; and these adaptations come slowly and not without discomfort. Perhaps the biggest change to be faced today is the large-scale entry of women into the work environment.

Large numbers of women have entered the workforce, and they will continue to demand jobs, opportunities, and pay commensurate with their qualifications. Also, the decline in the institution of marriage, optional parenting, and the women's movement have dramatically increased the number of working women, career single women, and female heads of household. Men have to deal with all their feelings about a "woman's place," their sense of rivalry, and their attitudes about women's abilities. Women, on their part, for some time to come will learn even more about competing with men in a previously exclusively male world.

Sometimes women feel themselves to be at a disadvantage because they are women. Some don't like themselves for being women, and they tend to overcompensate by intense competitiveness. That kind of competitiveness, usually resisted, undermines their relationships with their colleagues. They then blame their failure on prejudice. Although society is moving toward a state in which sex roles may become less distinguishable, the fact of the matter is that there are two genders, with physical, physiological, and culturally imbued differences.

Given the present male-dominated organizational structure throughout the American business world, the thrust to open up the promotion paths so that women have truly equal opportunities to reach the top will probably meet with an enormous resistance on the part of both some men and some women. The result of the collision of these two powerful forces is hard to predict; but it certainly spells upheaval in the current ways of doing work, of assigning responsibilities, of apportioning power, and of carrying on the everyday politics of business.

Expectations and Rules

The stress resulting from this conflict has evolved over a long period of time and cannot be solved overnight. During the 1950s and early 1960s, millions of white men took jobs in American corporations. These men went to work accepting the then given set of rules, expectations, and promises for their future. Within a decade, the black movement, stimulated by federal legislation and social pressure, called for the inclusion of blacks at every level of employment. Consequently, the original expectations and rules that existed when those white men went to work were changed as the degree of unexpected competition they faced increased.

No sooner had this generation of white men begun to adjust to all the changes the black movement brought to their career lives than the woman's movement began calling for equal employment opportunities for all women. The impact on the corporation was far-reaching. Many people felt confused, hostile, and bitter.

When we talk about the equal opportunity issue, it concerns expanding the numbers of people who will compete in a setting critical to every individual who has to work there. We are talking about a very human subject. It is a highly stressful topic that touches deeply the personal beliefs, assumptions, values, and emotions of every individual involved. Many women employed at lower levels of power resent having woman bosses, and the aggressiveness of some women who are overcompensating makes dealing with them abrasive for both sexes.

New Employees, New Stresses

Historically outsiders to American business life, women and minorities are now being assisted by a federal mandate to play a more vital role in the corporation. They bring with them new perspectives, different backgrounds, and sometimes new languages and customs. We know from group dynamics that the addition of each new person into a group changes the composition, status, and direction of the organization. As women and minorities enter new areas of industry, the stresses and adjustments called for are multiplied for both newcomers and old-timers.

In most organizations, the law controls the formal structure. But the informal structure is where the decision is made as to how equality is or is not implemented. The law opens the door to minorities and women. The informal structure determines how far they can go once they are inside.

Traditionally, the informal structure has been composed of and ruled by the typical white Anglo-Saxon Protestant male. Its forms, rules of behavior, style of communication, and mode of relationships grew directly out of the predominant white male culture. The different beliefs and assumptions women and minorities hold about themselves and others and about organizations and careers bring about changes in the organization. These changes are the result of different styles, different emphases, and very different ways of responding to situations and identifying problems on a day-to-day basis.

Still, many women and minorities find themselves obligated to act on the basis of deep-rooted assumptions, rooted in old perceptions and behavior. Because they do not share these assumptions, their working lives are stressful. The process of socialization of each culture has structured their roles, relationships, and individual personalities. Certain values are selectively emphasized and the rules and procedures to attain them established. For the relative newcomer to the corporate world, organization priorities and expectations may be new and strange. Unless one understands those priorities and expectations, one cannot decide how to accept, reject, or modify them, to negotiate them, or to trade them off.

Each person brings a different mind set to work with him or her. Each needs to cope with the cultural and social biases at work. Basically, four interrelated issues are particularly important in coping with problems of bias encountered on the job.

Employee self-concept
Employee perception of other's concept of him
Employee definition of the role he is to play
Employee perception of others' definition of his role

As mentioned earlier, a person's self-esteem is particularly important. Incongruities between self-image and others' perception of you cause difficulty for anyone. Similarly, difficulties in finding agreement in role definition pose problems in relations with others at work. It is in conforming to others' concept of the job role (manager, executive) that the particular person tends to lose his individuality and to become a social stereotype.

For instance, because the executive role is seen by many people as exclusively male, no matter who a particular woman is, she may be regarded first and foremost as a woman and therefore may not even be considered for the executive position. As a consequence, all too often, because of fundamental identity issues, her superiors may perceive little fit between her and the administrative position, no matter how well qualified she is.

Then there is a negative fit between the woman's ideological self-concept and her perception of herself as she really is: the inevitable result is concern, worry, and anxiety. Her self-confidence falters and she may become tense and angry when she feels that she is not seen as the person for the job only because she is a woman.

Many men and some women believe that women are biologically unfit for certain jobs. Women are stereotyped as emotional, passive, submissive, security minded, sustaining, and receptive. A perception of these characteristics as inherent may exclude them from the supposedly rational, active, risk-taking, creative, aggressive, and competitive behavioral requirements for succeeding in business.

Since society has traditionally agreed on the female stereotype, to deviate from the "norm" is considered unfeminine and negative. A successful businesswoman is commonly regarded as aggressive, masculine, hard, and cold. Such stereotypes appear to pit achievement against femininity and make the two mutually exclusive. Efforts to attain the best of both worlds create tensions and anxieties in some women who seek career advancement, because of their own conflicting role perceptions or their fight against the outside world's conception of what they should be.

The increasing numbers of women taking professional positions in business have had an enormous impact on the corporate world. Some men must deal with female bosses and peers for the first time, and women executives find themselves in pioneer roles for which there are no precedents and no models to emulate except men. Feelings of loneliness and lack of sufficient familiarity in any setting produce stress. Women who attempt to solve this problem merely by imitating stereotyped men may be as ineffectual—or uncomfortable—as men would be in imitating stereotyped women in the work world.

Changing Roles

Many people react negatively toward women in the professions as a result of the assumptions they hold about who men and women are supposed to be. Until recently, distinctions between male and female roles were rather clear-cut, and a cooperative or reciprocal relationship was presumed to exist. Today, women's liberation has added an incredible amount of pressure on both men and women as they seek to redefine their roles and relationships. Achieving some harmony on the differences and samenesses between men and women requires a thorough understanding of the biophysiological differences between male and female, an ability to cope with the conflicting role definitions, and an attempt to bridge the gap among the various points of view.

Certainly there are men and women who are prejudiced against women. There are also men who feel personally threatened by competent women and who will act to defend themselves. But their actions are typical of any person who perceives a threatening situation. Given the history of sex-role stereotyping, many men believe that it is unfair that work that has been defined as such a significant component of their masculinity can and is being done just as effectively by women.

As difficult as it is for anyone to succeed, women carry the additional burden of a cultural and social tradition in which they are not supposed to compete with men in the same way men compete with each other. Some women share this view or are stressed by the role conflict of what a woman "should" and "shouldn't" be doing. An increasing number of women today are motivated to succeed but are frustrated by the realities of the still male-dominated working world.

Ceiling to Success

Women are doing a far greater variety of jobs than they used to, but the upper reaches of success in American corporate life are still masculine. Some companies shy away from giving women upper-level positions because they fear the effect this will have on other employees—particularly men. Opinion is colored by the instinctive male fear of successful women. "If she were a man, the job would be hers. . . ." Frequently this is true, but social pressures block her from promotion to a more prestigious, more responsible, and better paid position "The stockholders don't like women in high-level positions. They just don't trust a woman with their money."

Women have generally found there is a ceiling to their success. It is easy for them to get to the $25,000 mark, possible for them to reach the $50,000 mark, but extremely difficult for them to rise above that. No matter how much money a company pays a woman or how much she makes for the company, when it comes to the long-term management of the company, the door closes.

Many of the critical decisions of running a business are still made over a drink at the golf course or in the steam room and a woman is excluded from these arenas. A competent woman may have great talent, but few people want to believe she has a real head for business. She is frozen out at the highest levels of management despite real or even very superior ability.

Women's median earnings are 57 percent of the median earnings for men. In 1978, 35 percent of women held clerical jobs, 18 percent were service workers, and 5 percent were managers and administrators.

FUTURE NEEDS

The reality of today and tomorrow is that most people who work will work because they have to in order to survive. As the pressure to work increases, the need to free employees from stereotyped roles will be imperative. The issue of including women and minorities in the ranks of higher positions, higher pay, and greater responsibility in modern organizations is not just an issue of social justice or legal justice. In the end it is an issue of economic justice that derives from the need of these people to support themselves and their families. Also, organizations cannot afford to overlook the great reservoir of much-needed talent among minorities and women.

Our society, and corporations in particular, can no longer afford to perpetuate social stereotypes that measure and maintain the differences between men and women or between majority and minority. American industry is confronted by the threat of legal action and social judgment; but perhaps more importantly, in the long run, by the economic needs of women and the minorities for survival. Today's equal opportunity employment means tomorrow's survival for individuals, families, and corporations.

A possible critical issue in the future is that more people may need jobs than there will be jobs available. The long-term drop in population after the postwar baby boom in the late 1940s may eventually ease the situation. However, no immediate relief is in sight from either competition in the job market or spiraling inflation.

Both situations are highly stressful. Consequently, corporations and individuals alike must deal with these critical issues of the future and be prepared to respond to the accompanying problems with viable solutions. The need for cooperation and a coalition of employees and employers, men and women, and majority and minority to resolve these challenges is clear.

We must find the strength in our common humanity. Working from that shared strength, we can reduce the tensions that threaten all our rights to a rewarding work life. If we can achieve rewarding work lives, everyone will benefit, including the corporation.

CHAPTER 8

Corporate Social Responsibility

The issue of corporate responsibility affects the thinking of execu-tives on the subject of business ethics. The two are intertwined in the complex of pressures that confront people in the work environ-ment today and produce health-damaging stress if not dealt with effectively.

Changes in all aspects of the organization's relationship with society and its local community, including the environmental im-pacts of its operation, challenge the basic values of the corporation as a sociotechnical system. In order to maintain the stability of the organization, changes must be anticipated. The organization can then work out strategic adaptations to the changes and follow constructive paths for planned change and stress reduction.

The previous chapters have explored some of what is happening in the country, in the work environment, and in the lives of most employees. Increased awareness of current circumstances is the single most important asset for bringing about adaptive change in order to build a quality of human life that befits twentieth-century society and that is increasingly in demand.

More and more, public attention is focusing on the forms of interaction between the corporation and its environment. Problems such as the pollution of streams and rivers, thermal pollution, landscape destruction, and possible extreme danger to population centers from nuclear power plants have caused intense feelings in the public, private, government, and business sectors of America. The effects of corporate activity are profound, and corporate responsibility has many dimensions (see Figure 5). The issues of corporate responsibility must be constructively dealt with in order to reduce stress to the organization and to individuals and society.

While society reaps the benefits of an industrialized nation, more

FIGURE 5. *Three major dimensions of corporate responsibility.*

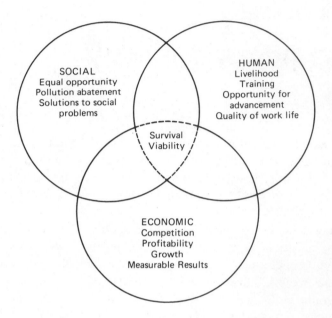

and more people are becoming aware of the price paid for all the progress. Many people are calling for a halt or stay in technological expansion until the costs to the quality of life can be determined more accurately. The basic criterion for filtering out certain technical innovations and applying others has been economic profitability. Increasingly, society is trying to learn what the long-term effects of new technology are and who profits from them.

The large corporation is a fact of life in the business world as we know it. As corporate power increases, the corporation's social responsibilities will increase in scope and complexity. It will be called upon to use its power and capabilities in response to societal needs and personal expectations.

Technological progress in the Western world has advanced a standard of living unparalleled in history or in any other area of the globe. The American people are better fed, clothed, sheltered, entertained, educated, and medically treated than our forefathers dreamed possible. American business has helped bring about this satisfaction of our basic needs, and people are looking to it to approach still higher planes of satisfaction on the levels of respect, recognition, confidence, and self-actualization.

These growing demands have brought about an increased sensitivity to the social costs of economic activity. The concept of corporate social responsibility focuses corporate power on objectives that are possible, but sometimes less economically attractive than socially desirable.

Today's corporate executive is challenged to meet the needs of five major publics:

1. Customers/consumers
2. Employees
3. Shareholders
4. Suppliers
5. Government and community agencies

In the past, the social responsibilities of business were simply to use resources efficiently and without deception or fraud. The dual purpose was to provide useful products and services to satisfy a public need and to make a profit. This definition has greatly expanded today.

A growing number of social activists see corporations as operating only in their own narrowly defined self-interests. They view the corporation as a selfish, greedy, profit-directed enterprise with little or no sense of responsibility or accountability to the country at large for the consequences of its operation.

Public awareness and distrust of business ethics are heightened by media headlines of collusion, price fixing, illegal payoffs overseas, bribes, and illegal political contributions. There is no question but that the credibility of business has been hurt by these disclosures. The public is cynical about a corporate president who expresses righteous indignation about the unethical business operations of others and announces what his or her company is doing to set standards.

Many critics suspect that while the corporation president is extolling selfless interests publicly, the corporation continues its self-seeking, often illegal, practices in private. Uneasiness increases when they contemplate the existence of corporate power in the hands of managers who (except in crisis situations) are answerable only to themselves or to boards of directors they have themselves selected.

SOCIAL RESPONSIBILITY AND PROFIT

The ever increasing demand for the corporation to make itself socially accountable for the sum total of its activities and operations is interpreted to mean that social responsibility ranks on a par with profit. Yet how much easier are the platitudes of virtue than the effective combination of profitable and socially responsive corporate action.

Over the past decade, many organizations have taken measures to make the total corporate enterprise fit within the overall need structure of American society. Nevertheless, others are bogged down in court battles defending their practices and operations, preferring to risk stiff fines rather than spend as much or more rebuilding their systems or relocating their factories.

The moral pressure on individual executives and their corporations is becoming unexpectedly and increasingly acute in today's highly competitive and more open business environment. Many executives are stress ridden because of a dichotomy between their business and their personal ethics. Tensions can arise from conflicts between an individual's ethical sense and the realities of business.

Few men in positions of authority and responsibility in the business world consciously breach the general code of morality. However, their consciences may be inoperative or relaxed. They may make their decisions without considering the moral implications of the course of action to which they are committing themselves and their corporations.

Specialists in the fields of accounting, personnel, engineering, and other phases of management bring their professional training to bear on corporate decisions. Businessmen immersed in their special fields frequently have little experience with social questions beyond their field of expertise and their own ambitions.

Still, social activists expect them to have the intelligence, knowledge of issues, compassion, and morality to factor social responsibility into economic decisions. But formal training in social problems and ethics is not a prerequisite for an M.B.A. Nor is the general public as skilled as critics would have the corporations be.

ETHICAL STANDARDS

The elusive character of ethics poses many stressful situations in the course of business. There are a lot of gray areas within which honorable men may differ. For instance, it is distressing for some people to deny a raise to a man who deserves it, to approve advertising copy that they believe to be misleading, or to conceal facts that they feel the stockholders or customers are entitled to know.

On a broader scale, the questions of numbers manipulation, padded expense accounts, and payoffs to foreign governments to secure contracts are some of the ethical dilemmas confronting businessmen today.

There is substantial disagreement among businessmen as to whether ethical standards have changed in the contemporary business environment. This disagreement is not surprising if we view the organization as a reflection of the shifting values, norms, and conduct of our entire society. The very nature of the compromises being made by some companies has often altered corporate behavior that once would have caused ethical discomfort but now frequently has become accepted as routine.

Like other professions, business is continually scrutinizing its behavior relative to the moral values and duties of the profession itself and the standards and expectations of the society around it. Because moral values are created by fallible people, they generally have some contradictions as they are put into practice according to each individual's information and belief.

Furthermore, standards and ethics may vary among the different sectors of society—business, church, family, political parties. Confusion, conflict, and uncertainty may arise as you move from one group to the next, from one set of standards and expectations to another. Thus, it is inevitable that businessmen face the stress of ethical dilemmas on a day-to-day basis.

CONSCIENCE VS. JOB

Superiors can cause a lot of stress by demands that produce ethical conflicts in the employee. Typical complaints are of pressures from superiors to:

Support incorrect or dangerous viewpoints
Sign false documents
Overlook superiors' wrongdoing or incompetency
Do business with superiors' friends

Employ marginally qualified minorities in order to meet affirmative action quotas

Where the action required is unqualifiedly repugnant to a person's conscience, distress is induced. Does he accept the judgment of his superior, carry out his instructions, and keep his objections to himself? Or does he breach the corporate chain of command and go over the superior's head, possibly jeopardizing both his and his superior's positions?

Of course, the third alternative is to quit. However, the consequences may be devastating, adding even more stress in his own life. The threat to his financial security, his reputation in the industry, the welfare of his family, and his career plans may be almost beyond his powers of coping. The dilemma of choosing between his job and his honor is particularly wearing on his body, mind, and spirit.

Clearly, ethical dilemmas do exist that are too often resolved in ways that leave executives dissatisfied. That is, when compromises are made that infringe upon a person's self-image as an ethical person, unexpressed feelings can accumulate that promote a damaging buildup of stress.

One way of coping with the question of unethical practices is to accept them as a routine part of doing business. Another is to accept general precept codes rather than formulate specific practice codes. A third is to become cynical about the ethical standards of others, remaining aloof from personal responsibility but at the same time giving lip service to supporting strict ethical standards.

When we stop to evaluate these subtle ways of avoiding the issues, we realize that the problem is not that there are not enough moral men in business; it is basically the problem of short-term priorities taking precedence over long-term considerations—myopic planning.

SHORT-TERM PRIORITIES

The incentive system in most organizations today focuses attention on short-term quantifiable results. Once strategic and operating plans are put into effect, managers are evaluated according to how much of the plans they implement. Conventionally, performance is measured by short-run economic or technical results inside the corporation. The manager is given high marks for current accomplishment, with no estimate of the charges against the future that may have been made in the effort to implement the plan.

Consequently, since career progress depends on favorable judgments of quantifiable performance, upward-oriented executives at lower and middle levels are motivated to do well at what is measured and to focus their attention on the internal problems that affect immediate results.

The more tangible short-term results are, the more unlikely it is that a qualitative evaluation will be made of such long-term intangible processes as:

The social role of the plants in other communities

The quality of corporate life in satellite offices

The augmentation of organizational competence

The progress of programs for making work meaningful and exciting

The qualitative evaluation of individual and management development

With individuals as with organizations, survival takes precedence over social concern. Employees' interest in compensation and their desire for the recognition and approval of their superiors direct their attention to the short-term results they are asked to attain. The outcome is that good works, the results of which are long term and hard to quantify, do not receive the attention they should in an organization using conventional incentives and controls and exerting pressures for ever more impressive results.

The pressures on the highly moral and humane manager are obvious. Society and his own conscience call for social involvement, but his job security depends on economic efficiency and measurable results. As we have said, corporate and humane goals are not mutually exclusive, but the present system of rewards and penalties does not provide incentives or stimulate creativity to formulate long-range economic policies that embrace social issues.

BUSINESSMEN'S VALUES
Leadership of the Chief Executive Officer

A growing number of chief executives are translating their concern, compassion, and conviction into a corporate strategy for social responsiveness. The power and influence of the chief executive are great. Therefore, the CEO's determination to act can go a long way toward resolving such specific problems as management development, pollution abatement, and the employment, training, and advancement of minority representatives. This is especially true when the organization is small enough to be directly influenced by the chief executive's leadership.

Efforts to further corporate responsibility are somewhat impeded in the large, decentralized multinational corporation. Here the chief executive's moral convictions and values are reinterpreted and diffused throughout the management hierarchy at divisional, regional, district, and local levels. It is difficult to make the social component of a corporate strategy credible and effective, especially when filtered through managers who may not share the chief executive's determination or fervor, believe that he means what he says, or be motivated to make more than economic contributions to society. Cynicism, a by-product of impersonal bureaucracy, is another impediment to the communication of corporate social policy.

Management Uncertainty

Today's managers are often faced with situations in which they are required to commit themselves openly or tacitly to an action with which they may not agree for moral or other reasons. Or they may be participating, willingly or unwillingly, in activities that are morally and ethically cloudy, questionable from a business point of view, and perhaps of doubtful legality.

There are innumerable unclear, ill-defined areas of activity in which people find themselves. They may discover that they are following a course of action they believe is wrong, although often they're not sure of the ethics involved.

Game Ethics

Popular books on corporate politics, success, winning, and gamesmanship point out the subtleties of business ethics as game ethics, commonly accepted operational standards that are unconnected to the ethical standards of private life or religious ideals.

The game is played at all levels of corporate life, down through the ranks from the executives to the managers to the employees. Most businessmen at one time or another are deeply involved, in the interests of their companies or themselves, in numerous strategies of deception. Avoiding outright falsehoods, normal business practice does include conscious misstatements, built-in obsolescence, concealment of pertinent facts, and exaggeration. The justification is that business, as practiced by individuals as well as by corporations, has the impersonal character of a game, one that demands both special strategy and an understanding of its special ethics.

Most businessmen are not indifferent to ethics in their private lives, but in their office lives they cease to be private citizens and become game players guided by a somewhat different set of ethical standards. The business strategist's decisions are as impersonal as those of a surgeon performing an operation, concentrating on objective and technique and subordinating personal feeling. The major test of every move in business is to look for profit wherever and however the law permits.

The Luxury of Conscience

However, many an executive with a well-developed contemporary conscience is troubled by efforts to maintain his drive for success while living up to his personal standards. A practical question arises: If a man in a responsible corporate position finds that certain policies in his company are socially injurious, what can he do? He may feel that he cannot afford the luxury of a conscience.

For instance, an executive might be branded as having a negative attitude if he voices concern over serious environmental contamination for which his company is responsible. If he argues for a change in policies that are helping to keep net earnings high, he might be labeled by his superiors as "unrealistic" or "idealistic" and either be overlooked for promotion or (if he pushes too hard) compelled to resign.

If the executive keeps his opinions to himself, he might lose not only interest and enjoyment in his work but also respect for himself. If he changes companies, he would merely be exchanging one set of moral misgivings for another.

An executive who adheres to ethical standards disregarded by his associates is asking for trouble. For example, the man who refuses to take kickbacks from suppliers in a purchasing department where graft is rife threatens the security of those who do. Unless he conforms, they will undermine his position and edge him out.

"Damned if he does and damned if he doesn't" goes along with situational ethics; the businessman is stressed beyond healthy limits. The conscience is never killed. When ignored, it merely goes underground, where it manufactures the toxins of suppressed guilt, often with serious psychological and physical consequences.

Within the accepted rules of the business game is to distrust others, ignore any claim of friendship given with kindness and openheartedness, and believe that it is up to the other fellow to protect himself from the other players. This defensive behavior is not infrequently carried over into private life. The transferral of business conduct can be costly in terms of interpersonal relationships.

As we have seen in the previous chapters, a strong support system is important to maintain personal well-being. When neighbors, friends, and family are kept at a distance and interaction limited by MBO criteria, warm, relaxed, and open relationships may not be cultivated. The climb to the top of the corporate ladder becomes progressively more lonely, with the chief executive officer often experiencing the greatest degree of isolation.

This isolation is potentially unhealthy for the individual who lacks a genuine support system or sounding board. Another effect is that the distance between the executive and those under him can lead to a weakening of his ethical leadership as it is filtered down the line and into activities beyond his scrutiny.

Adding to the stress is the fact that many wives are not prepared to accept the fact that business operates with a social code of ethics. A spouse's perception of a problem is generally in terms of moral obligation as conceived in private life. She does not understand it in terms of game strategy. These divergent perspectives can create marital conflict and raise the executive's stress score.

A by-product of the situation is a breakdown in communications between the couple and frequent complaints of "She doesn't listen to me or understand what I go through all day" and "He keeps his work a secret and never shares anything with me." For example, rather than risk the wife's questioning of the morality of firing a longtime employee, who at 52 will have a lot of trouble getting another job, the businessman says nothing about what happened at the office. Yet his stomach is tied up in knots, and he reaches for the liquor cabinet to dull his conscience and to keep himself from asking whether he couldn't have handled it another way.

He asks himself whether it is worth it. The corporation executive is popularly envied for his relative affluence and respected for his powers of achievement, but his ethics are suspect to many people and possibly a cause of anxiety and stress to himself. On whom did he have to step before he could afford the luxury of conscience after reaching the top? The unfairly but widely held belief that most businessmen would try anything—honest or not—for a dollar is a significant clue to public opinion.

ORGANIZATIONAL VALUES

The concept of organizational values is one means by which to bring together complicated and sometimes confusing economic, social, and human issues. These values are the prevailing norms that guide, direct, or constrain the attitudes and actions of employees. They are just as real and operational as the organization's basic charter, plans, and formal policies.

The employees of the organization perceive these values, consciously or unconsciously, and react to them accordingly. The ethical dimension is present in a continuous, day-to-day way in actions and attitudes.

It is sometimes difficult for the employees of a company to adhere to ethics of honesty and fair play on the job when their top managers seem to bend the rules of ethical practice. By their combined actions over the long term, the top managers of an organization communicate the values they hold about the organization, its people, its mission, and its relationship to the surrounding society.

The extent to which businessmen are able to make progressive and constructive efforts in response to the new ethical imperatives in the decade ahead may have a decisive influence on the future of the free enterprise system, of the corporation as a viable sociotechnical force, and of the general quality of human life. In these days of strained credibility, American businesses must prove themselves against a widespread skepticism. The solutions the corporation chooses can improve the quality of life within the organization. If it does that, it will improve its functioning in a number of ways that will reduce long-term chronic stress and its damaging effect on human health and well-being. This will also have the cyclical effect of making the organization realize that what's good for the people is good for the company.

Eight key organizational values, when promoted in policy and procedures, can strengthen the overall health of the organization and its people:

1. *Equal employment opportunity and affirmative action programs*. The continued commitment to recruit, employ, and advance people who are qualified or qualifiable on the basis of merit and ability, regardless of race, religion, color, sex, handicap, or national origin can provide valuable resources to the corporation and reduce tension and frustration in the workforce from inequitable employment practices.

2. *Occupational safety and health*. Recognition of the company's obligation to protect the integrity of its human, physical, and financial resources is essential. To fulfill its obligation the company may have to design new facilities or redesign existing ones so they have the maximum health and safety features and activities.

3. *Rewarding of accomplishment*. A company whose policies take into account the entire range of ongoing and future compensation and benefit programs provides incentives for high levels of accomplishment. Salary and retirement systems that are competitive and responsive to changes in economic and social conditions provide financial security for employees.

4. *Human resources development*. A company committed to the training and education of its employees provides opportunities for them to challenge themselves, to grow and develop, and to perform meaningful and productive work. These opportunities are basic to a humanistic environment.

5. *Open communication*. An open communication system that solicits employees' opinions, answers their questions, and keeps them informed about the plans and progress of the company can greatly reduce distrust and misunderstanding in an organization. It can also reduce the stress aroused from uncertainty by clarifying goals and procedures and elevate self-esteem and respect by valuing what all levels of company representatives have to say.

6. *Employee health*. Recognizing the importance of physical health and well-being to the effectiveness of the organization

requires responsive programs to meet the needs of employees. Physical fitness, stress reduction, and drug and alcohol rehabilitation programs, if added to standard medical services, might head off many serious health problems.

7. *Social awareness and responsibility*. Company encouragement of employee involvement in the community supports its obligation to society. Many companies encourage their employees to respond as individuals to the concerns of energy conservation and traffic pollution, through financial and administrative sponsorship of commuter busing, van pools, and car pools. Civic action programs give employees opportunities to become active on a voluntary basis in civic and community affairs, charitable enterprises, politics, and government during the workday.

8. *Setting a good example*. The character of a company is simply a reflection of how its people think and act. The corporate reputation reflects the integrity and good judgment of all its employees in day-to-day activities. Top executives and their immediate second-level executives have the visibility, sense of direction, and control of resources to set the standards. However, in the final analysis, every individual is accountable.

CONCLUSION

There is increasing evidence that business managers see the corporation as a social, as well as economic, entity. Social responsibility, for both businessperson and the corporation, tends to be defined in terms of the social arrangements and obligations that make up the structure of the society. Ethics are the rules by which these responsibilities are carried out; it is difficult to separate the rules of the game from the game itself.

The meaning and consequences of a sense of social responsibility are frequently so vague as to render it essentially unworkable as a guide to corporate policy and decisions. This uncertainty is particularly stress producing for those called upon to bring social responsibility to the operating level without first having the corporation's role clearly defined in reality rather than in rhetoric.

Business executives and the companies they serve have a personal and vested interest in the resolution of ethical and social responsibility dilemmas. General precept codes, statements from business media, specific practice codes, social audits, and other measures help in meeting the challenge. Sensitivity to the social cost of doing business must be embodied in a strategy that makes a consistent whole of private economic opportunity and public social responsibility. The concept of corporate efficiency needs to be broadened to include social values in the context of long-range profitability.

The corporation is the dominant force; an integral part cannot be divided from the whole. In order to improve business, business will be impelled to improve society. The results will be profitable for both.

Part II
STRESS AND DISEASE

CHAPTER 9
The Physiological Results of Stress

We all possess the technical ability to reduce and control stress arousal and thus prevent stress-related illness. This potential is far from being fully developed, but great progress is being made in understanding the stress response and in developing useful techniques for achieving and maintaining a high level of health.

In Part III we present an overview of various methods that have gained some degree of acceptance in dealing with stress. Among them are progressive relaxation, systematic desensitization, autogenic training, the relaxation response, guided imagery, and numerous forms of medications. It is important to understand the potential of these and other methods for influencing the activity of the body's functions and for mobilizing our native physiological defenses.

It is helpful to review the chain of biological events touched off by our conscious and unconscious efforts to adapt to situations or pressures. These stimuli may appear as physical or symbolic external or internal threats. The physiological changes that take place in the body processes and electrochemical system are the same whether in response to joy, fear, anger, hunger, pain, or disease. Dr. Hans Selye defined them as "stress responses" in terms of a three-stage general adaptation syndrome (GAS) of the body's adaptive process.

By Selye's definition, stress is the nonspecific response of the body to any demand made upon it. As explained in Part I, stress occurs when there is a basic need to maintain life and to resist or adapt to changing external and internal influences. When the body is called upon to adjust in order to maintain normal stasis, it undergoes the general adaptation syndrome in response to the stressor. As we have discussed earlier, a stressor is any stimulus—positive or negative—that induces stress. Almost all living processes imply constant interaction between man and the environment and demand unremitting adjustments in order to survive.

Whatever the change within our environment, an enormous amount of physiological machinery comes into play. The whole body is involved. We have the effective central nervous systems that enabled our forebears to meet physical emergencies. However, contemporary man's conditions differ from those of his ancestors; physical activities are de-emphasized in favor of mental dominance, tool usage, and social organization.

The pathway from complex social environment and physical restraint to ill health is a complex one and involves total brain integration with bodily functions. Every system of the body is affected at some time in the stress response by nervous stimulation of an organ or nervous stimulation of the endocrine glands.

The stress reaction, first referred to in Chapter 1, is the process through which the human organism responds to any stress of any magnitude or duration.

STRESS AROUSAL

Briefly, a stressful event or chronically stressful condition produces a physiological and emotional response. First, let us examine the physiological response. A small collection of nerve cells in the brain, called the hypothalamus, perceives and picks up what is going on in the environment through neural pathways not yet fully identified. According to recent work, the hypothalamus, part of the limbic system, is a control center for the major regulatory functions of the autonomic nervous system and immune system. This major area of the brain provides the link between the nervous system and the endocrine system. Once the hypothalamus is stimulated, it prepares for possible action by increasing the discharge of hormones.

The hypothalamus produces substances known as endorphins or enkephalins, which activate the pituitary gland at the base of the brain. The pituitary gland, the body's "master gland," receives input via both neural and chemical processes. The function of the pituitary gland might best be described as one of integrating all hormonal activity of the body. Although the mechanism of this action is unclear, the effect of hormonal excesses as well as of deficiencies on the development of malignancy and other diseases has been fairly well documented. Severe depression from learning you have a terminal disease can start the circuit of limbic–hypothalamic–pituitary activity, resulting in an imbalance in hormone secretion or uptake and a decrease in the immune response.

In the activation of the pituitary gland, the chemical ACTH (adrenocorticotrophic hormone) is discharged into the bloodstream. When this hormone reaches the adrenal glands located just above the kidneys, it sets off a characteristic reaction in them. ACTH induces the external cortical portion of the adrenal glands (adrenal cortex) to secrete corticoids. These hormones elicit shrinkage of the thymus simultaneously with many other changes, such as atrophy of the lymph nodes, some of which can be felt in the sides of the neck, the armpits, or the groin. In addition, inflammatory reactions are inhibited, as is the production of sugar for a readily available energy source. These hormones can also lead to the development of peptic ulcers in the stomach and intestine, a process facilitated by the increased level of corticoids in the blood and mediated in part by the autonomic nervous system.

The second part of the adrenal gland, called the medulla, is the inner section of the gland and is surrounded by the adrenal cortex. The medulla receives an impulse from the hypothalamus via the sympathetic nervous system, and it immediately releases the hormone epinephrine, commonly known as adrenaline. The effect of this hormone is the "fight or flight" response that brings the body up to a highly aroused or active state.

Specifically, there is increased cardiovascular and metabolic activity. Heart rate and volume of blood increase and the body makes more efficient use of the available blood supply by constricting blood vessels in organs like the intestines and stomach that serve no function in the fight-or-flight response; thus, digestion is temporarily impeded. This allows an increased flow of blood to go to essential organs, such as the heart and skeletal muscles. Breathing becomes deeper, faster, and generally more efficient through expansion of the bronchials. The pupils of the eyes enlarge, making eyesight keener. The rate of salivary secretion decreases.

The secretion of adrenaline and other hormones reinforces and prolongs the sympathetic effect. Two of these primary hormones, secreted by the adrenal cortex when it is stimulated, are corticoids—cortisol and aldosterone.

Cortisol stimulates a metabolic process of the liver to release more blood glucose (by gluconeogenesis) either to fuel the body more efficiently during the accelerated period of activity or to recover from an extreme period of overactivity.

During the process of gluconeogenesis, both fats and proteins are mobilized in the blood. Prolonged stress can promote muscular wasting and impair the immune system by depleting the stores of protein in the body cells available for the formation of mature white cells and antibodies. Also, taking fat from the fat cells and circulating high levels of fat in the bloodstream appears to promote arteriosclerosis (hardening of the arteries). Furthermore, during the process of gluconeogenesis, cortisol decreases the use of glucose by muscle and fatty tissue, probably by making the system insulin resistant, thus producing a mild diabetic effect.

As a result of the increased amounts of aldosterone secreted during the stress response, the body makes certain other adjustments. These prepare it for increased muscular activity and improved dissipation of heat and waste products. For instance, the body retains extra sodium (as salt), which results in increased water retention. Also increased are blood volume, blood pressure, and the amount of blood the heart pumps out with each beat.

Because the bloodstream is the common communication and transport system for the entire body, these stress chemicals soon reach every cell in the body—journeying to the farthest point in less than eight seconds. Simultaneously, messages traveling throughout the nerve pathways alert heart, lungs, and muscles for increased action.

Short-lived physical arousal can be advantageous for man's survival when its biochemical by-products are dissipated through physical action. However, physical arousal of a chronic or highly intense nature when the physical defense mechanisms and processes are not dissipated or the supplies exhausted is physically detrimental to the system. Continuation of this stimulation–biochemical response–nondissipation process over a period of time can produce extremely dangerous effects on the body.

THE NERVOUS SYSTEM

It is essential to understand the concept of stress arousal by examination of the involvement of the central nervous system

(CNS). The brain cells (gray matter) and spinal cord are interwoven into a complex relay system that collects, stores, and transmits sensations and information throughout the human organism. The brain is always involved in the stress response, because each of the brain areas is responsible for the control of a particular part of the body or for a particular group of sensations or impulses.

The function of the brain is twofold: a voluntary system that we consciously control, and an automatic system that we cannot control easily, if at all. Understanding the function of these twin nervous structures supports better understanding of stress and how to control it.

The actions or behavior governed by these parts of the brain are natural, open, and direct, without learned inhibition. The basic instincts are stored in the hindbrain (lower brain center; see Figure 6). The physical boundaries of the brain can be delineated as three distinct layers, for the sake of simplicity and for our purposes here. These three layers are:

1. The brain stem or hindbrain
2. The limbic system interbrain
3. The cerebral cortex or forebrain

These structures, and their functions, include the spinal cord, the cerebellum (center of muscle coordination), the medulla oblongata (which controls the heart rate, circulation of blood, and breathing), the pons (a network that sends nerve impulses to various parts of the brain), the thalamus (the switchboard that sends incoming signals to proper brain areas), and the hypothalamus (which regulates hunger, thirst, body temperature, rage, pain, and pleasure).

The actual response of the brain to stress is outlined in Figure 6. Stressors, internal or external, stimulate the secretion of a chemical by the hypothalamus (11), which activates the sympathetic nerves (13) and the pituitary (12). This master gland discharges ACTH into the bloodstream, which stimulates the adrenal glands (7). Their secretion of adrenaline stimulates the heart (2) and increases the pulse rate and the blood pressure, the muscles, and the lungs (16), improving the blood flow, oxygen consumption, and strength. Additionally, the secretion of corticoids by the adrenal glands and other hormones activates the liver (3), spleen (8), and other organs, and inactivates some others, such as the digestive system.

The basic instincts that exist in lower animals as well as in human beings are centered around activities for keeping alive and reproducing. They include:

Preparing a homesite
Establishing and defending territory
Hunting
Homing/nesting
Hoarding
Mating
Forming simple social groups
Doing routine daily activities

The interbrain enables man to modify or refine his basic instincts. This second layer of the brain wraps around the hindbrain and is called the limbic system. It contains tracts (bundles of nerve fibers) that connect it with both the higher and lower brain centers and with the spinal cord. This group of brain structures is associated with the sense of smell but, more importantly for our discussion here, also with other activities such as autonomic functions and certain aspects of emotion and behavior.

The limbic system embodies not only the basic survival instincts but also the ability to think and act on feeling and emotion. Researchers have been able to locate the brain's "feeling good" circuit in the brain. They suspect that this circuit may involve the chemical norepinephrine, which the brain uses for passing messages around this and other circuits.

The importance of this work in stress management is that it is significant in helping us to gain insight into how our personal computers allow us to think, reason, and feel emotion. What impact these activities have on the individual biologically and socially are indicative of how successfully or unsuccessfully he or she is coping with life. Feelings such as fear, anger, and love guide behavior. A person's actions tend toward that which protects or rewards and away from that which threatens or punishes.

We hope that mapping different circuits within the brain will reveal which cells are talking to one another and will perhaps eventually uncover what messages are being transmitted in the complex brain language we are unable to interpret at the moment. These and other brain studies can be particularly beneficial in

FIGURE 6. *The stress reaction: real or perceived threat leads to increased alertness and physical strength.*

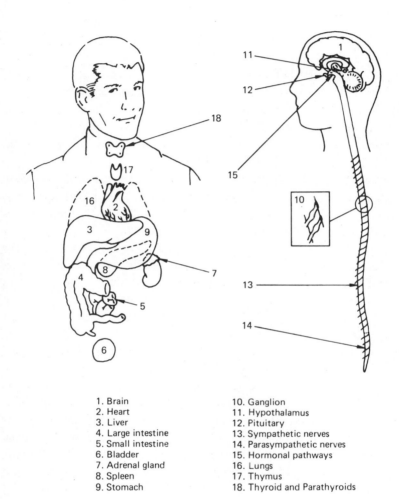

1. Brain	10. Ganglion
2. Heart	11. Hypothalamus
3. Liver	12. Pituitary
4. Large intestine	13. Sympathetic nerves
5. Small intestine	14. Parasympathetic nerves
6. Bladder	15. Hormonal pathways
7. Adrenal gland	16. Lungs
8. Spleen	17. Thymus
9. Stomach	18. Thyroid and Parathyroids

finding ways to activate the brain's reward circuits without using such maladaptive coping measures as alcohol and drugs.

For instance, the particular brain cells that use norepinephrine to carry their messages seem to start in the "satisfaction center" region of the brain; that is, in a group of nerve cells on which signals converge to register the fact that what the person is doing or has just done is satisfying. The implication that various chemicals or chemical reactions exist that can lead to distress or inappropriate behavioral response is obvious. The concepts of reward–pleasure and punishment–displeasure are important in the development of stress, as will be shown in Chapter 10.

THE CEREBRAL CORTEX

The third layer of the brain is called the cortex, neocortex, or forebrain. It consists mainly of the cerebrum, which is divided into two hemispheres—the right and left brain. In human beings, in the majority of cases, these two cerebral hemispheres are specialized for different judgmental (cognitive) functions: the left for verbal and analytic thought, the right for intuition and for understanding patterns. Also, empathy, fine motor control, additional emotion, memory, learning and rational thought, problem solving, and survival abilities are stored in the cortical cells.

It is in this higher center of the brain that reactions can be more than reflex responses. That is, an individual's reality can be determined largely by his own perception and by his language, as Alfred Korzybski showed. Behavior can be weighed against possible outcomes. Symbolism, goals, motivation, and anticipation are part of the functioning human being.

THE RETICULAR ACTIVING SYSTEM (RAS)

Stress involves the integration of virtually all components of the brain. The brain is responsive to stimuli through the reticular activating system (RAS; see Figure 7). The RAS carries messages from the brain to the body and the body to the brain. These messages are general as well as specific. For example, in the process of hearing a sudden loud sound, the specific arousal alerts the brain for increased attention to the sound and the nonspecific impulses cause a general arousal of the cortex.

This general arousal stimulates the limbic system and the hypothalamus, thus possibly activating emotions such as fear, lowering body temperature, and speeding up heart rate. These responses prepare the body for potential action even before the cortex appraises the potential threat of the sound and makes the decision to act. These and other increases in bodily functions are sensed by the RAS, which further alerts and arouses the system.

FIGURE 7. *Operation of the reticular activating system (RAS).*

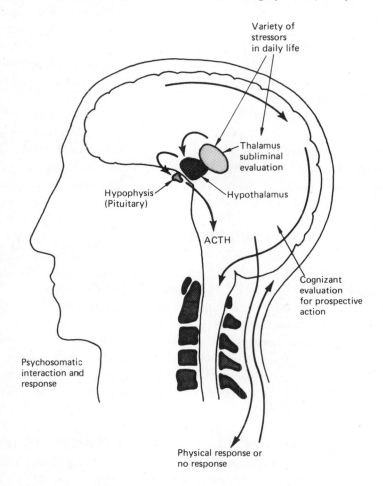

The state of arousal continues until action expends the biochemical consequences of stress. However, action may not be pursued because the stressor may not consciously be appraised as a potential threat or because circumstances seem to indicate that action is not warranted or appropriate. In this situation, the system has become stressed for no useful purpose, and the biochemical products of stress must circulate throughout the body until they can be reabsorbed or otherwise used up. The reaction, therefore, can be physically detrimental to the human organism, with increased or prolonged arousal causing excessive preparedness.

The RAS has the capacity for prolonged vibration of an impulse and prolonged response; it can adapt to frequent arousal by staying aroused. For example, if your lifestyle is hurried and pressured, exposing you to frequent stressors, chances are your body responds to your stressful life by remaining in a constant state of arousal or readiness for the unknown—fast heartbeat and breathing, tense muscles, and so on.

On the other hand, the RAS also has the capacity to recruit impulses from other brain structures, and it will adapt to a familiar stimulus—regardless of whether it is pleasant or unpleasant. This ability to adapt to repeated situations mitigates such stress as city noise more for the permanent resident than for the visitor; the novel noises are more stressful for the latter.

THE AUTONOMIC NERVOUS SYSTEM

The autonomic (voluntary) nervous system mentioned earlier in this chapter is that part of the central nervous system primarily responsible for such basic, elementary bodily functions as hormone balance, metabolism, vascular activity, and reproduction. These day-to-day operations work without much conscious thought, although the processes can be influenced by the higher, conscious centers. One of the major areas of the brain that regulates the autonomic nervous system and influences the stress response is the hypothalamus. This was already demonstrated in the prior section on stress arousal.

THE SYMPATHETIC AND PARASYMPATHETIC SYSTEMS

The sympathetic and parasympathetic systems carry the impulses that arise from the autonomic nervous system to the body. The sympathetic subdivision reacts to stimuli with a mass discharge to activate the fight-or-flight response that prepares the body for physical battle or rapid escape from a perceived danger.

By contrast, the parasympathetic subdivision has no mass reaction to stimulation. Rather, it is responsible for the day-to-day functioning of organs and is relatively specific. For instance, this system will increase the action of some organs while inhibiting the action of others. Whereas the sympathetic system might constrict the blood vessels and enlarge the pupils, the parasympathetic system would have the opposite effect. It would expand the blood vessels and constrict the pupils of the eye.

Although most bodily organs work with both subdivisions acting on them, some organs are stimulated by only one of these nervous systems. In this case, the fluctuation between the two systems determines whether the organ is activated or inhibited. The stress reaction begins to subside once the stressor disappears or the individual has revised his evaluation of the threat to his well-being. The sympathetic branch becomes less active. The body begins to metabolize or dissipate the stress chemicals, and the parasympathetic system begins to restore the inner workings of the body to its normal low arousal state and to repair the effects of its previous excitement.

Up to this point, we have referred to several elements of the nervous system that contribute to the stress response. It is difficult to generalize how the nervous system affects stress-related disorders because either stimulation or inhibition can alter the body's function. Also, the action of the nervous system is influenced by the action of the endocrine system, which will be examined next; the emotions will be explored in Chapter 10. It is important to remember that stress induced by direct trauma to the body and stress induced psychologically both provoke an identical biochemical reaction in the body.

THE ENDOCRINE SYSTEM

The endocrine system is a major control system of the body. It consists of all the glands in the body that secrete hormones into the bloodstream. All these glands within the body are involved to some extent in the stress response: the pituitary and adrenal glands are the most significant.

We have already mentioned in the section on stress arousal the intimate relationship between the hypothalamus and the pituitary gland. As the hypothalamus is stimulated, it in turn stimulates the pituitary, and thoughts, anticipations, and general nervous system responses convert to hormonal actions. Some portions of the hypothalamus stimulate the parasympathetic nervous system and inhibit the stress response, while others activate the sympathetic nervous system and increase the response.

The adrenal glands are responsible for most of the physical response to stress arousal, as previously explained. The effects of adrenaline, ACTH, corticoids, and other chemicals released into the bloodstream to a large extent constitute the stress response. Their secretion in increased amounts during arousal demands that the body make certain adjustments to prepare for action of many kinds. The body has many sensitive responses to stress: muscular, gastro-intestinal, mental, neural, cardiovascular, epidermal, and emotional.

MUSCULAR RESPONSE

A muscle is a mass of millions of specialized cells that have the ability to shorten (contract) when stimulated by nerve impulses carried from the motor cortex of the brain via the spinal cord and a cable of neurons called the pyramidal tract. These muscle contractions move bones, skin, and some organs, and work is accomplished. We cannot move toward pleasure or away from danger without muscle action. In addition, every mode of expression—speech, eye movements, facial expressions—and every feeling and resolution of an emotion is accomplished through the movement of muscles.

Muscles have two natural states: contraction and relaxation. The state of relaxation is the absence of contraction. As the muscles make up such a large portion of the body's mass, the achievement of muscular relaxation can represent a significant reduction in total distress.

Tension develops between these two functional states. That is, often an incomplete or partial contraction occurs—and no work is done. There are many examples of muscle tension in our daily lives. For instance, how often have you found your knuckles white from the grip you hold on the steering wheel when driving fast or in rush-hour traffic? You may recall the tension in your neck, back, shoulders, face, and back of your head.

The muscle tension we are talking about is excessive and needless muscle action. It is far more than needed to accomplish the task. This excess muscle tension is both a response to stress and a secondary cause of stress. Chronically tense muscles complete a feedback loop and further stimulate the mind, thus perpetuating and perhaps intensifying the distress. We know that such stress can consciously be reduced by our altering our perceptions, objectives, or muscular actions.

Unfortunately, many people spend a great deal of time in unproductive preparation to defend themselves against imagined or potential physical or symbolic threats. Their bodies adapt to anticipated stress by increasing general muscle tension. Signals from the hypothalamus and upper limbic area via the extrapyramidal motor pathway cause a variety of unconscious postures and rhythmic movements.

If a chronic state of muscle tension exists for an extended period of time, a wide variety of physical disorders may be produced or exaggerated. Among the numerous psychosomatic disorders are such conditions as:

Tension headaches
Backaches
Spasms of the esophagus
Spasm of the colon
Limited range of movement
Posture problems
Urinary problems
Dysmenorrhea
Limited range of flexibility
Susceptibility to muscle injuries
Insomnia
Asthma or hay fever
Tightness in the throat and chest cavity
Lockjaw
Some eye problems

The breadth of the repercussions of chronically tense muscles should not really be surprising, because the muscular system is involved in every active body process and in every feeling and expression of emotion.

THE GASTROINTESTINAL RESPONSE

Although the gastrointestinal system serves no function in the fight-or-flight syndrome, responses to stress arousal have been clearly established as causative factors in many gastrointestinal disorders. Difficulty in swallowing due to the spastic contraction of muscles in the esophagus, lack of salivary control, ulceration of the stomach lining, diarrhea, constipation, and inflammation of the pancreas are but a few of the results of repeated or continuous stress arousal in the structures along the alimentary canal.

The gastrointestinal system breaks down food by churning it in the stomach, moving it through the intestine by a rhythmic movement (peristalsis), and supplying digestive enzymes to break down the food particles into amino acids, blood sugar, or simple fatty acids that the body uses for building tissue or energy. This system is governed by numerous automatic reflexes to control its rhythmic movements, its emptying, and its secretaion of digestive enzymes. Feelings of anxiety, anger, frustration, fear, and depression—all manifestations of undue distress—can trigger either under- or over-stimulation of the system, which may result in some of the diseases previously mentioned.

THE BRAIN'S RESPONSE

As we explained earlier, the brain and the endocrine system play important controlling roles in the chain of biological events related to coping and adaptation. The brain can also be viewed as a response system, because its electrical activity can be analyzed. The cells of the brain emit a constant electrical charge, which in turn produces wave patterns of different voltage and frequency. Billions of cells simultaneously perform thousands of functions. It is impossible for the entire brain to produce activity at any one frequency at any given time. Rather, there is a complex pattern of mixed wave forms occurring at varying frequencies. Nonetheless, at any given moment there does appear to be a dominant frequency emitted from a specific section of the brain, as measured on a brain wave instrument, the electroencephalograph (EEG).

The analysis of brain wave patterns is used to diagnose abnormal brain states and to describe various states of activity. It is an extremely complex process, with such general applications as biofeedback, the conscious control of vital functions. Research has begun to associate brain wave patterns with cognitive functioning, emotion, and states of consciousness. Its application to the management of stress is obvious.

Brain waves represent a continuum of frequency and activity that seems to parallel the continuum of mental alertness. Although recent research shows that sharp behavioral lines do not exist, there is a four-state classification of brain wave patterns: delta, theta, alpha, and beta. In each of these brain wave states, there are some recognizable characteristics. However, these are not necessarily the exclusive functions of each state.

Delta-dominant brain wave states are usually associated with sleep. This is the slowest wave pattern and signifies a state of consciousness that is not interacting with the external environment.

In the theta state, the mind is active but not actively involved with specific external events. The thoughts are not directed by the will, as they are in daydreams. The theta state is often associated with fantasies and daydreams in which thoughts are original bursts of images that are not related to external events. These imaginings are not "controlled" by learned inhibitions that may prevent the acceptance of new ideas. Consequently, the theta state is believed to be a highly creative state of mind.

The nondominant hemisphere of the brain, which processes ideas rather than factual pieces of information, can be trained in the drowsy, dreamlike, theta state to change certain types of stressful patterns of thinking. In Part III, one can see the practical application of this knowledge of the brain in the use of biofeedback, autogenic training, self-hypnosis, meditation, and other mental coping techniques.

The current media focus on the alpha state has given rise to the popularity of yoga, meditation, and time and energy conservation. Many people attribute pain control, increased IQ, improved sleep, improved intuition, accelerated healing, and even weight loss to their ability to control their alpha state.

Everyone experiences this slow, synchronized, nonprocessing brain wave. It is the relative absence of sustained ego-involved thought process that is responsible for the alert but peaceful state. We have alluded throughout this book to examples of stress triggered or augmented by ego-involved arousal thoughts such as guilt, insecurity, or failure. These are not present during the typical alpha state. As stated earlier, feeding information back to the individual about the general activity of the brain can promote the ability to decrease potentially stress-producing thought patterns. Physiological arousal seldom occurs during the alpha state.

Arousal almost always occurs during the fastest of the major brain wave patterns, the beta. During this state, the brain is more active than in the other three states and is usually considered to be involved in more quantitative, analytical thought. This thinking, problem-solving state may include a feeling of challenge and un-stress rather than a feeling of being threatened and distressed. Certainly, not all thinking activity means arousing the stress response; however, when physiological arousal does occur, it is most likely during the beta state. Aside from these measurable physical responses of the brain to stress, there are psychological or mood responses. These will be explored in the next chapter.

THE CARDIOVASCULAR RESPONSE

Years of research have made it practically impossible to exclude the role of stress in the long-term development of cardiovascular disease. Exactly how prominent a role stress plays in this chronic disease is widely discussed and debated. It is generally believed, however, that a chronically stressed person bears a higher risk of contracting hypertension, atherosclerosis, migraine headache, heart failure, and other heart and vascular problems.

The cardiovascular system is very responsive to stress arousal. The heart is constantly receiving impulses from the brain, and its inherent rhythm is continually influenced by the central nervous system. The heart receives impulses from both the sympathetic and parasympathetic nervous systems. Its activity is a balance between these two major divisions of the nervous system. You will recall from an earlier section that the sympathetic nervous system stimulates the stress response, and the parasympathetic counteracts, or slows down, this arousal. It is responsible for the day-to-day functioning of the organs.

Every day the heart pumps some 2,000 gallons of blood, circulating the body's 10.5 pints again and again throughout a network of arteries, veins, and capillaries 60,000 miles long. In an average lifetime, the heart will beat some 2,500 million times. The adult heart beats about 70 times a minute, which is roughly four times for every breath under normal circumstances. Higher speeds may occur during the stress of exercise, pain, fever, asphyxia, anxiety, or intense excitement or pleasure. It can pump as many as 12 gallons of blood a minute, or eight times as much blood as in a period of relative relaxation, adapting as necessary to a short- or long-term increase in its workload.

The heart pumps the blood containing essential sugar and oxygen for the nourishment of every living cell in the body. Vital centers such as the brain would suffer severe damage if their blood supply were to cease for more than two or three minutes. The pumping is done by the alternating contraction and relaxation of the heart muscle. Various centers of the brain signal the metabolic and physiological demands of the body through the central nervous system.

In addition to this neural regulation, the heart can also be influenced by the hormone adrenaline, which can increase the speed and strength of the contraction. As explained earlier, when the hypothalamus is stimulated, the endocrine glands are involved; specifically, the adrenal gland releases epinephrine (adrenaline), which increases the heart rate. One of the most commonly recognized signs of a distressed individual is rapid heart rate, "flutter," or palpitations. Awareness of this cardiac activity may heighten general stress and anxiety and serve in a negative feedback loop to intensify or prolong the stress response. Techniques for reducing this condition are set forth in Part III.

During the fight-or-flight response, the heart increases action in anticipation of physiological and metabolic demands of the body. However, this increased cardiovascular activity is inappropriate when final action is not actually required or taken. As previously mentioned, the stress response in man was intended to end in physical activity. When it does not, the preparatory products and sensations wear down the body's systems and erode good health.

Chapter 14 explores the importance of perception—how the individual sees and interprets the world—as a major stress factor. Anger, anxiety, change, ego threats, and novelty frequently elevate the heart rate and can overwork the heart. Obviously, the fewer times a heart must contract or beat to fulfill the necessary supply functions, the more incremental rest it will get.

Like other muscles, the heart can become stronger through appropriate activity. When it is strong, fewer beats are required to do its job efficiently. The benefits to important physiological processes that may result from vigorous aerobic-type exercises are explored in more detail in Chapter 16.

HYPERTENSION

Another cardiovascular problem in which stress is strongly implicated is hypertension. Approximately one third of the population over 50 in the United States suffers from high blood pressure, usually considered to be a pressure above 160/95. The average normal adult male reading is about 120/80; it is slightly less for females.

There are two basic types of hypertension. One is attributable to such organic causes as hardening of the arteries, excessive aldosterone secretions, or kidney obstructions or ailments. Another is known as "essential hypertension" and has no apparent cause. Approximately 90 percent of the cases are of unknown origin. Nevertheless, either the heart is pumping too much blood or the blood vessels are too narrow, making the heart pump harder than normal.

We know that one of the body's responses to stress is to constrict the artery walls, which raises the blood pressure in the artery. Since the primary work of the heart is to overcome the pressure in the arteries, through which the blood must flow, the increase in blood pressure due to constricted artery walls may cause the heart to enlarge, weaken, and lose efficiency. This condition can also weaken the arteries, making them less elastic.

Other consequences of hypertension include greater risk of stroke, hemorrhages, or blindness (from the weakening of the small blood vessels in the eyes) and impaired ability of the kidneys to clear waste from the blood.

Like the heart, the blood vessels have an inherent tone that can be altered from moment to moment by both the sympathetic and parasympathetic nervous systems and by the hormones norepinephrine and epinephrine.

Psychological as well as somatic states can alter the diameter of the blood vessels, producing a physical response to either real or imagined physical or symbolic threats. These will be discussed at greater length in the next chapter.

Repeated stimulation of the stress reaction accounts for a coronary insufficiency with ischemia (inadequate blood supply to the heart), which becomes a factor in any number of ailments—for example, heart attack and angina pectoris. The lack of enough nourishment to meet all demands can cause these and other ailments related to the heart and blood vessels.

THE SKIN'S RESPONSE

The complex function and intricate nervous system control of the skin make it a sensitive response system to stress arousal. Basically, the skin has two response patterns: electrical and thermal.

Each of the millions of cells that make up the skin system contain chemicals whose activity changes as the skin cells change, producing different patterns of electrical activity. These changes in electrical resistivity of the skin are found to be fairly reliable indications of stress. Police authorities and health authorities use detector systems to help them understand emotions, motivations, and problem-solving techniques.

Temperature change is the second basic response system of the skin. A drop in the skin's surface temperature is due to the constriction of the small blood vessels under the skin that change in response to emotion. For instance, when you are under stress, the activation of your sympathetic nervous system diverts blood away from your fingers and toes, according to a suddenly revised system of priorities. This causes the skin to appear pale and the skin temperature to decrease.

At other times, the blood vessels open and allow the skin to flush with blood, increasing the skin temperature and causing the red color associated with rage or shame. Prolonged emotional responses to stress can cause abnormal blood flow or an excessive amount of fluid exuded by the skin cells and can result in malfunction and disease. Eczema, hives, psoriasis, and acne are among the skin conditions being studied in connection with psychological response patterns to stress.

CONCLUSION

We have examined the body's characteristic patterned responses in human functioning. They are an extremely complex interplay of chemical secretions, physical functions, and electrical messages. To summarize: At any one moment a person experiences both physical and psychological stress and has a certain momentary level of reactivity. This reactivity level may be influenced by any number of experiences, feelings, and thoughts and by conditioning and coping abilities. How the individual responds to the momentary level of challenge initially is imprinted in the alarm reaction.

During the resistance stage of the stress response, there is a marked decrease in ACTH, and "specificity of adaptation" occurs. In other words, efforts at self-preservation mobilize specific vital resources to enable the body to resist and adapt to the stressor. The stress response is channeled into the specific organ system or process most capable of dealing with it or suppressing it.

For example, the body can adapt to high blood pressure without constantly eliciting general arousal. During the resistance stage, the kidneys and heart will be pressed into service for the adaptation process. However, these organs may eventually fatigue and start to malfunction if hypertension is chronic. The body then goes into the third stage or exhaustion phase. The constant pressure can promote kidney and heart damage, which can ultimately kill the individual.

Adaptation may be considered a life-saving process when the body can overcome the virus or injury and regain homeostasis, a state of healthy balance between body systems achieved by the organism through its own regulatory mechanisms. Adaptation can also be recognized as a type of disease process when chronic resistance diminishes the ability of the system to function, resulting in disease, malfunction, or even death.

A central theme of this book is that increased awareness of the complex social, physiological, evolutionary, and psychological processes that constitute life as we know it can substantially illuminate the intricate mechanisms of stress. From this information base, individuals and organizations are better equipped to identify the stressors in their environment and to mobilize their resources constructively. They can then deal responsibly with the important issues of stress and distress in their own lives and in the lives of those around them.

CHAPTER 10
The Psychobiology of Stress

The psychobiological implications of stress lead to the study of mental health and behavior in relation to other biological processes. Increasing laboratory and practical experiences have shown irrefutable links between emotional stress and physical distress.

Incidents in which the famous are victims of their own emotions are headline news; but one need not be a politician or other public figure to suffer from the normal demands of living. People in all stations in life can literally worry themselves sick. Dr. Marvin Stein of the Mt. Sinai School of Medicine in New York states that "There is considerable evidence that grief and stress retard the body's ability to fight disease."

PHYSIOLOGICAL RESULTS

In an attempt to illustrate the physiological consequences of environmental events on man, many different variables have been pointed out. These include life cycle, family, social events, time, work, and other events. When a situation is perceived as being stressful, the physiological variables that are measurable in blood and urine samples, for example, usually include either some output of the pituitary–adrenal system or some function of the autonomic system, as explained in Chapter 9.

Therefore, in order to understand the stress–disease relationship, it is important to recognize how the disease processes are interwoven. In the study of mind–body interaction, stress has been implicated in diseases ranging from the common cold to cancer.

ORGANIC DISEASE

Chapter 9 examined the physiological responses to stress and alluded to several organic diseases that adversely affect the struc-

[167]

ture and function of the body. Microorganisms, pollutants, or some natural degenerative process can cause infectious or noninfectious diseases of short and severe or persistent duration. Highly stressed people are more susceptible to illness, and their conditions can be aggravated by poor coping abilities, as suggested in Part III.

CONVERSION REACTIONS

Conversion reactions such as deafness, blindness, the inability to speak, and paralysis are functional physical disabilities that may subconsciously be used as coping mechanisms in the face of unbearable stress. When such functional impairments occur without any underlying organ destruction or other structural impairment to explain it, they may be considered neurotic mental disorders.

Extensive physical examinations may confirm legitimate functional physical disabilities yet uncover no organic cause. Sometimes when a person is faced with overwhelming stress, the body responds with an unconscious maladaptive coping mechanism. When the stressor is eliminated or the emotional conflict is resolved, the conversion reaction subsides.

PSYCHOSOMATIC DISEASE

A third type of disease, termed "psychosomatic," refers to bodily symptoms or bodily and mental symptoms stemming from mental conflict. The basis of this concept is that the mind plays an important role in many different diseases. All psychosomatic illnesses affect the function and structure of the human body. They fall into two basic categories: psychogenic and somatogenic.

Psychogenic Disorders

Psychogenic disorders are physical diseases caused by emotional stress. In such cases, there is actual structural and functional organ damage, yet none of the usual underlying physical causes of organic disease is present. Conditions that fall into this category include bronchial asthma, skin reactions, backaches, peptic ulcers, and migraine headaches. These disorders may manifest themselves when a person is not coping adequately with life. Fear of failure, rage, grief, the frustration of not living up to expectations, or anxiety from deadline pressures can be translated into these and other disorders.

Somatogenic Disorders

The somatogenic phenomenon has far-reaching implications for health and the strength of the mind–body relationship. Research is continuing to show that emotional disturbances such as anger, anxiety, fear, and frustration increase the body's susceptibility to organic diseases and infections. Many virulent microorganisms exist in our environment and persist in the body without causing obvious harm under normal circumstances. However, when a person is under more stress than he is able to handle, latent infection can be converted by stressful disturbances into organic disease.

A healthy body can usually fight off many invading organisms by natural defense mechanisms, but distress impedes this defensive role, and the result becomes physical breakdown. Intense or prolonged stress may give organic disease a foothold in the body or may accelerate the rate at which it spreads throughout the body by hampering the body's natural immune system.

A person's psychological makeup, lifestyle, and attitude toward life affect his physiological condition. Numerous accounts exist of incidents of spontaneous remission or relapse of diseases such as multiple sclerosis and cancer. The removal or appearance of stress in the patient's life may be the deciding factor in warding off or bringing on disease. Chapter 9 analyzed the total bodily response to stress. In this chapter the interrelationship between thoughts and feelings and physical reactions reveals itself more clearly.

MIND–BODY INVOLVEMENT

Almost all diseases have some mind–body involvement. It may be concluded from the information given thus far that the two are a cooperative and interlocking unit. What affects the body will affect the mind, and vice versa. The human organism is a complex of neural, chemical, electrical, and biological processes in which the whole far exceeds the sum of its component parts.

The brain receives information from all the senses and decides what is important and how to react. The brain's job is to produce action that fits the situation. This reaction may be one of a long series that eventually will make some plan for the future work out. But the eventual function of the brain is to control muscles and, as explained in Chapter 9, the control of muscles starts at the cerebral cortex.

All the input from the nerve cells and dendrites in the cerebral cortex are interwoven and intertwined, with some hundred billion nerve cells in the whole brain, affecting one another and drawing on a lifetime of images and memories to work out strategies for dealing with each situation that arises. Man's unique possession of foresight and his ability to learn from experience make the human instrument a most exceptional creation.

It is obvious from all the evidence presented that physical malfunctions can drastically interfere with mental performance. Severe physical pain, a cold, a hangover, or extreme fatigue can seriously impair the performance of mental functions—attention, speech, comprehension. Conversely, Western medicine is coming to realize that mental and emotional states such as grief, rage, or fright can substantively contribute to physical disease. The concept of "mind" is that of a complicated network of behavior resulting from the presence of the brain and nervous system in the body.

A strong relationship exists between behavior and emotional distress and the wear and tear on physical processes. The vicious cycle of stress weakening the system and making someone more vulnerable to further emotional strain is evidenced in a variety of mental and physical breakdowns.

STRESS AND MENTAL HYGIENE

A single thought can increase or de-escalate our internal arousal. This remarkable process holds the key to understanding emotional well-being and suggests opportunities for stress management and a high level of emotional tranquility. Balance between the environment and man and within the person himself is becoming increasingly important.

There is a growing interest in maintaining psychological and physiological stability rather than being willing to sacrifice one for the other. Many people have always centered their activities around pleasure, happiness, and ego gratification, often at the expense of mind–body health. New methods of treating illness recognize that a person may have lifestyles with habits and activities that affect his or her overall well-being. In Part III, we explore possible methods of coping. These are designed to end, alter, or prevent the detrimental effects that a person's environment, perception, and imagination have on the arousal of his or her body's control system.

APPRAISAL PATHWAYS

Of the different pathways that process the millions of messages from various parts of the body, we will concentrate on the subconscious and conscious pathways.

The Subconscious Appraisal Pathway

The subconscious appraisal pathway contains physical and emotional reflexes that act to prepare the body for action. The preparation is independent of the final action, as noted in the last chapter's section on involuntary action. This pathway is stimulated by the autonomic nervous system, and if the higher thought centers determine that the action is appropriate, the subconscious pathway has already begun to mobilize the body's resources.

The Conscious Appraisal Pathway

The conscious appraisal pathway is responsible for voluntary action. This system includes perception, evaluation, and decision making. These judgments are based on one's characteristic concept of self, ego strengths, attitudes, imagination, value systems, heredity, and prior experiences. Chapter 14 elaborates on the issue of perception and how it relates to behaviors and arousal level.

Much of stress is determined by the meanings a person assigns to the events in his life. Different people are likely to interpret the same situation differently or assign unique meanings or significance to it. As stated in Chapter 1, this explains why each person's pattern of stress response is unique. One person may be angered or frightened by events that another will find pleasurable or relaxing.

Because of the unique nature of stressors and the resultant stress, there is a rich variety of coping strategies for every situation. These strategies will depend, at least in part, on antecedent conditions (see Figure 8). For example, the psychological characteristics of the person and a complex interaction with other people set the conditions under which the coping skills will be used.

Various psychological factors interact with physiological systems to produce the final strategy used for coping. The same physical stressor can have different consequences, depending on such considerations as predictability. It might be met with surprise or shock or be expected, and therefore met with some degree of preparation.

It appears from current research that psychological factors are often more important in influencing certain outcomes than physical

FIGURE 8. *Mind–body involvement: the link between psychosocial events and psychophysiological changes.*

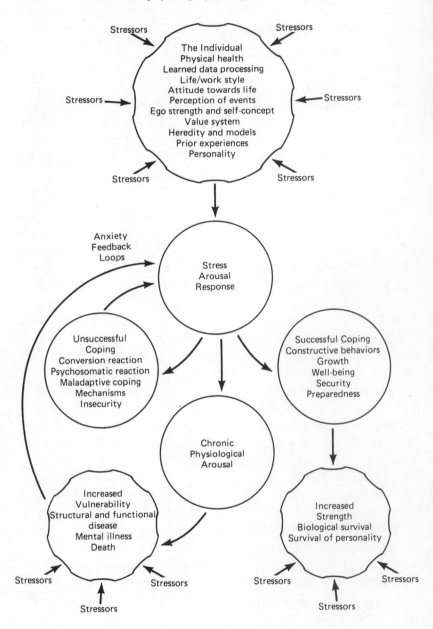

stimuli themselves, even if those stimuli are intense and noxious. Among the psychological variables that have a significant influence on the response to noxious stimuli are:

The ability to offer a coping response
The ability to escape from the stressor
The predictability of the outcome of the reaction to the stimuli

The ability to make a coping response is based on awareness of the problem and previous knowledge of alternative actions that can be taken. Part I indicated many sources of possible problems, and Part III provides information concerning a range of constructive actions that can be taken to mitigate stress. Instructions about how to develop a stress reduction program are outlined. These plans take into account whether or not one is able to escape the stressor.

The predictability of the outcome of an event is important to a person's security. When overloaded with demands, people tend to lose sight of the light at the end of the tunnel. This myopic, negative viewpoint further intensifies the stress response and decreases a person's ability to think clearly and take constructive actions. The interaction between psychological and physiological variables is a complex feedback system between the brain and the rest of the body. Although there are general patterns of responsiveness, there are also unique patterns that account for a large portion of the variance of individual differences.

Whether a situation is personally evaluated as unpleasant or threatening may be the primary mediator for hormonal release and the degree to which the arousal reaction is detrimental.

Changes from predictable to unpredictable events, and vice versa, are enough to cause increased or suppressed pituitary–adrenal activity, respectively. It remains for further research to discover whether the bidirectional nature of the pituitary–adrenal reaction is also true of other hormones released in response to changes in expectations and resulting stress.

HABITUATION AND COPING

Habituation is usually defined in terms of a response to relatively neutral stimuli, such as sudden loud noises that initially cause arousal but are not themselves intrinsically aversive or life threatening. When someone is presented with an unexpected stimulus such as a loud noise, he shows an alternating or orienting reaction. The physiological components of the orientation response include:

A general activation of the brain
Cardiovascular changes
Changes in the electrical resistance of the skin
Increases in the circulating adrenal corticoids

If the loud noise of a door slamming or of an explosion is repeated frequently, all of the above reactions diminish and eventually disappear in the general process of habituation. This process is based on a matching system, in which the human organism mentally matches immediate events with a central nervous system representation of prior events. Thus, man has a set of prior expectancies with which to deal with the environment. If the environment does not contain any new components, a person will no longer show physiological responses related to arousal. If a noise continues, it is in a sense expected; hence less surprising or threatening.

Our modern world exposes us to repeated aversive stimulation, such as air pollution; yet man does not overtly respond continually to these stimuli. This fact has led to the development of the concept of coping. Coping differs from habituation in that the stimuli that elicit the coping response continue to be threatening and aversive, but the human organism no longer responds to them fully. This is in contrast to the process of habituation, in which the stimuli themselves are relatively neutralized.

Coping is a function of what the person learns about his real or probable status in the stressful situation. It relates not only to task performance but also to a series of intervening psychological variables. They include:

Resources	Role identification
Interests	Expectations
Motivation	

These and other psychological variables mentioned earlier in the book are important for a significant reduction in internal physiological activation. This reduction, in turn, depends not only on performance and feedback from the environment, but also on each person's experience and evaluation of the situation. Coping can be learned. Habituation is a less conscious adaptation.

ENERGY RELEASE

Some researchers have proposed that all behavior has a common dimension of energy release, its extent governed by the degree of effort the person feels is required in the situation. One of the tasks of adaptive behavior is to avoid disruptive secondary effects. These are disorganizing feelings such as anxiety, confusion, frustration, and anger, which can seriously hamper competent coping. If the system is unable to maintain its balance—for example, if a headache develops—coping response is impaired. Over a prolonged period of maladaptive or inappropriate responses to life situations, a person may subject himself to more catastrophic ailments.

Cancer

There is a statistically significant association between psychological patterns and susceptibility to cancer. For example, consistent suppression of anger can affect carcinogenesis through determination of behavior or stimulation of the endocrine system. Patients who respond to the diagnosis with stoic acceptance or feelings of helplessness and hopelessness may also adversely affect the outcome of the disease.

Some very exciting things are happening in the fight against cancer. Some physicians are involving the patient in his own fight for life through a technique called visual imagery. This method involves the utilization of relaxation techniques two or three times a day for brief periods of time. The patient is taught to use thought control to mobilize his innate healing abilities and strengths.

During the relaxation periods, the patient visualizes in the mind's eye the cancer and its medical treatment. He pictures the radiation or chemotherapy entering the body and destroying the cancer cells. He also visualizes his white blood cells carrying away the dying and dead cancer cells. Finally, the focus is on seeing first the cancerous area and then the whole body as well and healthy. The patient pictures himself as more active and vital.

The results after several weeks of practicing this visual imagery technique have been encouraging. Physicians have frequently discovered a more positive outlook on life, less pain, more energy, and increased vitality in many of their patients. In some cases, there has been a complete remission of the disease. Overall, it appears to prolong life a few months to a few years and to improve the quality of life for the patient and his family.

This is but one example of how the mind–body interrelationship has the capability of altering health or disease. Pain and other disturbing symptoms can be managed by changes in attitude. Physicians have realized for a long time that the human spirit is essential to recovery in any illness and in major surgery. Those who "give up" have a greater chance of more serious illness and even death.

Heart Disease

The circumstantial evidence is increasingly convincing that psychological experiences can trigger a heart attack. Some physicians now believe that it may be emotions, not blood clots, that cause the heart attacks that kill 400,000 Americans each year. As shown in Chapter 9, stress can retard the body's ability to fight disease.

Stress-related illnesses may result from the frantic effort of the mind searching for answers to a problem when it lacks information. This lack of information can result from ignorance of social realities (how others think and feel, how they respond to us) or from ignorance of the inner state of the body. When the mind fixes on external realities, it engages neural circuitry that would otherwise be regulating internal processes.

In stress reactions, when the cortex is preoccupied with identifying the source of the stimuli, the mind distorts perceptions and fails to recognize different mechanisms, even for pain tolerance. Such maladaptation is less likely in people who are not stressed.

As a result of emotional arousal, purely cognitive processes can lead to the neuroendocrine changes of stress diagrammed in Chapter 9. Several psychosocial and physiological changes develop, depending on the predominant emotion. A sense of loss of control, anger, fear, and uncertainty are among the feelings that can arouse the sympathetic adrenal–medullary system as well as the pituitary–adrenocortical system in the fight-or-flight response.

The highly competitive, time-conscious, ambitious, dominating personality not only runs a greater risk of coronary heart disease than a milder person does, but he also shows biochemical differences in his responses to appropriate social stimulation.

Feelings of social acceptance and high personal worth, which commonly accompany effective coping defenses, are associated with decreased activation of the pituitary–adrenocortical mechanism. In contrast, feelings of lack of self-worth are found to preoccupy the mind and body defensively and to keep a person tense and aroused for action.

Stress is identified with the physiological consequences of emotions aroused by various sources of anger, fear, depression, or frustration. As already pointed out, regardless of whether or not someone experiences these feelings consciously, they are accompanied by nervous system and hormonal changes. Unconscious or sublimated emotions can wear away a person's resources, quicken the aging process, and lead to a shortened life span.

Everyone is subject to the aging process. The heart, for example, may deteriorate with time, regardless of what we do. But that deterioration can be significantly hastened by behavioral factors such as smoking, drinking, poor nutritional habits, and negative personality traits. There are psychophysiological reactions to environmental stimulation that can retard or accelerate the aging process.

An awareness of man's psychological, physiological, and social processes and their limitations can significantly contribute to a person's ability to interact more effectively and in a more health-enhancing manner with his or her environment.

Some of the prerequisites for developing resiliency and health include:

1. The physiological capacity to mobilize energy reserves under stress, to utilize the "second wind" phenomenon.
2. The flexibility with which to see things differently, to modify defenses, and to develop the capacity to change.
3. The self-esteem basic to the whole orientation toward the quality of life one pursues.
4. The survival instinct, which can reduce pressures through the drive to change either the situation or the person's relation to it.

These characteristics and their practical applications are explored at greater length in Part III, which should provide a better understanding of yourself and stress and prepare you to develop stress reduction programs for overall health enhancement.

CHAPTER 11
Male and Female Psychobiological Differences

The battle between the sexes, or the conviction that it is important to determine the superiority of one sex over the other, is a source of highly stressful interpersonal relations. The emotional nature of this issue often clouds and distorts the few facts there are about maleness and femaleness. To complicate matters further, we are not even very sure what the questions of sex-linked abilities involve.

Very few members of either sex are well informed about the actual intellectual, social, biological, and mental traits that are uniquely characteristic of the male or female of the species. Ignorance of differences between the sexes causes breakdowns in understanding and discomforting interactions.

We are concerned here not only with the recognition of the mechanics and elements in stress and distress but also with opportunities to prevent, cope with, and manage distressing factors in our lives. In an endeavor to develop an increasing awareness of the interacting dynamics of life today, this chapter deals specifically with some of the basic dissimilarities between the sexes. Through the illumination of this dichotomy, both men and women will be able to increase their awareness of interpersonal relations and reactions between the sexes. They can then manage their own behavior more effectively and realistically and reduce unnecessary distress in this area substantially.

Changes in the sexual, social, and economic roles of women have cast aside familiar guideposts of what has ordinarily been considered basically masculine or feminine. The resulting tension between the sexes is seen at home and at work as a sign of our contemporary confusion in a rapidly changing world. In our family forms, economic dealings, and business and social relationships, we are forced to cope with the conflicts between routine and nonroutine, predictable and unpredictable, and known and unknown in male–female interactions. The novelty and uncertainty of role definitions and "appropriate" behavior can present a distressing crisis in adaptation to the changing mores of twentieth-century America.

There are significant differences between men and women that extend beyond obvious sexual and physical variables. The harmonization of these differences requires a thorough understanding of the psychobiological differences between males and females. Understanding will help in coping with the conflicting role definitions and attempting to bridge the gaps between the differing points of view in order to achieve cooperative enterprise in business and social environments.

BIOLOGICAL BIASES

Biology initiates and sets limits on behavior. But we are not entirely limited by our biology—unless we fail to understand it. Though exceptions do exist, there are great differences between the predispositions of the sexes in motor, sensory, and some intellectual abilities. Several of these differences are apparent from birth, but it remains to be seen which behavior precedes which subsequent development, the order in which sex differences in advanced psychological processes unfold, and how powerfully the forces of culture accentuate them.

Gross Motor Skills

Boys from birth are significantly more active than girls; they are awake more, show more low-intensity motor activity (head turning, hand waving, twitching, and jerking), and more facial grimacing than girls.

Rough-and-tumble play is almost exclusively male throughout life. The male's larger muscle mass (40 percent of body tissue at maturity as opposed to 23 percent in the female) and superior integration of sight and motor skills give rise to excellence in fast gross motor action.

Males characteristically explore their world, manipulate objects by taking them apart, and show superior performance in reaction time and tracking tasks. Their love of gadgets and machines can be seen clearly as early as one or two years of age. As they grow up, male superiority in strength, speed, and accuracy in sports generally increases.

Men have better depth perception and grasp spatial relationships more quickly, giving them an advantage in mechanical and mathematical work. They are less sensitive than women to extreme heat but more sensitive to extreme cold.

Women are generally shorter and have much smaller bones and weaker muscles than men. However, women can bear physical pain far better than men and are readier to risk their lives for loved ones. From early childhood, they are more interested in people than in things and have more empathy in emotional and social situations.

Fine Motor Control and Speech

Females excel in fine motor control and in a facility for sequential motor acts, such as are used in needlework, typing, and brain surgery. This aptitude is also present in the speech process. Consequently, girls have a tendency to speak sooner, with greater fluency and grammatical accuracy, and use more words per utterance than boys. Women are more skilled in expressing themselves verbally. Male difficulties with stuttering and the inability to produce certain sound combinations usually decrease with age. The inability to sing in tune is six times more common in boys than in girls.

Girls and boys differ in the quality and the intentional use of speech to communicate. Females tend to develop a consistent mastery of language in both reception and execution. They also talk more for contact or signs of affiliation.

Girls also consistently show superior tactile sensitivity with their fingers and hands, as well as an overwhelmingly greater sensitivity to pressure on the skin in every part of the body. However, males and females do not generally differ in distinguishing the distances between two points of pressure. Females, therefore, have a heightened ability to detect the presence of a stimulus, but are no better than males at the acuity of their touch.

Hearing

When it comes to hearing, females exhibit particular discernment in hearing high-frequency sound. High frequencies provide information about the quality and clarity of sound, such as of consonants in speech and of the timbre of voices and musical instruments. This information also allows females to locate the source of sound more easily than males.

The sexes do not differ in their ability to detect the direction, duration, or pitch of a sound, but females are consistently superior in detecting changes in the volume or intensity of sound and are less able to tolerate loud sounds. Their sensitivity to volume and intensity of sound also makes them better able to discern the inflection or emotional content or mood of a speaker.

Sight

Wide differences exist between the sexes in their ability to see. Females adapt more rapidly than males to the dark and also continue to see the afterimage of a spot of light longer than males, but only when they have adapted to the dark. This changes in the daylight. Women have better nighttime vision than men, and men see better during the day.

Males show a greater ability in detecting differences in contrast and in detecting rapidly moving targets. Men see afterimages longer in bright light and consistently choose lower levels of brightness than females do.

Although no sex differences emerge in any other range of the color spectrum, females tend to be more sensitive than males to colors at the red end of the spectrum. More males than females are color blind.

Females process more general information about the total visual field but with less detail about an entire image or pattern than males. They have greater imagery and superior visual memory, while males have superior visual acuity.

General Differences

Females are more efficient than males at coding and seem better able to remember names and faces. Boys code nonsocial stimuli faster than girls do, are more easily distracted by novelty, and are more willing to explore a new environment.

At all ages, males tend to be oriented toward objects and nonsocial events, and females tend to respond most strongly to social cues and to people. These abilities enable women to grasp the nuances at a meeting communicated by voice tones, body language, facial expressions, and implied suggestions. This phenomenon is often spoken of as female intuition, but it is actually heightened sociopersonal perception.

Threshold sensitivity to all sensations and response to intensity are generally biologically fixed and untrainable, so consistent sex differences cannot be explained away by cultural influence. Although researchers are a long way from mapping sex differences for each aspect of every sense, they have found differences that seem to match the specific abilities of each sex, as we have seen in the areas of touch, hearing, and sight.

Our understanding of the differences between the sexes is far from complete, but there are enough data to piece together some of the puzzle. Males and females appear to learn about the environment differently and have qualitatively different patterns of behavior, which are in turn strongly influenced by the social setting. The great plasticity of the human brain allows a correspondingly great variation of traits, predispositions, aptitudes, and sensitivities, which are integrated in complex behavior.

By and large, society reinforces traits that are already present, and when it does so, its male and female members develop widely different interests, attitudes, and categories of intellectual skills.

Intelligence Quotients

Intellectual abilities reflect the activity of brain control mechanisms that operate on information in the sensory systems. In any intelligent or creative act, these capacities are also linked to motor efficiency. Intelligent behavior involves memory, planning, attention, and the ability to monitor and integrate appropriate information while discarding inappropriate data and taking appropriate actions.

National surveys have concluded that female and male adult IQs are just about equal. However, more men register at high and low extremes.

The more we know, the more we are struck with the innumerable innate differences between the sexes.

Dreams

Women dream more than men, and they report more of their dreams are in color. It is interesting that 80 percent of men state that they enjoy their dreams, as opposed to 72 percent of women. Therefore, it is not surprising to discover that more women have frequent nightmares. Women are far more likely to experience anxiety dreams and dreams about the sea than men. Sexual dreams are somewhat more common in men (85 percent) than in women (72 percent).

Seventy percent of all people report having recurring dreams, the majority of these being women. In most cases, recurring dreams are vaguely unpleasant and are almost certainly caused because the person has a problem of significance that cannot be resolved in waking life. Solving the problem almost always leads to the disappearance of the recurring dream. Interestingly, more men report dreams about finding money. This statistic presumably relates to the fact that men are more likely to be preoccupied with money matters than women, although real wealth and property interest many women.

Men and women require approximately the same amount of sleep and generally awake refreshed after a night's sleep. Women are far more likely (44 percent) to suffer from insomnia than men (35 percent) and have a greater tendency (17 percent) to use sleep-assisting drugs than men (10 percent). These studies seem to suggest that women on the average have more to worry about than men or at least are more likely to carry their worries to bed with them.

We have explored some of the sleeping and dreaming habits of a large cross section of normal men and women because dreams can offer interesting gateways to the unconscious mind and reveal new personality insights.

Reactions to Crowding

Another apparent difference between male and female behaviors is in their reactions to crowding. There are at least four subtle differences in men and women's relationship to space.

1. Males tend to become more competitive and aggressive in close proximity to others and are considered naturally more "territorial" than females.

2. Males are generally larger and more physically active than females and therefore need more space around them. They also feel more comfortable, creative, and likeable in proportion to the amount of "personal space" they have.

3. Women seem to prefer smaller spaces and regard close physi-

cal contact as a condition of friendship and intimacy. They respond more positively and warmly and maintain more eye contact with others when placed close together.

4. Men and women respond differently, not to crowding as such, but to members of their own sex. Men tend to attempt to create a psychological distance between themselves and others by averting their eyes. Close physical contact tends to create threatening or homosexual overtones among men. In contrast, women are quite comfortable and enjoy the psychological closeness of looking directly into people's faces more often.

CHANGING ROLES

The industrial revolution, the human potential movement, mass education, inflation–recession complexes, several global wars, and woman's liberation, among other social influences, have disturbed the old equilibrium of the social roles of men and women. As a result, our society is a crazy quilt of contradictory values, practices, and institutions.

Not only have we failed to anticipate the changes; we were slow to recognize them. Now, we are having to cope with them long after they have exacted a high price in human suffering and social waste. Many of the stresses experienced by men and women in their personal and professional lives persist because they lack the imagination, understanding, and skills to cope with social change and the sex-related differences that affect men's and women's roles in business and government.

Chapter 5 explored the revolution in the family cycle and pointed out how the typical cycle of life has changed radically since the turn of the century. Women are having no children or fewer children later in life, so that the time and role of motherhood have changed. Motherhood is for a shorter period, and the mother is older when the last child leaves home.

The "empty nest" syndrome has been added to the family cycle, and not only with current longevity figures. A man and wife might hope to live together for 41 years, spending a third of their life together after their children are grown. Also, the average woman is younger than her mate and can be expected to end her life as a widow.

Changed conditions of life and new aspirations have created new problems and demands for adaptation. The difficulty of anticipating social problems stems from the fact that they often emerge as unintended by-products of former decisions. The difficulty of foreseeing problems does not account for our failure to cope with them when their impact is fully realized.

Sex-role ambiguities in the modern marriage may be the result of man's trying to live up to an unrealistic and no longer attainable model of masculinity. Disappointment and contempt may be the woman's reaction to the same discrepancy between outmoded expectations and reality.

Under the influence of old attitudes, men today continue to expect too much of themselves in a world that no longer gives them their former advantages. Legislation has opened up opportunities for women in schooling, legal protection, responsibility, economic rewards, employment, and political participation in formerly masculine spheres.

MALE VULNERABILITY TO STRESS

Many sociologists and medical researchers have attributed the difference in longevity between the American male and the American female to the comparative amounts of pressure they experience. On the average, men in the United States die almost eight years earlier than American women. Whereas men have gained an average of about 21 additional years of life expectancy since the turn of the century, women have gained almost 27 years. The average life expectancy for men is 67.1 years; for women, 74.8!

Men are less moody, more prone to ulcers and heart disease, and 82 percent prone to baldness. They are also more apt to develop antisocial personalities.

With women being transformed into independent, self-sustaining people who get a great deal of emotional support from others of their own sex, some men can find themselves quite alone and cut off from nurturance. In turn, men are learning to cultivate male friendships, aside from business associates and contacts. They are learning to work through some of their fears and to realize that they do not have to be all things to all people.

People with few social contacts are two to four times as likely to die from major causes as those who maintain strong social ties. Lonely people with bad health habits (smoking, excessive alcohol consumption, obesity) are five times more likely to die prematurely. Being married, having good friends, and belonging to church or community groups, professional associations, or other sources of togetherness and identification seems to mitigate against heart disease, cancer, and several of the other leading causes of death.

Men, in particular, are slowly realizing the importance of non-competitive, mutually supportive relationships to their overall health and well-being. As we mentioned in Part I, strong social support is health enhancing. The reverse is also true: Social isolation can lead to headaches, ulcers, sleep disorders, depression, and suicide.

MEN'S LIBERATION

There is a growing recognition of the stress inherent in the stereotype a man accepts through the socialization process from childhood through adulthood. The American male is taught to be stoical and brave, to hide pain and fear. He is expected to know where he is going in life and to be competitive, aggressive, and successful. His conversation is expected to encompass such "approved" topics as business, cars, sports, sex, and politics. He does not generally confide self-doubts or discuss the traumas of problems at work or a troubled marriage for fear of being thought weak or unsuccessful.

Thus, the American male shuns emotional or physical closeness and suppresses his anxiety or manifests it through acceptable male channels, frequently reinforcing the aggression he needs to escape, thus robbing himself of a healthy outlet. Basically he hangs on to learned poses and roles and expresses whatever anger he feels indirectly. Detached behavior, forgetfulness, courtly "politeness," proneness to accidents, excessive use of tobacco or alcohol, psychosomatic ailments, and impotence can all be expressions of male anger.

Women's liberation has added an incredible amount of pressure to both sexes. In addition to society's expectations that men be performance oriented, successful, powerful, and take-charge oriented, men are also asked to be warm, loving, gentle, and expressive. Yet the typically male characteristics that traditionally attract the opposite sex frequently are thought to preclude development of the other qualities—which men are then criticized by women for not having.

The resultant dilemma of how to balance these traits without losing the benefits derived from each is distressing for many men. The apparent conflict in values and priorities between work and personal life is a great source of tension in both arenas. New rules for social interaction in the office create confusion, lead to repressed irritation, and make some men feel that they no longer fully understand how to compete with the supposedly weaker sex—or whether they are allowed to!

STRESS AND WOMEN

Women's changing social roles may account for the perceptible increase in their deaths from heart disease. New cultural values and expectations pressure women from all sides as they decide on such issues as higher education, marriage, family, and career. The broadening of women's choices has also broadened their chances of contracting stress-related ailments—cardiac infarctions, gastric ulcers, and hypertension, for instance.

Women have greatly benefited from medical advancements in this last century, through the eradication of disease, a reduction in accidents, a decrease in infant mortality, and the improvement of birth control methods. However, the rate at which contemporary women exhibit stress-related illnesses, enumerated in Chapters 9 and 10, is now almost equal to that of men.

Studies seem to indicate that women have two distinct advantages in dealing with stress. First, on the whole they appear to react better physiologically under stress than men because of the female hormonal mechanism for responding to stress. Second, many physicians contend that women have been more conditioned to be in tune with their bodies, which perhaps enables them to recognize the signs of stress more easily.

Nonetheless, incidents of cardiac infarction are increasing among women. There has been no conclusive evidence that the stress engendered in the business world is the main culprit. The fact remains that women are entering formerly male bastions and are being subjected to the traditional pressures of those areas besides the unique set of problems created by virtue of the novelty and prejudice of their presence in the work environment.

Women are increasingly making decisions, taking on responsibilities, and worrying about their lives and the lives of dependents and other people. As more and more women enter the business arena, they will be challenged by high-pressure jobs, deadlines, competition, conflict, and hostility. There are more working women, married and unmarried, in the United States today, whether out of choice or economic necessity, than ever before. Researchers are discovering a slow rise in the Type *A* personality pattern that appears to go hand in glove with big business. These are but two of the conditions contemporary women are facing.

Women not only have the daily pressures of dealing with the demands of the workplace, but they also frequently face overt or covert rejection. Women are not yet in the psychological position of being viable equal partners on the active team. They are often not "seen" by others as the kind of person who should have a particular position.

Not only are women not accepted by men in blue-collar or managerial jobs but frequently they don't even have the acceptance of other women or themselves. The legal drive over the last decade to enforce equal opportunity has legitimized the inclusion of women in all areas in the business world. However, these laws cannot ensure that women will immediately or naturally be able to demonstrate the ability to take advantage of the opportunities that do exist.

The people who must make room for the newcomers, sometimes by curtailing their own opportunities, are becoming hurt, angry, and resentful. Chapter 7 illustrates the distressing aspects of prejudice and discrimination.

Much of the stress experienced between men and women has to do with fundamental differences in perception. They hold different views about themselves and each other and about organizations and careers. They recognize, interpret, and act on issues from different perspectives. These differences result in different styles, emphases, and ways of responding to situations. Men understand their own mind sets but not those of women, and vice versa. In such cases, stress breeds a state of confusion, misunderstanding, and misinterpretation.

Although the results of female and male stress are basically the same, the dynamics that cause that distress sometimes differ. This generation of working women has some guilt and anxiety about success. The emotional ambivalence of today's young career woman creates problems in coping with family, femininity, assertiveness, happiness, and success.

Many women are slightly defensive about their experiences, developing independent, stiff-upper-lip qualities to make themselves appear more sanguine about their experiences than they truly feel. In earlier chapters, we explained how suppressing emotions can be dangerous to health: The unvented arousal turns on the individual and is likely to show up through headaches, indigestion, clammy hands, excessive eating, drinking, or smoking, ulcers, sexual promiscuity, and a variety of other ills.

AGGRESSION

Throughout history, warfare has been found to be almost exclusively a male occupation. The male uses his aggression, physically or intellectually, chiefly to master the environment. Men see aggressiveness as a positive trait, a sign of self-confidence and of conscious commitment to going after what they want by progressively mastering new tasks and the environment.

Women, on the other hand, have been nurtured in passivity, which may obscure initiative, particularly in the business world. The socially sanctioned behavioral prescription for women has been an accepting role that was passive, sustaining, security minded, gentle, and receptive. Conflicts arise within the woman when she sees herself as restricted and confined by this role, which she perceives as only a part of her.

Another significant difference between men and women is in their traditional attitude toward work. Men report that their career motivation derives in large part from knowing since early childhood that they would have to work all their lives. They also feel the pressure to achieve in the business world from knowing that they are responsible for the support of a family. They make a conscious commitment to advancement over the long term and take an active role in making things happen.

Men see their careers as a progression of jobs leading upward in level of responsibility, authority, prestige, and money. For a man, a job has both a present meaning and a future importance. He recognizes that a job can mean money, challenge, utilization of skills and talents yet to be discovered, a game of chance, and many other things. A man sees his career as an integral part of his life, his personal goals, his very identity. Society tends to prepare him by legitimizing and supporting his ambitions.

On the other hand, for many women, a career decision comes much later than a man's. Women have a tendency to think of work as a nine-to-five position and a means of earning a living. They frequently lack the male assumption of movement, a set of assignments to be fulfilled and then left to go on to something else. Men recognize a job as part of a career; women sometimes have problems seeing a series of jobs as a career path.

Women seem to concentrate on the here-and-now tasks, responsibilities, and influence—sometimes to their own long-term advantage. Whereas men define their careers in terms of where they are going, with recognition and reward implied, women's attitudes are quite different.

For a woman, a career involves personal growth, self-fulfillment, satisfaction, making a contribution to others, and/or doing what she wants to do. These goals may be shared by men, too. However, the priorities are in a different order. For men, the goal is all-important. For women, the path or the means to the end may be more important.

ROLE RECONCEPTUALIZATION

Working mothers are in a particularly stressful position. They may feel guilty about not being able to take care of the home or be with their children, and at the same time work with daily aplomb, effectiveness, and satisfaction.

To compensate for this guilt, many women develop the attitude that they must be superwomen. They try to prove that they can handle work, household chores, and family responsibilities, and handle them all well. They may ignore signs of fatigue when they get home at night and overextend their energy supply in an effort to get everything done, not just well, but perfectly. They also have a tendency to do too much so that no one can accuse them of being "bad" wives or mothers.

If the husband is not enthusiastic about his wife's working, the situation is particularly acute. The stress of carrying on two full-time careers, one at home and one in the office, may leave a woman constantly fatigued and exhausted. When her body and/or mind is depleted of adaptive energy by unremitting demands, a breakdown in mental or physical health may follow.

Failure to fulfill either role according to expectations, internal or external, is particularly frustrating. Restructuring priorities, reassessing goals, and using some of the time management techniques outlined in Chapter 3 can be helpful in coping with the problem. In order to survive as a person and maintain a positive self-image, today's woman may have to separate her identity from her conditioning. She may have to change homemaking practices and delegate duties. The internal conflicts created by her natural insecurities as she goes against a traditional lifestyle are a major source of tension.

Our chapter on the family pointed out some of the stress-producing factors in today's nontraditional working couples. Of the 48 million couples in America, more than 40 percent are two-income families. Forty percent of these wives in the labor force have children under three years of age. These and other social factors have brought about modifications regarding family responsibilities.

These modifications do not always come easily. Many people feel betrayed, unloved, or threatened by a break in deeply rooted sex-role stereotypes. "His" and "her" jobs are deeply rooted in our culture and consciousness, and the emotional weight of traditional roles and activities burdens both mates with anxiety and resentments.

Women who feel the husband is "supposed" to be the breadwinner and men who feel the wife is "supposed" to do the laundry may feel a real strain on the relationship when the responsibilities cross over or are neglected.

Additionally, men's work was supposed to come first; but today's women are taking their careers very seriously. Decisions about who uses the only running car for transportation, who takes the child to the dentist, who waits for the plumber to replace the hot water heater, or whose job would take precedence in deciding where to live are not so clear-cut today for most working couples. Both sexes suffer from the strain of trying to adjust contemporary realities by necessity, if not yet by conviction.

Role ambiguity, where there is no clear-cut agreement about who should and will do what, challenges the stability of marriages and adds stress that impacts on a person's total effectiveness. The man has traditionally served as the family's link to the world of work, and the woman's status and prestige have been determined by the husband's status and prestige. The woman, in turn, has been in charge of the expressive side of the family. She has always been the one to nurture others, ease emotional crises, orchestrate the family's social life, and "be there" to meet the needs of her husband and children, often sensing their worries and problems before they could identify them.

What will happen to individuals, families, children, and society as these roles are switched, weakened, or eliminated is hotly debated. There are house husbands, women executives, and women military officers who outrank their male mates. There are more lifestyle options available than many people can recognize and assimilate into traditional beliefs, attitudes, and behaviors.

The conflict between the new and the old often spills over into the workplace, where men and women act out their defensiveness and anger about who "belongs" where, doing what. Men may resent female promotions, feeling that women have an edge and have shouldered aside men who provide for their families.

The issue of leadership illustrates the multifaceted nature of the dilemma. Generally speaking, men have a difficult time knowing how to relate to female leadership. Cultural overtones and lack of experience in dealing with women in this role can challenge both sexes. Men may treat women like a sister, wife, girlfriend, or pal, or they may take out their unresolved conflicts with their mothers on the female superior.

For women, the lack of female role models and lack of familiarity with how the male business network operates can make them overanxious, domineering, confused, and disoriented. They are not always prepared for the criticism and competition of the work environment. Most women are conditioned to seek out approval, particularly from men, and when they do not receive the type of approval they have come to expect they perceive themselves as failures or men as oppressors.

It is difficult for many women to comprehend that they do not have to like or be liked by the people they do business with in order to get the job done. Admittedly, amiable relations with co-workers and business associates are desirable, but cultivating friendships that might be pursued outside of business hours is not a prerequisite to effective interaction on the job.

Women tend to view relationships as ends in themselves, and they overlook the different styles and roles that may be necessary in a given setting. Their responses to others center on who one is rather than on the demands or expectations of the situation. They have a tendency to take things personally and lose sight of their long-term self-interest. Men apparently have learned greater flexibility and have developed a way of behaving that makes it seem simpler to get what they want. They know how to put up with, tolerate, and use each other to a degree that women often find incomprehensible.

Corporate manners and career goals may dictate that two people who dislike each other intensely work together and support one another. Men recognize this as a matter of survival; women may consider it hypocrisy. A man may make friends as a means to an end and consider any lasting friendships that develop as a side benefit. For a woman, the quality of relationships may be her most important priority, and she may be oblivious to the subtle informal side of the organization that makes the system work and provides the groundwork for upward mobility.

Women have a tendency to rely on the formal structure of roles and policies—the way things "should" be—as the critical factor determining career advancement. Men, on the other hand, recognize the informal system of relationships, favors granted and owed, information sharing, connections with influential people, and the like as an important and morally acceptable element in the organizational process. Women are oddly apt to be more blunt, less "political," more direct, less subtle, more personal, less self-protective.

We have mentioned only a few of the patterns of differences between men and women. These and other insights may help cut down on the stresses and strains, irritations, and work-robbing attitudes in the organization.

As we have pointed out, men and women do not share the same experiences, assumptions, perceptions, physiology, or behaviors. As a consequence of all these factors, both men and women have tended to define themselves in part by their differences. Many feel confused, fearful, hostile, bitter, and angry and are prejudiced against one another. Feelings of anxiety, resentment, insecurity, lack of control, and frustration all work against the individual by stifling productivity, limiting effectiveness, draining energy, and potentially damaging health.

In order to contribute to an improvement in the quality of life, it is important to understand what our biological and cultural inheritance has been. It does not take very much to translate these differences in mind set into the implications they hold for behavior in the business environment and society at large.

Studies in psychology, biology, physiology, and personality theory reveal a broad range of sex differences. We have only given a few examples. There are intellectual, physical, glandular, motivational, sexual, and actuarial characteristics that bear investigation as a means for dealing with one another more effectively in the world of tomorrow. Awareness of general beliefs, assumptions, values, and emotions can improve the way we relate to one another and enable us to make coping adjustments. We can then reduce the damaging effects of intense or prolonged unnecessary stress due to innate or acculturated sexual differences.

CHAPTER 12

Adaptation
and Contemporary Life

The human body has numerous mechanisms that are constantly shifting to maintain a healthy balance in its biological functions in the face of the demands of everyday life. The human organism is a magnificent creation in its ingenious capacity to trigger intricate general adjustments to regain homeostasis when any challenge threatens to disrupt the consistency of the internal environment.

Nevertheless, there are limits to man's ability to adapt, both psychologically and physiologically, and hence culturally. People have unique elastic limits beyond which their tolerance threshold and recovery ability break down. The need for adaptation is obvious; understanding the dynamics of the process is important in order to preserve and assure the quality of life and well-being we wish to attain.

The speed of change in the last part of this century is not as favorably related to man's ability to adapt as it was in the past, when life was simpler and moved at a slower pace. Adaptation takes time. When conditions develop more rapidly than the species can adapt to them, they are not as easily tolerated and are more detrimental to functioning than if they evolve gradually, over a long period. Modern man's environment has changed quicker and more radically than he has been able to change himself. The species has taken 500,000 years to evolve to its present complex state; the great changes in life conditions that relate to stress have taken two or three centuries.

Adaptation is a dynamic, evolving, unending process of adjustment. As circumstances change, so must people, if they are to survive. From a biological point of view, the reproductive success and genetic development of a population depend upon adaptation to the demands of the environment over hundreds of generations.

BIOPSYCHOSOCIAL INVESTIGATION

We are using the word "adaptation" in terms of the evolutionary biopsychosocial system of our existence. This concept takes into account the biological, psychological, and social components of the life cycle. In our interdisciplinary approach to dealing with stress, we talk about adaptation, defense mechanisms, skill mastery, and coping techniques. As has been said, both internal and external environmental stimuli initiate an equilibrating process in man in all instances. This process can lead to avoidance or attack, to accelerated or compensatory changes, to novel solutions, to regressive patterns of denial, or to other behaviors.

There are many ways in which common human experiences can be distressing and result in failures of adaptation. We have previously illustrated that the variation in impact of severe stress is wide indeed. The hazards of living in the twentieth century reflect the consequences of our evolutionary heritage. Some repercussions are crises associated with normal developmental changes during the life cycle. Others reflect major features of the new environmental demands that are related to social and technological change in a rapidly changing industrialized techniculture.

RADICAL CHANGE

Ours is an era of radical change, ever widening, ever accelerating, affecting every part of life. It is estimated that 25 percent of all the people who ever lived are alive today; that 90 percent of all the scientists who ever lived are living now. The amount of technical information available doubles every 10 years. Throughout the world, about 60 million pages of scientific and technical literature are published in more than 60 languages, and the number doubles every 15 years. As Charles de Gaulle once said: "The world is undergoing a transformation to which no change that has yet occurred can be compared, either in scope or in rapidity."

Psychosocial man is undergoing a cultural mutation, not necessarily in the Darwinian biological sense of genetic structure, but rather in the emergency of homo humanus, the "human man," out of homo sapiens, the "rational man." There is a growing sense of awe and apprehension about what all the revolutionary social, technological, and economic changes throughout American society mean to us and where they are leading us, our society, and our world.

The present gets replaced by the unfamiliar future at such a rapid rate that we are forced into a state of continuous struggle to adapt. In addition to the stress loads caused by everyday living and working, the anxiety of accelerating changes engenders a level of physiological stress arousal that increases man's vulnerability to health breakdowns and to a loss of emotional well-being. Consequently, man is turning his attention to improving the quality of life and health, on and off the job. He is looking not only for a better life, but also for a better lifestyle.

The ingredients for survival are very different now from those of earlier evolutionary eras. Scarcity of living space, the proliferating consequences of urbanization, the population explosion, a sedentary way of life, environmental damage, pollution, and resources depletion are comparatively recent problems of man.

Our species has been in existence for about 500,000 years, but the industrial revolution only began just over 200 years ago. The biological equipment of man is very old by comparison with the forces that challenge him today. In addition to obvious physical characteristics, some of our emotional response tendencies and learning orientations reflect the biological equipment developed in man because they worked well tens of thousands of years ago. Man's present life is largely the product of the accelerated and cumulative impact of science and technology in the wake of the industrial revolution. In view of all the social changes that have taken place on an evolutionary-time scale, there has been relatively little time for man to change. It has been estimated that for 99 percent of the time since man's emergence as a distinct species, human biology evolved under conditions requiring adaptation to the social structure of hunting and gathering societies. Consequently, we really do not know how well suited we are to the world in which we now find ourselves.

SUITABILITY OF RESPONSE PATTERN

Since cultural change has moved at a more accelerated pace than genetic change, the emotional and biological response patterns that have been built into man may turn out to be less suitable for some present environments than for those of the past. As we have stated earlier, the fight-or-flight response pattern was most appropriate to prepare for physical action at a time when the conditions of life and threatening challenges were physical in nature. However, in contemporary America, usually very little, if any, physical action follows intense physiological arousal.

The changes to which we are exposed are usually perceived as threats to self-esteem, to relations with significant other people, to what we consider our rightful place or vested interest. Confronted with what we believe to be a threat, our whole circulation and metabolism are mobilized—in preparation for physical action that never takes place. Chapter 9 explained how these reactions can become harmful and produce disease, especially when they are mobilized many times in the course of a day. As we have pointed out before, stress is not just an isolated part of life; it is a constant factor in everyone's life situation. There seems to be no escape from stress.

In Chapters 9 and 10, we examined how the body and mind respond to stress. From this information, it may appear that mental and physical health are based largely on the ability to maintain a state of internal equilibrium and balanced lifestyle. This healthy balance of mental and physical processes is called homeostasis. Throughout the last 11 chapters, we have presented many examples of stress-producing agents in society and the individual. As you now know, these stressors disrupt the body's natural balance and force it to restore homeostasis through adaptation. Regardless of the positive or negative consequences of the change, both stress and adaptation develop.

GENERIC STRESS

Thomas Holmes and Richard Rahe focused their research efforts on the concept of generic change as a stressor—that is, how change resulting in either positive or negative life events contributes to the stress reaction and affects human health. They found that undesirable or distressful events are usually the most harmful when they are disruptive for a longer period of time. Undesirable events such as arguments, death, or job loss seem to stimulate negative thoughts that stay in the mind temporarily, producing a secondary effect. This effect may stimulate concern, doubt, and doomsday projections and imagery. The negative feelings may in turn maintain the body in a prolonged state of alarm and physical response. From the section on the general adaptation syndrome, it is clear that even-

tually adaptive energies—the ability of the body to regain homeostasis—are used up, and survival itself may be at stake.

ADAPTIVE RANGE

Each person is believed to have an adaptive range below and
above which his ability to cope breaks down. Both understimulation
and overstimulation can lead to anti-adaptive states.

When the mind and/or body can no longer handle the demands
placed upon it, the final stage of exhaustion sets in. There may be
evidence of confusion, disorientation, distortion of reality, fatigue,
anxiety, tenseness, or extreme irritability. The person may seem to
lose the will to live and become dull and listless, apathetic and
withdrawn, and display a generalized overall drop in mental and
physical abilities.

There are limitations to man's adaptability. These are individual
in nature but can be categorized in a broad sense. In Part I, we
focused on eight areas of social forces that tend to cause stress.
Each person has his own tolerance level in each of these areas. The
social forces can operate up to this level without the person
suffering a physical or psychological breakdown.

FACTORS IN ADAPTATION

Diseases of adaptation are ailments in development to which
biological stress has contributed. The same stressor—chemical,
physical, or nervous—can produce different manifestations in different people or in the same people at different times. Diverse
internal and external factors condition the effects of the stressor.

Adaptation depends greatly on the psychological skills of taking
things in stride. These include observation, self-appraisal, a general
level of maturity, problem-solving skills, and a general level of
personal adjustment. A person's reactivity level—his characteristic
response to pressure—correlates with these skills. The higher the
reactivity level and the lower the coping skills, the greater the
limitations on adaptability.

A person's ability to cope with sensory input depends on his
physiological structure and to some extent on learned patterns. The
nature of his sense organs and the speed with which impulses flow
through his neural system set biological bounds on the quantity of
sensory data he can accept. The human brain has approximately 100

FIGURE 9. *Basic functions of the brain.*

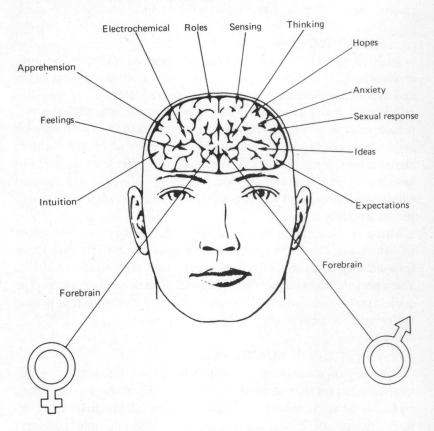

billion neurons (brain cells) and 1 million billion synapses (connections). Heredity, environment, and the sex hormones modify, alter, influence, or control all mental activities, through the network of brain cells which ultimately create differences in behavior patterns. The neurons are in a constant state of chatter with each other by way of chemical messages (neurotransmitters) that cross the synaptic gap between them (see Figure 9).

Man is unquestionably among the most adaptable of creatures. Yet, even in man, the boundaries of the nervous system and sense organs are imposing. Many of today's environmental signals are too novel, unpredictable, disorganized, and irregular to follow; we are reduced to sampling experience at best, and our image of reality is distorted.

Man's behavior depends upon his ability to predict, to a certain extent, the outcome of his actions in his environment, on the basis of information he receives from the environment. In our rapidly changing world, the individual needs to process more data in order to make effective, rational decisions. As there are limits on how much sensory input he can accept, there are also built-in constraints on his ability to receive, collate, abstract, classify, and code the information.

Sensory, cognitive, and decisional overload can impair a person's ability to think and act clearly and may lead to the breakdown of performance. It may also be related to psychopathology in ways we have not yet begun to explore. For example, both managers and highly skilled technicians, plagued by demands for rapid, incessant, and complex decisions, can pay a high price in psychic costs and generate distorted images of reality.

New needs and novel emergencies and crises demand rapid response. The individual may detach himself, be noncommital, and lose sight of the overall project. He may fight against the demands to make faster and more complex decisions by tabling the issue, referring it to committee, losing it in the paperwork, or assigning blame for the delay on red tape. There are several other strategies people employ to ward off the confusion, self-doubt, anxiety, frustration, and fear often brought about by too many choices and too many demands in too short a period of time, plus a high price tag on failure.

SOCIAL LEARNING

Social learning seems to be crucial in the development of adaptive behaviors. The skills of observation, exploration, organization, setting of priorities, and communication are but a few learnable processes that can bring about and maintain a healthy match of the person to the environment.

Social behavior in meeting such fundamental adaptive tasks as finding food and water, avoiding predators, procreation, and caring for the young is a function not only of individual people but also of the entire social system. The ability to cope effectively with the specific requirements of a given environment is vital in the shaping of evolutionary change.

In times of such rapid technological and social change, old

guidelines for behavior become uncertain or discredited. These established guidelines are difficult to change, even when they may be poorly suited to new conditions. Achieving self-managed change is difficult for a person in his lifetime, because his self-esteem and close interpersonal relationships depend on his behavior patterns. Yet the need for new adaptive behaviors is called for in view of the social and health problems we face today.

The preceding chapters have detailed the pervasiveness of the stress problem. We can detect a sense of urgency for dealing with stress. With the vastly different patterns of social organization current today, adaptation requires a high premium to be placed on the individual's learning, self-sufficiency, autonomy, foresight, and planning. Each person must also be capable of organizing institutionally into cooperative group efforts.

When the environment is stable in its main features over long periods of time, guidelines for behavior emerge that are, on the average, useful for the population. Such guidelines for behavior tend to be learned or assimulated, as we have mentioned before, very early in life. They are shaped by rewards and punishments, are emotionally charged, and are supported by norms important for group cooperation in meeting developmental needs.

Such early learning of guidelines for adaptive behavior tends to induce lifelong commitments. These guidelines are geared to prepare the young to meet the adaptive requirements of the environment by fulfilling the roles of adult life. That they don't always work these days is reflected in the high tension, alienation, and lopsided maturity of American adolescents, some of whom appear to reject the world of stress. This withdrawal may be a protective adaptation of the species, but it does not solve the problems of the majority, for whom there is no escape.

ADAPTIVE GUIDELINES

Evolutionary research has taught us that when there is a drastic change in environmental conditions, some genes and behavior that had formerly been of little adaptive utility may become exceedingly important. Successful adaptation means the ability to utilize environmental opportunities and to avoid catastrophes.

The capacity to evoke help, to use help, to relate to new objects, and to accept support is important to the maintenance of mental health. There is a need to focus on current and future reality and to anticipate and rehearse new behaviors and forms of social encounter. Relearning means changing the interaction between personality dispositions and situational requirements in problem-solving situations.

Perceptual and cognitive processes are significantly related to adaptive behavior. They affect a person's positive self-image under the most adverse social realities. The concepts of personality functioning and social dynamics in their adaptive aspects help point up the demand characteristics of a situation, and they offer some insight into the appropriateness and effectiveness of the defense preferences and coping styles that will influence choices and overall stability.

The role of differentiation and cognitive mastery is in limiting stress, in clarifying to oneself that it is this, but not this or this; or "I've lost this and this, but I still have this." To circumscribe stress it is important to hold on to resources that are still positive and allow them to contribute to resilience.

Reinforced hope, expectations for the future, readiness to use support, and new constructive defenses can add ego strength and lower the threshold for recovery.

I'm a new me.
I got stronger through it.
I can put up with a lot.

Processes contributing to recovery include:

Eliminating stress
Eating and self-gratification
Indulging in self-fulfilling visual imagery
Changing the pain–pleasure balance (being good to yourself)

PATTERNS OF VULNERABILITY

Besides hereditary factors, birth difficulties, and the consequences of severe illnesses, specific patterns and interaction tendencies can also interfere with the capacity to cope with the environment and with the ability to maintain enough equilibrium to support optimal functioning. The impact or stress of specific or combined pressures, frustrations, or pains differs with the individual, depending on constitutional and acquired sensitivities, affective and autonomic ability, consequences of previous trauma, conflicts, anxiety, or suspicion, the subjective or objective mitigating factors, and the effectiveness of defenses. A wide range of organic and psychological factors affect the stress to a person of any particular experience.

Resilience can be seen as an active psychophysiological push to restore a satisfying state of balance. This includes being supported by the physiological capacities to resolve disruptions of smooth autonomic functioning by returning to optimal levels and by the physiological capacity for self-healing.

Man's capacity for orientation, differentiation, organization, and integration of perception with action is basic to his dealings with both the impersonal (cognitive) and human (social) environments. It is also characteristic of his coping style. Man is uniquely capable of imagination, foresight, and choice and of using his culture to cope with the stresses of environmental change rather than to end up shattered by them. In Part III we deal with some creative means by which man has learned to adapt to and cope with his stressful environment.

Part III
MANAGING STRESS

CHAPTER 13
Goals and Principles of Coping

Throughout Parts I and II, attention has been directed to four forms of stress: behavioral, emotional, intellectual, and psychological. This increased awareness of the pervasive effect stress has on you and others may in itself produce stress. That is, your stress level may increase if you feel overwhelmed by the inescapable nature of stress. Please be reminded, however, that not all stress is negative. By learning the goals and principles of coping, you can use stress constructively to promote good health and self-development.

Chapters 14 through 18 present the means by which the five goals of coping can be attained. The ends toward which this effort is directed are to:

1. Realize potential of self-direction.
2. Assume self-responsibility as a major factor in health and sickness.
3. Minimize detrimental effects of distress.
4. Restore sense of harmony with environment.
5. Achieve and maintain a high level of health.

In order to accomplish these goals, you have to follow some basic principles. These will be elucidated.

First of all, stress is the product of an entire lifestyle, whether personal or organizational. It is not the product of an occasional crisis. Rather, it is the unrelieved state of arousal many people experience in day-to-day verbal battles with co-wrokers or spouse; television viewing of violent and unsettling programs; news reports of inflation, terrorism, crime, and disturbing national and international incidents; traffic congestion; computer errors; and other high-stimulus situations. Consequently, each person must learn to monitor his or her internal arousal level. Managing your stress better is related to the psychosomatic concept of illness discussed in Chapter 9, which pointed up the interrelationships among the mind, the body, and the entire environment.

Also, people need to find ways to relieve stress, often simply to allow the body to carry out its biochemical repair work. You can protect health and well-being by using constructive coping response to balance the episodic stress experienced. For example, you can simply stop what you are doing for about five minutes and relax. As pointed out in Chapter I, a stressor can be environmental or internal.

THE SYNERGISTIC APPROACH

By the synergistic approach we mean using a combined action or operation such that the total effect is greater than the sum of the individual effects. In an era of specialization, one person may be treated simultaneously for various complaints by a dentist, psychologist, urologist, ophthalmologist, and gastroenterologist. The problem—poor health—may be broken down into manageable parts. However, most people, including physicians and other health experts, overlook the mutually supporting, synergistic relationship among the six aspects of well-being:

Physiological	Emotional
Nutritional	Spiritual
Environmental	Lifestyle values

In stress reduction programs, these factors are treated as integrated aspects of good health. Such an approach requires a balance of the multifaceted dimensions of living and working in order to achieve a quality of life which is productive, nurturing, and satisfying. What you do in one area supports, enhances, and capitalizes on actions in the other areas. Conversely, if one or more aspects of your life go unattended or awry, your equilibrium is thrown off balance, often with unfavorable results.

For instance, poor eating habits may increase your stress level in the following ways: An unbalanced diet lacking in sufficient nutritional content frequently leads to weight problems and lack of vitality. This lack of energy may slow down productivity and lead to increased pressure at home and at work to get things done. The pressure can lower your self-esteem or defensive behaviors, thus throwing your entire lifestyle out of balance and increasing your stress to unhealthy levels.

Medical professionals need to look at the whole person, including analyses of physical, nutritional, environmental, emotional, spiritual, and lifestyle values. We need an expanded health care concept which emphasizes personal responsibility to bring into harmony the body, mind, emotions, and spirit.

THE WELLNESS CONCEPT

Health is regarded as the natural order of things, the condition of being sound in body, mind, and spirit. It is a positive attribute that man can acquire if he governs his life wisely. As a rule, unfortunately, he has found it easier to depend on professionals, drugs, and surgery to cure sickness rather than to attempt the more difficult task of living wisely to prevent disease.

Although both professional and individual approaches may be necessary in the treatment of disease, it is increasingly apparent that the acquisition of coping mechanisms is essential to prevent the probability of such diseases as essential hypertension, various cardiac diseases, and ulcers. The benefits of prevention as opposed to treatment are obvious.

Among the environmental and lifestyle factors that have been associated with individual health are:

Work environment (Chapter 2)
Quality of nutrition (Chapter 16)
Social support networks (Chapter 7)
Industrial pollution (Chapter 8)
Substance abuse (including food, alcohol, drugs, and tobacco) (Chapter 16)
Exercise and recreation (Chapter 16)
Emotional health/self-awareness (Chapter 15)

Each of these factors affects the amount of stress someone experiences and how he or she deals with it. Many studies have shown the relationship of poorly handled stress to a wide variety of diseases and debilitating conditions. However, stress, when properly managed, may lead to "eustress," providing opportunities for the enhancement of health, personal growth, and well-being. Like the Chinese character for "crisis," stress can signify either danger or opportunity, depending on how it is perceived and dealt with.

Optimum health is an attainable goal for every individual. The process of obtaining physical and mental well-being is a learning process. You can develop and maintain behaviors consistent with good health if you:

1. Stop doing things that are detrimental to your health, such as smoking.
2. Engage in health-producing behaviors, such as relaxing at regular intervals.
3. Are provided with self-regulation and self-control information, such as time management and thought stopping.
4. Receive experiential training in health promotion strategies and technologies, such as self-hypnosis and biofeedback.
5. Have appropriate incentives, such as increased vitality.
6. Increase involvement and responsibility for your own health, such as developing a stress reduction program.

THE STRESS REDUCTION PROGRAM

The stress reduction program emphasizes enhancement of health and well-being through appropriate recreation, nutrition, and therapeutic and preventive care. In addition, employees can receive stress management counseling and learn new ways to manage distress and promote eustress in their personal and professional lives. They can learn to make positive lifestyle changes in a supportive program environment.

Health consequences are determined, to a large extent, by choices made by people. In order to measure a person's quality of life, we must include behavioral and social parameters as well as meures of functioning ability, wellness, and goal setting.

Our approach to health enhancement is multidisciplinary, with the goal of extending the productive lives of employees. Health is a complex mosaic of proper nutrition, exercise, and mental fitness, components of a person's total lifestyle. Stress reduction training is a form of human resources development that focuses primarily on a person's own well-being as an avenue to improved organizational operation.

Stress reduction training centers on the person—his or her unique situation, reaction pattern, and lifestyle. It is based on two principal concepts:

1. A great deal of stress is unconsciously self-induced by a high level of reactivity.
2. A great deal of stress is avoidable through self-monitoring and self-regulation.

THE VICIOUS CYCLE OF STRESS

With the health procedures now available, the vicious cycle of distress can be broken. Coping mechanisms can reverse the bleak pattern of vulnerability and the debilitating physical and psychological effects of stress overload. Immunity to adversity and resistance to impaired functioning can be heightened by the physical and psychological skills of controlling the stress in life. With proper education, reinforcement, a plan of action, and behavior alteration, everyday stressful situations can be turned into positive stress—eustress—and opportunities for growth.

The last part of this book focuses on how to prevent stress from obstructing health by coming to terms with the all-pervading nature of the problem as examined in Parts I and II. The program is a combination of prevention, intervention, and treatment. It encompasses a multitude of factors, including differences in biochemistry, physical strength, psychological and emotional makeup, values, attitudes, behaviors, social history, health history, environment, dietary habits, sleep patterns, and drugs.

SUSCEPTIBILITY TO ILLNESS

Effective coping mechanisms address the state of well-being of the whole person, combining common sense with medical experience. Breakthroughs emerging from the field of psychophysiology are helping to explain why 10 to 20 percent of us almost never get sick and why the others do. Although no one can avoid the stresses of living, those who understand how both good and bad changes in life can accumulate and compound to influence susceptibility to illnesses and accidents can respond more positively to a given input. That is, they have developed a variety of coping behaviors to handle the inescapable day-to-day events and to minimize those stressful life changes that are not under their control.

COPING RESPONSES

People who get along well in life can respond to any given situation with appropriate behavior. Coping behaviors include a variety of responses:

1. Emotional—humor, anger, sadness, excitement
2. Personal habits—eating, smoking, sex, physical activity, drinking
3. Unconscious habits—nail biting, sighing, finger drumming
4. Absorption in job, family, hobby

Flexibility and a creative range of coping behaviors enable people to handle the considerable amount of life change experienced. A limited coping repertoire may be harmful. It lacks adaptability and the behavior initiated to handle the stressor may have negative side effects. For instance, if eating or drinking is the primary coping response to stress, obesity or alcoholism is likely to present its own problems.

Maladaptive Coping

Illness itself may be a form of maladaptive coping. Other potentially destructive responses include violence, procrastination, drug abuse, overwork, poor sleeping habits (sleep disorder), compulsive spending sprees, total withdrawal, and caustic remarks. They make a problem worse or initiate a new one rather than solve anything. They cause internal harm or they hurt other people.

Conscious and Unconscious Coping

If you react automatically to stressful situations, with little awareness or deliberate choice, your coping response is unconscious. On the other hand, if you react to stress in ways you have chosen because they work for you, and if you are aware of what you are doing, you are coping intentionally and consciously. Lack of conscious awareness of your responses to life's situations can perpetuate losing, destructive behavior that undermines your health and well-being.

A LOW-STRESS LIFESTYLE

A low-stress lifestyle is a combination of adaptability and balance. It is a matter of choice—what the person does that contributes to or minimizes the stress that he experiences. The process of controlling stress promotes change in many aspects of your life. There are five broad approaches to coping with life's difficulties. Within each of these responses, there are a number of specific methods that can be used to strengthen your stress filter and soften the impact of future stressors.

Living with the Distress

This is perhaps the least acceptable approach to dealing with stress. It may be necessary for short periods of time, but it does not promote health over the long haul. For instance, the intensity with which a concert pianist prepares for a Carnegie Hall appearance is both invigorating and grueling. The temporary sacrifice is made to reach a goal, but does little lasting harm.

Unfortunately, many people are almost addicted to distress and perpetually go to great lengths to create distressful situations. These people not only live with the distress, they wallow in it, playing out "loser" and "poor me" life scripts or showing how tough they are.

Withdrawing from the Stressor

There are several coping responses that enable one to get away from a distressful situation when other approaches have not reduced the distress.

Leaving the scene for a while by recessing a meeting or taking a walk, a day off, a nap, or a vacation can be healthy responses to restore vitality and relieve overload. However, like other coping responses, this approach can be constructive or destructive, depending upon when and how it is used.

It can provide a change of pace and renewal or it may merely be a means of escape and, in fact, create more stress. Chronic procrastinators and hypochrondriacs typically react to stress by running away from the problem rather than tackling it head-on. Frequently, this avoidance technique creates further problems.

A more permanent move—changing your job, place of residence, or relationship—should be considered as a last resort in most cases.

The decision to remove the stressor permanently must be considered within the total stress picture. Will this in fact eliminate the chronic overload, excessive role conflict, or incompatible relationship, or should you explore what you do to cause yourself conflict and tension in different settings? Are you the problem, or is someone or something else the cause of your distress? Chapter 15 will provide insight into understanding yourself as the most important approach to bringing balance into your life.

When the stressor cannot be changed—for instance, the crowding and noise of city life—and to remain in the same environment would mean living with perpetual distress, withdrawal may be the most viable coping response. But usually there are alternatives by means of which you can moderate the negative stressors in your life without leaving the stressful situation.

Changing How You Relate to the Stressor

Changing how you relate to the specific stressors in your life means altering the pattern of interchange between yourself and the demands or aspects of your lifestyle that cause you problems. Recognize that the source of your tension may be an overdemanding employer who chronically gives you a new project too late in the day to complete and who then berates you for not being conscientious or for falling behind schedule. Being more assertive and candid with your employer about your work schedule and time demands, suggesting alternatives, and being empathetic about his scheduling problems can defuse the daily tension. Other ways of relating to the stressor differently include:

Developing new skills
Establishing a support network of close friends
Being more diplomatic
Being tolerant of others' imperfections and your own
Broadening your perspective

Changing the Stressor

Although some situations are beyond your control—for example, stormy weather or the death of a loved one—this is not true for all stressors. You can change many features in your environment that adversely affect your health and self-development. For instance, you can change others' actions toward you to the degree to which you alter your behavior. By changing the thermostat, lighting, or music in your office you can alter the distractions or discomforts in your micro-environment. Also, there are social and political approaches to help reduce the number of stress-producing features in society and the world at large.

Reducing the frequency of stressful life-change events can markedly reduce tension in a fast-paced life. As pointed out in Chapter 5, there are many changes inherent in the adult life cycle to which most of us must learn to adapt. When you double the demand for adaptation by frequently changing jobs, cities, homes, or sweethearts, you could be overloading your coping mechanism.

The underlying dynamics are the same: awareness of the problem and conscious choice of a constructive coping response to improve the quality of life by reducing destructive features. The idea is to change those things you can change but accept those you cannot, tolerating them by recognizing your own limitations.

Accepting the Situation and Lowering Stress

There are several ways to lower the stress experienced when the situation cannot be changed:

Moderation
Relaxation
Exercise
Communication with confidant
Professional counseling and therapy
Rest
Religious faith and practice

We shall look at each of these techniques more closely in the ensuing chapters. As we have seen here, the selection of specific ways of managing stress is a matter of individual choice and circumstances. The two guiding considerations are these:

1. In what ways will a particular choice or action promote your own good health and self-development and minimize distress?

2. In what ways will your efforts promote the health and development of others and reduce distress?

It is vital to create conditions in which your limited energies (and those of others) are directed toward activities that are healthful and important to you, so that stress is mobilized as a positive force.

CHAPTER 14

Perception and Communication

The level of stress a person experiences is determined to a great extent by the closeness of the fit between the perceived and actual situations. His perception or consciousness is a result of his interpretation of the elements in his environment as screened through physical sensations, attitudes, and experience.

Whether a situation is a threat or a challenge is largely a matter of how a person views it. There are as many reactions to stressors as there are people experiencing them. People who cannot handle adversity collapse, while others meet the same threat with equanimity. Still others actually thrive on challenge and are stimulated by it to achieve great things.

These differences in reaction to stressful circumstances are partially accounted for by such factors as:

Culture	Habits
Biochemistry/heredity	Social context
Physical strength	Personal experience
Psychological constitution	Aspirations
Emotional makeup	Interests
Value system	Education
Attitudes	

By and large, most events are neutral. You give them meaning. You make them what they seem. Your expectations, knowledge, and anticipation of a situation will have a critical bearing on the event's impact. An event of which you are aware is not necessarily the same as your perception or interpretation of it. First-order experiences from sensory input are different from the second-order experiences relating to the thoughts you have of those experiences. The mental categories, ideas, concepts—the meanings you give to the world you experience—shape your behavior and your inter-action with your environment.

COMMUNICATION SKILLS

Practically everything we do involves the use of words, including letter writing, reading, giving and taking orders, speaking at meet-ings, and listening to people. What is not so obvious, however, is that we depend on words to digest what is going on around us and to pass this information on to others. The language we use directs our attitudes, controls our thinking processes, and modifies our behav-ior to a certain extent. How you name what you see—that is, how you describe your observations—leads to conclusions, yours and those of your listener. Since 70 percent of a typical day is spent communicating with other people, it is imperative to develop effective communication skills to minimize distressing experiences brought about by misunderstandings.

General Semantics

Behavioral scientists and philosophers have achieved, through the discipline of general semantics, amazing results in understand-ing the way man thinks. General semantics cuts across boundaries of neurology, psychology, philosophy, psychiatry, chemistry, biol-ogy, biochemistry, sociology, anthropology, and other natural sciences.

The late Alfred Korzybski, in his monumental book *Science and Sanity* (1933), drew from generations of knowledge to formulate an engineering approach to creating new methods of thinking that can be utilized in communicating, training, problem solving, human relations, personal adjustment, and creativity.

The system of general semantics points up the interrelationship of factors such as personal experience, culture, feelings, purposes, mental set, and physiological conditions on the meaning of words and symbols. By teaching you to emphasize thinking and under-stand your emotional reactions, general semantics can increase your effectiveness, your productivity, and the overall quality of your life.

Figure 10 illustrates schematically a person's overall response to any stimulus. The four overlapping ellipses illustrate the principal elements of man's interactive nature and indeed serve to define man as a *thinking, feeling, self-moving, electrochemical organism-as-a-*

FIGURE 10. *Man in his environment, as described by the system of general semantics.*

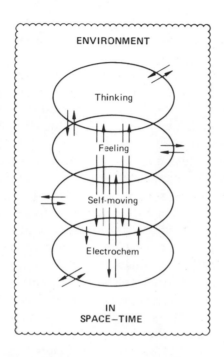

whole in continuous interaction in an environment in space-time. The top two represent activities that are within the usual range of observation. The other two, *self-moving* and *electrochemical,* deal with activities that are revealed by scientific instruments and techniques such as EKGs (electrocardiograms), EEGs (electroencephalograms), EMGs (electromyograms), use of anesthetics, insulin, and vitamins, studying biofeedback, and measuring blood pressure.

The thinking ellipse includes ideas, language, symbols, writing, reading, talking, problem solving, planning, and related activities. A letter, a newspaper, a sales graph, and a report are means we commonly use to communicate our thoughts.

Included in the feeling ellipse are pleasure, joy, anger, fear, desires, regrets, and wishes. Feelings reach lower on the evolutionary scale and are more apparent in children than in mature adults.

Involuntary body movements and organ functions are called

self-moving activities. That is, the heart pumps, the lungs breathe, the whole body grows, the nerves react to touch.

These various activities overlap and interact. When something happens in one section, something happens in all others. When you think hard, you become tense. When you are emotionally upset, your thinking goes awry. When you are given an anesthetic, you stop most thinking and feeling, but not self-moving.

If our reaction to a stimulus takes place principally at the feeling level, it is an emotionally governed reaction. When a reaction is governed by the thinking level, it is considered to be controlled by the reasoning process.

The dictionary meaning of words and the semantic reaction to words are often two entirely different things. The first belongs to the world of words; the second belongs to the world of nonwords. These two worlds overlap when a word is taken into the stream of life and acquires a unique meaning for the person who hears it or uses it at a particular moment under particular circumstances.

One further feature of semantic reaction is that the reactions of each individual are different from those of all other individuals. This is illustrated in Figure 11, which represents three people: the first, a physician; the second, his patient; and the third, a research technician who keeps records in the hospital.

Above these diagrams we write a statement from the pathologist: "It is cancer." The words are clear enough. We can assume that all three people agree on the meaning. But do they react to it in the same manner? Evidently not. The event that the word described does not mean the same thing to all three. It is easy to realize that their semantic reactions are different at all levels of activity.

For example, the technician who made a slide and identified the cancer cells is confronted with the technical requirement of doing it a second time for confirmation. In the face of his long-anticipated date with a strikingly attractive young lady he has attempted to romance all week, "It is cancer" means the cancellation of that opportunity, since he will now have to work overtime to prepare another slide.

To the specialist who brought the patient into the world many years before and has had to break the bad news, it is a most unfortunate interruption in a young life.

To the patient with two children and a loving family, the diagnosis portends an end to all this, a sad and dismal event.

FIGURE 11. *Individual nature of semantic reaction.*

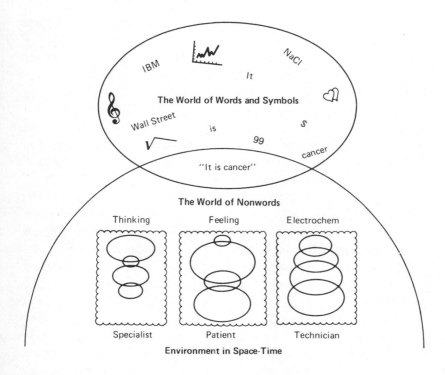

And so you see, "It is cancer," as with other linguistic exchanges, has a multitude of possible and different meanings for different people.

In a business, how often do people react differently to simple key words such as "incentive," "grievance," "cost control," "delegation," and "planning"? You don't relieve stress by referring to the dictionary. Tension can be released by using language effectively, evaluating complex semantic reactions in yourself and in others, and developing the skill of dealing with these reactions. Training is required for this skill, because our semantic mechanisms are often so well integrated with daily life that they are difficult to recognize or deal with.

The Effective Use of Language

The effective use of language represents one of the most important objectives of general semantics. Language is more than a means of reproducing or voicing ideas. It is itself a shaper of our ideas and of action. This is perhaps the most important and original contribution of general semantics.

Problems of communication, poor analysis of problem situations, and other difficulties that plague us can often be traced to built-in structural deficiencies in our language, deficiencies of which we are largely unconscious because we take language for truth.

One of the objectives of general semantics training is to sensitize people to these difficulties and to help them to use language more effectively. One of the reasons most frequently given for the breakdown in business or personal relations is poor communication. Alternatively, good communication can make a business or marriage function smoothly and enjoyably.

In general semantics, it is postulated that any happening in the world outside our bodies (weather, a chair falling), as well as any happening inside our bodies (thinking, feelings, emotions), happens on the nonverbal or silent level. These happenings involve electrocolloidal processes in the nervous system to which we may react verbally. It is at this point that choices are made, skills are utilized, and the importance of semantic self-regulation in the reduction of stress is realized.

The main sociocultural role of language seems to be intercommunication about nonverbal experiences. Communication is the imparting or interchange of thoughts, opinions, or information by means of speech, writing, signs, or symbols. These forms convey your interpretation of what you perceive. Yet whatever you may say that something is, it is not what you experience on the silent levels.

Also, what you experience is unique to you; there is no such thing as an external, "real" world out there that is exactly the same for all of us. Our methods of thinking and feeling are powerful agents in the building of our personal worlds, the only "real" world to each of us. Anything that threatens the hanging together of our own personal world is apt to provoke the stress alarm in us. We feel challenged to defend our world as we know it.

Therefore, our choice of words is an important means of shaping experience and hence of limiting stress under many circumstances.

How we express ourselves is related to methods of fact-finding, methods of reaching conclusions, ways of keeping preconceptions from distorting the understanding on new data, and pitfalls of language.

In order to develop better communication skills, we must begin with more effective habits of thinking. As we have seen, only when we have a fairly clear idea of what is to be expressed can we draw verbal maps that adequately represent the territory of our observations. In our fast-changing world, about which our knowledge is incomplete, no one is able to say the final word or have an omniscient point of view. Making sweeping generalizations causes antagonism. No one has all the facts in any given situation; information is appropriate and complete only up to a point.

Recognize the human equation in knowledge. Statements speak only for the speaker and reflect how he sees the situation:

As far as he knows
Up to a point
Personally
At a particular point in time
Under a particular set of circumstances

We do not deal with people in a categorical way. We deal with people individually. When we do this, we assume we know all about someone and may close our eyes to what is actually going on in this time and place. Lack of accurate information leads to false knowledge, which is known to breed maladjustments.

Prejudging or projecting what a person is going to say or do blocks effective communication and may cause distressful interpersonal relationships. Chapter 7 explores social stereotyping, bias, and prejudice in more detail.

Self-fulfilling prophecy can add to stressful relations when a person expects the worst of himself or others. When he preconditions his mind against a task or situation, his actions usually follow this negative outlook, and his expectations are realized. Such counterproductive thinking patterns can cause a range of negative emotions and tax a person's ability to cope with his life.

If we want to react to people as they are, we must remember that they may act differently with the passing of time. People and circumstances change; they are really never the same. Into every interaction, each person brings his or her own experiences, needs, and aspirations. The distressing aspects of personal relationships often stem from the simple fact that when two people come together, it is like two widely different worlds interacting. The

Figure 12. *Diagram of a dynamic interaction between two people.*

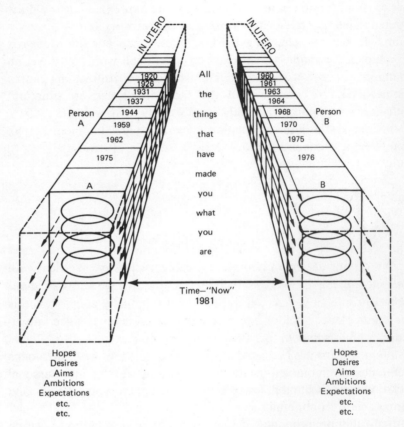

ever changing dynamic nature of people, relationships, and organizations constantly creates novel situations. (See Figure 12. The four ellipses shown for each individual correspond to the ones described in Figure 10.)

Yet many people continue to react to others and their ideas as though life were static and immutable. We have seen throughout Part I that this is not the case. People, relationships, and organizations go through cycles of change. We are constantly called upon to update our information in order to maintain our equilibrium in this fast-paced life.

Expanding your vocabulary does not necessarily ensure improved communication, just as increasing your palette of colors does not automatically improve your painting ability. In order to improve your ability to communicate with other people, you must develop your capacity to think straight. As you know, broadening your perspective, opening your mind, and listening actively are important.

One of the major barriers to interpersonal communication is the tendency to evaluate, judge, and approve or disapprove of statements made by others. This tendency is heightened in emotionally charged situations, in which feelings are deeply involved. The stronger the feelings expressed, the more likely it is that the respective points of view will be deepened and that there will be no mutual understanding or agreement in the communication.

An effective approach to good communication and good relationships is to develop an empathetic understanding of the other person. We must enter his private world and see the way life appears to him, without any attempt to make evaluative judgments. To do so, we have to see the expressed idea and attitude from the other person's point of view, to sense how it feels to him, and to achieve his frame of reference, thoughts, and feelings with regard to what he is talking about.

When the parties to a dispute realize that they are being understood, that someone sees how the situation seems to them, the statements grow less exaggerated and less defensive and it becomes unnecessary to strike the pose of being "right," with the opposition "wrong." The influence of such an understanding catalyst in a group permits the members to come closer to the objective truth involved in the relationship and reduce the pressure. The defensive distortions, lies, false fronts, exaggerations, and critical behavior that characterize almost every failure in communication are avoided in small groups by empathetic understanding. One of the members of a group or even a neutral third party can initiate empathetic understanding to foster further understanding and cooperation.

Empathy depends on a person's capacity and willingness to see and accept points of view different from his own. It is an emotional as well as an intellectual achievement. Useful tools in developing empathy include active listening, attention to body language, and an awareness of whatever background and personal life might influence the person's perspective and actions in the particular situation.

For instance, you may tell an employee to do a special rush

project for you within the next 48 hours. You become irritated at his response, "It can't be done." To your way of thinking, it has to be done, and his refusal indicates insubordination, lack of initiative, and perhaps lack of competency. You have told him what needs to be done by when, but you have not also told him that doing it will reflect well on his promotion possibilities and that you have selected him especially for this opportunity.

From the employee's viewpoint, this is just another rush job that could have been planned ahead. His family has been complaining about his long hours at work, and he questions whether or not the company appreciates his dedication. His daughter is graduating from high school, and he is worried about being financially able to send her to college. He knows he will ultimately have to do the project or possibly lose his job. Unfortunately, chances are the project will not be done as well as possible, which may reduce his promotion opportunities.

Had the manager approached the employee from a more empathetic understanding of his position, they both could have gained. For instance, if he had acknowledged the time the employee has been putting on the job and admitted that he realized the rush would mean the employee would have to reorder his priorities, the manager might have gained a more attentive listener.

Under pressure, many people become defensive in the face of more demands being placed upon them. If the manager had shared his hidden agenda with the employee and had told him how important the project could be to his career, he might have won an enthusiastic ally. The employee–manager relationship could also have been improved by the employee's awareness of the manager's confidence in him and interest in his career. The stress produced in the situation could have been channeled into a motivating, constructive effort. Instead, it became distressful to both parties through a lack of understanding of what was being said.

Out twentieth-century world of the Concorde and satellite and laser transmissions has made us aware of different cultures with their own views of the world, theories to account for what happens, and methods of reacting to the world in which we live. It is readily apparent that we are very different in our thinking, values, and purposes. As a consequence, a completely objective view and understanding of oneself or of any other person can never be reached. Perfect agreement as to what is and what is not is impossible.

Nonetheless, the situation is not futile, and we all have some control over the success of communicating. If we make the necessary distinction between an agreement with the other person's ideas and the acceptance of him as a distinct individual, we will have an awareness that could be the source of valuable communicative encounters.

A person is a complex of interrelated systems:

Nervous system (including the brain).
Circulatory system.
Chemical system (glands, hormones, metabolism, and so on).
Habit system (sensory and motor activities, talking, listening, walking, writing, gesticulating, and so on).
Semantic system (values, attitudes, purposes, prejudices, and so on).
Linguistic and symbol system (native tongue, acquired languages, mathematical and professional modes of thinking, and so on).

Each is interdependent on the others. Out of this complex symbiotic bundle of patterned energies emerges the personality of the individual, his style of living, and his perception of the world.

Basic training in general semantics fundamentals can help people to acquire better emotional control and maturity with less explosive behavior. These results contribute to strengthening our stress filter, developing positive coping behaviors, lowering the overall level of stress experienced, and increasing overall health and well-being.

Straight thinking can ease the impact of stressors on the mind by reducing confusion and frustration in exchanging meaning with another person. It also aids in listening actively to what the other person has to say, which improves the possibility of reaching mutual understanding, if not agreement.

The use of language directs the listener's perception. Adjectives and adverbs describe how we compare, rate, or value something. Without attentive listening, these value terms will not be heard, and the listener will get an incomplete picture of the message being sent. Recognition of the facts, inferences, and judgments in a speaker's statement will provide information for feedback and for checking out the message. This procedure can minimize guesses and assumptions that might lead to misunderstanding or misinformation.

Statements in which one or more terms are undefined or convey a different connotation to different people cloud the issue and can lead to endless controversy and distress as the sender and receiver go off on separate tangents based on the "facts" as they perceive them. Moreover, not all the facts are identical in significance. The interpretations you make of what has been said depend on the information your senses provide you and the thoughts you already have, as well as on the immediate feelings, wants, and desires you bring into the situation. Because of this, it is not surprising that two people can reach very different conclusions from the same sense data.

With this in mind, consider treating your interpretations, conclusions, impressions, and evaluations as tentative. This flexibility strengthens your stress filter and prevents a forced conclusion based on incomplete data. Furthermore, making an interpretation too quickly, and immutably, can preclude the possibility of employing a valuable coping technique in seeing things in a new and different way.

Before drawing any conclusion, check out your understanding of what has been said with the other person. Try to understand his evaluation of reality as relevant, valid, and consequential. What is a fact for you may not be a fact for him. Make sure the words and the symbols you use to communicate with him (and he chooses to use with you) have a similar content for both of you. Often blood pressure is raised by someone's taking offense at the use of a particular term that has a negative connotation for the receiver but not for the sender.

Once feelings and emotions get in the way, a person does not function at his best. We cannot behave sensibly if we are under stress—angry, afraid, or overenthusiastic. In a group, an emotionally charged situation leads to the outcropping of defense mechanisms, political ploys, and personality displays. If the situation is curbed by authoritarian methods, members feel frustrated. The strong ones become hostile; the weak ones lose all initiative.

When an emotional disturbance spreads throughout the nervous system of a person, he functions at his worst. If your stress filter malfunctions and magnifies rather than minimizes a stressful challenge or your perception indicates a threat where there is none, repetitive disturbances will weaken parts of the organism. Eventually they will cease to function. The result may be a whole gamut of psychosomatic troubles, from nervous breakdowns to peptic ulcers or high blood pressure.

The problem that faces us is to learn to control our semantic reactions, so that we can achieve the three purposes of any self-regulating system:

Save ourselves from excessive wear and tear, and eventual self-destruction.

Keep functioning within an optimum range of efficiency.

Remain oriented to our objectives though they are pursued under changing conditions.

At the same time, we must learn to apply a self-regulating control system to accomplish the positive results of effective group dynamics.

Stated simply, semantic self-regulation in terms of feedback control is a technique by which an individual continuously analyzes what he is saying or writing while he is doing it. If he finds himself too far over on the emotional scale, he can compensate and swing back to the intellectual side. Similarly, a person can recognize emotionally controlled behavior in the speech and writing of others and thus make adjustments for dealing with them. Emotional reactivity to language is a learned response. By the use of relaxation training, self-management techniques, and a logical thought process you can learn to minimize the harmful effects of stressful experiences.

CONSTRUCTIVE THINKING

Another technique for stress reduction is constructive thinking. Up to this point, we have looked at developing your thinking ability, broadening your awareness, and improving your means of communicating with others and yourself. Constructive thinking basically focuses on the latter, on what you tell yourself.

There are basically five approaches to dealing with self-defeating destructive thoughts. They are rethinking, thought stopping, mental diversion, rehearsal, and desensitization. The names suggest the various processes.

The first skill is rethinking. This technique can prevent the energy drain you experience from dwelling on the frustration or anger you feel under stressful circumstances. For instance, you are detained in a meeting, then slowed down in traffic, and are circling the parking lot for a space as your airplane takes off without you. You might slam on your brakes, pound on the steering wheel, and yell something out loud as you realize you have missed your flight.

Turn your attention from the frustration of the past (the incident is over; the plane is gone) to decide rationally what to do next. Acknowledge what happened, vent your anger healthily if you need to for a moment, and then decide what to do next. Accept the frustrating, angry feelings for a short time, but do not get caught in an anxiety-sustaining negative thought pattern.

For instance, going over in your mind who talked too much at the meeting and dragged it out, what the transit department should be doing with taxes to alleviate traffic jams, and other angry thoughts only perpetuates distressful feelings, prolonging the stress response and filling the mind with the problem rather than looking for a solution.

Rethinking moves your attention from what has happened to what you want to happen or how you are going to deal with the facts of the situation. To continue our illustration, you have missed your plane to Los Angeles. You are due at an 8:00 A.M. meeting tomorrow. You begin to move on what needs to be done: see the ticket agent, notify people of the change in your schedule, and so on, to meet your original objective. Your energy is used productively, and you are once again in control of your emotions and mental processes.

Monitoring your thoughts from time to time may lead to an awareness of negative or counterproductive thinking. With conscious awareness, you can literally call a halt to these troublesome thoughts. Practice this out loud when alone: Actually direct yourself to STOP thinking unproductive thoughts.

Feeling sorry for yourself, belittling others, or worrying about failing in a task serves no useful purpose and may have nonproductive side effects. Many people seem to underestimate their ability to control their thoughts and choose how they focus their attention. The technique of mental diversion is one by which you give your brain a positive thought or activity to tune in and replace the negative or anxious thought that is troubling you.

If there is nothing you can do or you have done all that can be done at this time in terms of the problem, you should give your mind and body a rest. Indulge yourself in mental activities that bring you positive feelings. Sing, recite a poem, practice your French, keep your mind too busy to worry about giving an important presentation or having a job interview. The pause will refresh you and make you feel better and generally do better.

You can also handle challenging situations by mentally rehearsing an event or situation until you are comfortable with it and confident in handling it. Visualize any problem that may arise in as great detail as necessary to deal with it and solve the problem.

This technique will enable you to overcome some fear and anxiety about particularly troublesome situations, such as flying or an impending problem. It is true that anxiety or anticipatory stress can facilitate the process since it alerts a person to impending danger or challenge and prepares the body's resources to meet the situation. However, either one can also be destructive. With anxiety, for example, what you get anxious about determines whether the anxiety is normal or abnormal, disruptive, and long lasting. Furthermore, its intensity is related to prior adaptive experiences and reactions.

By carefully rehearsing a situation in your mind, you become more familiar with it and lessen the uncertainty. Thus, you can gradually reduce your anxiety by preparing yourself to do a good job and seeing yourself do it. Once you know you can handle something, your confident, calm, relaxed attitude enables you to do it effectively, keeping your stress level to a reasonable minimum.

Man's brain and central nervous system are in a constant state of activity, receiving, interpreting, collating, and transmitting messages, storing some away in his memory for future use and safekeeping. The habits and patterns of functioning he has acquired can either lower his efficiency or raise it to unexpected levels in an inverse relationship to the amount of stress experienced.

Thus far we have seen the interrelatedness of most everything in our lives. To be is to be related. Our heritage, time, space, behavior, mind, and body interact in some way. Human behavior is a function of the senses as well as of aspects of the environment. A change in shapes, people, spatial structure, sound, and so on, when perceived by man, brings about a corresponding change in his total reaction, behavior, and level of stress. It does something to him, it affects him. This is the affective influence of the environment.

There is a functional relationship between men and the affective influence of their environments. Function is a matter of the inter-dependence of those factors. An effective stress filter makes use of all the apparent functional relationships between man and his environment and man and man.

The world in which we live is a world of relative values, not of absolutes. There is no single dogmatic way of solving a given problem, and in the final analysis what is going to matter most to you is what you think, whether you think, and what you do about it.

LISTENING
Poor Listening

The results of poor listening habits frequently show up in little incidents that accumulate daily. They may result in useless or duplicated work effort, irritation, wasted time, poor interpersonal relations, misunderstanding—in other words, distress. Most executives and supervisors spend the major part of each workday trying to communicate with others. On the average, listening takes 45 percent of our waking time with others; speaking, 30 percent; reading, 16 percent; and writing, 9 percent.

Face-to-face talk gives us more information on both the subject to be discussed and the attitudes of people than a letter or a memo. A telephone conversation comes next. No wonder three-fourths of our communicating is by word of mouth. Speaking to the point is important indeed, but effective listening is also a great time-saver. If we improve our listening comprehension by 25 percent, as the experts in this field claim we can, we increase our overall communication efficiency by an even higher percentage.

To review, the communication process means the transmittal of information, views, opinions, ideas, and attitudes from one person to another. In written communication there is a writer and a reader; in oral communication there is a speaker and a listener; in sign communication there is a sender and a receiver. In all cases there must be a code that both communicators interpret according to the same rules.

The message may be shortened, distorted, or stopped anywhere in the process—at the starting point, in the transmission, or at the receiving end. To ensure effective communication there must be agreement on what the words mean.

At the sending and at the receiving ends of the process, matters are not so simple. In spoken communication particularly, and in written communication also, the sender and the receiver have semantic reactions that are more complex than the code can transmit. This is where communication often fails.

Roadblocks to Listening

There are basically four categories of roadblock to good listening: intellectualizing, bias, boredom, and apathy.

1. Listening intellectually for the verbal statements alone many times excludes other means of information gathering such as the speaker's tone, gesture, posture, and facial expression.

2. Bias against a speaker's message may be due to some physical characteristic, manner of speech, or choice of word, phrase, or idea. Another form of prejudiced listening is to distort the speaker's message by hearing only those parts of it that seem to support your own point of view. In all cases of bias, the listener may be precluded from hearing the full message and gathering sufficient data on which to act.

3. Boredom sends you off on your own tangent of thought away from the speaker. Inattention can be due to self-defense, lack of a reason for listening, too simple a subject matter, or dull presentation.

4. Apathy is another reason for not listening. It occurs most commonly when the subject matter is too difficult or the speaker is not making his point clearly.

If a person has not learned listening skills, either through experience or training, his ability to understand what he hears will be low. This can lead to a breakdown in communication and breed stressful situations. Since effective communication is based on the transmission of an idea from a speaker to a listener, mutual understanding cannot be achieved when the message is not received. Confusion, frustration, and other counterproductive emotions can grow when the initial exchange of information breaks down. This misunderstanding can block productive interpersonal relations and personal effectiveness, resulting in poor working relationships and low productivity.

How to Improve Your Listening Skills

Like all skills, listening requires self-observation, time, patience, humility, and practice. In a group that has the advantage of having an appointed moderator, the feedback may be left to him. But no one can really progress until he takes it upon himself to check on his own performance as he goes along.

1. Listen to understand what is meant, not to reply, contradict, or refute.
2. Be aware that "what is meant" is more than the dictionary meaning of the words that are used. It includes, among other things, what is transmitted by the tone of voice, the facial expression, and the general behavior of the speaker.
3. Look for clues that may help you achieve closer correlation between the unexpressed views of the speaker and your own, clues as to what the speaker is trying to say.
4. Put aside your own views and opinions for the time being. Know that you cannot listen to yourself inwardly at the same time as you listen outwardly to the speaker.
5. Put yourself in the speaker's shoes, as it were. Try to see the speaker's world as the speaker sees it. Accept the speaker's feelings as facts that must be taken into account.
6. Control your impatience. Listening is faster than talking. The average person can speak about 125 words a minute but can listen to about 400 words a minute. So, the effective listener does not jump ahead of the speaker; he gives him time to tell his story. What the speaker will say next may not be what the listener expects or wants to hear.
7. Do not prepare an answer as you listen. You want the whole message before deciding what, if anything, to say. The last sentence of the speaker may give a different slant to what was said before.

8. Look alert and interested. By being attentive, you can stimulate the speaker to a better performance.
9. Expect the speaker's language to differ from the way you would say the "same" thing yourself. So do not quibble on words, but try to get at what is meant.
10. Follow the main ideas and try to construct a mental outline of what is said.
11. Do not interrupt. Ask questions when the time comes, and then to secure more information that is needed, not to trap the speaker into a corner.
12. In a conference, listen to all participants, not just to those who are on your side.
13. Before giving an answer, sum up what you understood was meant. If the interpretation is not accepted, communication stops at this point. Clear it up before proceeding further.
14. When you are not sure what is meant, ask questions. To ask a question is to show knowledge, not ignorance.

The Benefits of Effective Listening

The benefits of effective listening are many:

1. We take away from a conversation or a conference more than the indifferent listener does for the same amount of time spent.
2. We refrain from snap answers that tangle the communication in knots, and we save the time it takes to unravel these knots by lengthy and laborious explanations.
3. We stand to make better decisions based on the information, opinions, and attitudes expressed.
4. We differentiate descriptions from inferences and assumptions, facts from value judgments.
5. We reconstruct vague speaking into clear communication.
6. We stimulate better speaking in people who try to communicate with us.
7. We learn to speak more effectively by observing how people convey or fail to convey their own messages.
8. We learn by observation what language the other person will understand best when our turn comes to speak.
9. We are better prepared to make our own viewpoint fit with the

knowledge, the language, the views, and the feelings of those with whom we are communicating.

Effective communication, free communication between men, is always therapeutic. Effective listening, constructive thinking, and the principles of general semantics substantially improve the process of productive communication.

Effective communication is one of the most important coping abilities man can develop in managing conflict and lowering his overall level of stress.

Low-stress communication is both an approach to enhancing communication and a problem-solving process. It enables you to cope with situations that might make you feel and act defensively. By following the techniques described here, you can increase your understanding, improve your personal relations, and lower your stress level (see Figure 13).

When communication channels are blocked or misused, miscommunication can promote game playing, waste time, stifle creativity, and prevent effective decision making.

Awareness of your personal communicating style is the first step in communicating nondefensively. If the majority of your transactions are relatively rewarding and positive for the other people, conflict is kept to a minimum. The skill of putting and keeping others at ease through the course of a business transaction is due in part to their reaction to the way you treat them.

There are ways of affirming others' self-esteem so that they react

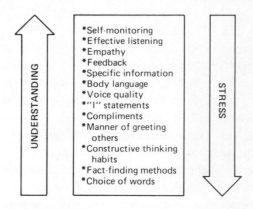

FIGURE 13. *Low-stress communication techniques.*

positively to you, seek you out, and share ideas and points of view with you.

You express respect for the values and opinions of others by listening attentively and hearing them out. By giving others a chance to express their views or share information, you encourage open and honest communication. This in turn enables each person to state his needs and desires as well as to make constructive suggestions.

These and other techniques may not be particularly new to you. However, practicing what you know is what makes the difference in maintaining your composure and preventing negative stress in potentially difficult or demoralizing situations. Chapter 15 will explore more deeply your understanding of yourself and the stress you experience and/or generate.

DEFENSIVE COMMUNICATION

Defensive communication is due in part to poor listening, habit, fear, and a lack of creative problem solving. The conflicts that frequently arise out of reactionary confrontations are often based on a lack of awareness of what is really going on in the environment and of how the lack of perspective or information limits options.

Routinely disagreeing, flying off the handle easily, refusing to level with others, and pushing others with "should" language are some negative behaviors that present difficulties in dealing with others. Other counterproductive actions that cause conflict, disagreements, and distressful personal incidents are:

Displaying negative or apathetic body language
Monopolizing the conversation
Using verbally abusive, ridiculing, or insulting language
Refusing to negotiate or compromise
Talking down to or patronizing others
Finding fault or being excessively critical

You can easily add others to the list. Begin to develop your overall awareness of stress-producing styles that thwart a cooperative atmosphere and lead to adversary interrelationships. High-stress settings nurture opposing factions within a group and an every-man-for-himself attitude that leaves people uncomfortable, relatively depressed, and less likely to want to interact.

How a person perceives a situation, reacts, and communicates within a particular setting is diverse and unique to that person. However, this does not mean that we have no control over steering our interrelationships into productive, positive experiences.

By the employment of the principles of general semantics, "conscious" awareness, active listening, and constructive thinking, we become more sensitive to our own attitudes and feelings. We can then analyze more objectively what is "really" going on around us and control how it affects what we do.

CHAPTER 15
Understanding Yourself and Stress

Understanding yourself and stress is a complex but rewarding task. Throughout Parts I and II of this book, we have examined many relevant dimensions of your existence—that is, many factors that come into play in determining who and what you are. For most people, they involve the assumption of different roles—employer, employee, citizen, parent, spouse. Sometimes these roles are in conflict or there are conflicting dynamics interacting on your lifestyle. For instance, the intertwining of the various life cycles—personal, marital, career, physical—can converge on a person all at once, culminating in intolerable levels of demands.

The Holmes-Rahe life-change scale referred to earlier is indicative of many of the personal dynamics going on and reminds you that the wear and tear on the body, mind, and spirit is cumulative. It is not so much one particular life event (for example, change in job or spouse) that causes the heart attack or breakdown, but rather the manner in which the person has handled his daily pressure (for example, at home, in traffic, and during the sales meeting) that leads to the total effect his life circumstances have on him.

We referred to balance and most of us are familiar with the reference to a "well-rounded" person. This term is not meant casually. Research and life observations indicate that well-being depends on an integrated lifestyle. There is little doubt that either too much stress at once or a little stress for too long can impair physical and emotional well-being.

We are living in an age when we don't want merely to be told what to do; we want to know why we should do it. A successful management program has to be realistic and applicable to the employee's way of thinking and style of living.

Even with the newfound knowledge and methods for self-application in this chapter, certain methods may not be for you. As we have said, stress is a highly personal matter, affecting each individual differently. Throughout the pages that follow, you will be informed of many of the coping techniques available to deal with stress and change.

INDIVIDUAL RESPONSIBILITY

The psychological attitude toward health prevalent today plays a considerable role in motivating people to control and improve their lives and the welfare of others. Maintaining wellness means more than following doctors' instructions when you are sick. It goes beyond a crisis-oriented approach of intervening with treatment after the symptoms are evident. Building and maintaining good health means: (1) becoming aware of the precursors to health breakdown; (2) doing things to prevent the onset of disease; (3) actively promoting health through effective stress management; and (4) consciously eliminating those things that are damaging to your well-being.

At the risk of redundancy, stress is caused by many situations and combinations of events. For example, you may have an argument at breakfast with your wife over charge account spending and then be delayed in traffic on the way to the office so that you are late to a meeting. If your secretary then goes home sick, all of these problems accumulating before lunch, your stress tolerance abilities are loaded.

One effective way to handle these and other stressors during your day is to have a personal preventive and treatment program that attacks stress from several dimensions. The four forms of stress—behavioral, emotional, intellectual, and physical—can be dealt with through techniques such as personality engineering, physical activity, relaxation training, social engineering, and mediation. Examples of various intervention and management strategies are presented in this and the following chapters.

TOTAL HEALTH CHECKUP

For you to understand yourself within a health context, a complete physical examination can be helpful. It will increase your awareness of certain risk factors in your health profile. It is suggested that a healthy person between the ages of 20 and 35 have a complete physical every five years. The older one gets, the greater the chances for weakening or failure to some vital body part, and the warning signs become more discernible after age 35 or 40. Therefore, those between 35 and 45 should have an examination every two to three years. After 45, the usefulness of data collected from an annual examination can make the difference between life and disability or death.

The necessity for a yearly checkup becomes increasingly apparent when you consider the potential ramifications of the sedentary lifestyle most people settle into. Furthermore, many people begin to experience a "middle-age" crisis as they feel edged out of our youth-oriented society by the aging process and sense that time is running out for achieving their goals. Lack of exercise, emotional upheaval, aging, alcohol and drug usage, and the weight of other social factors can threaten a person's well-being and suggest as you get older that you should be more aware of changes taking place in your health.

Modern technological advances in diagnostic instruments have made possible the early detection of some of the major "killers." The "silent sicknesses" like chronic obstructive pulmonary disease and some heart problems display few discernible signs until they have progressed past the point of no return. Early detection of symptomatology related to degenerative diseases, when pointed out in the context of a person's total lifestyle, can encourage him to engage in certain health-enhancing practices with the prospect of postponing or warding off the illness.

A growing number of physicians are recommending that in addition to the customary resting electrocardiogram (EKG), people should take an exercise tolerance stress test, usually done while they are undergoing strenuous levels of activity on a treadmill. Stress electrocardiograms are detecting coronary abnormalities in about 15 percent of patients with normal resting EKGs. Additionally, portable EKGs, developed for the space program, are becoming available for measuring everyday routine activities while at home or in the office.

A complete health workup can provide for an overall health forecast while pinpointing particular conditions that may require some specific attention by the individual or treatment by a professional.

IMPORTANCE OF A PERSONAL PHYSICIAN

Regular visits to a family doctor can provide continuity in health care aside from the annual physical. An open, personal relationship between the patient and his physician serves many purposes.

For one thing, continuous contact can reveal subtle changes in a person's coloring, attitude, or health habits that a one-time examining physician might miss. As we have state earlier, the interpersonal dynamics in the family, workplace, and environment are important factors in a person's well-being. Sometimes a person's state of health affects his behavior and daily functioning ability, task performance, and approach to life. Therefore, continuity in health care and a close relationship between the caretaker and the care given are in the patient's best interest. Chapter 18 will examine in more detail the need for and selection of professional health care services.

PATIENT INVOLVEMENT

However, even the best doctor, medication, hospital, or other health enhancement program can do little to reduce the harmful repercussions of stress without the patient's daily commitment to control the stress in his environment. Time management, regular exercise, pacing activities, and low-stress communication techniques are some of the daily means by which someone can cope effectively with the pressures and strains of today's world. Without such conscious effort, the person who takes a tranquilizer, for instance, to get him through the day is only dulling the awareness of, and not eliminating, the stressor. Alcohol and drugs only temporize; they do not solve the stress problem.

Central to man's capacity to cope is the fact that he is a problem-solving animal with the potential to define and choose his problems and to plan ahead. He has the ability to meet life's crises creatively, independently, and, if possible, without resorting to temporary crutches such as cigarettes, alcohol, or drugs.

The fact is, most people can learn to cope with stress by understanding, acceptance, and commitment. Coping behavior has importantly among its considerations: (1) the effectiveness with which a given task is accomplished and (2) the cost of this effectiveness to the person who is coping. The cost of using artificial stimulants such as cigarettes is well publicized.

In place of the temporary neutralizing effect of taking stimulants, man can learn to control his physiological and psychological stress responses by the means introduced throughout this book. He can learn to use stress as a positive factor in his life and to defend himself on a long-term basis against the excessive wear and tear that result in disease and mental turmoil.

ACHIEVING SELF-MANAGED CHANGE

In this chapter, a variety of very specific skills such as meditation, active listening, biofeedback, personality engineering, and environmental alterations are suggested to reduce stress in your life. Although you cannot eliminate all the stressful features in your life, you can substantively alter the sources or their influence. This power can help control the variables in your life, of which behavior is a function and eustress or distress the by-product.

An array of expectations, assumptions, physiological reactions, beliefs, values, and environmental stimuli all make it difficult for a person to cope with stressors. In order to achieve self-managed change, choices must be made to reconcile the differences between your perception of the way things are or should be and the way others see things.

For instance, what you expect your job to provide and what opportunities the position in fact offers may be different. Furthermore, how you see your performance and how your supervisor evaluates it may be in conflict. How you respond to these conflicts may have different consequences. That is, if your behavior is defensive and hostile during your performance review, you might engender more distress than understanding between yourself and your manager.

On the other hand, if you listen attentively to your manager's evaluation and then communicate your feelings on the points raised, you may reduce the tension between the two of you and within yourself. This low-stress exchange of ideas is more likely to lead to a workable plan of action to resolve differences than the former behavior. How you respond to work-related and other life stressors involves the same basic choices between adaptive or maladaptive behavioral responses.

ADAPTIVE AND MALADAPTIVE STRATEGIES

Each of us uses a wide range of coping skills to avoid, combat, and respond to stress. These skills are learned, first from family members and later from our own experiences. You may not even be aware of the coping strategies and tactics you employ for adapting to the changing conditions and stressful events of daily life—for example, sleeping more than usual, being boisterous or otherwise calling attention to yourself, looking for someone to blame, or taking long drives. Whatever your method of coping, it generally falls into two categories: adaptive or maladaptive.

Adaptive strategies reduce anxiety and increase your confidence in being able to deal effectively with stress. Successful coping is a way of making the best of a situation and getting what you want out of life. On the contrary, maladaptive tactics neither reduce anxiety nor resolve stressful situations. Such responses as excessive smoking, overeating, overdrinking, or temperamental outbursts often isolate you and compound your problems.

As you know from Part II, about how the body and mind respond to stress, maladaptive coping can have very serious effects on your mental well-being and physical health. Acute stress can cause susceptibility to physical illness, ranging from colds to cancer, hypertension and psychoneurosis, psychosomatic illness, and other symptoms of impaired mental functioning.

We all know problems don't usually go away by themselves. Decisive action must be taken to reduce the frequency of the stressful situations that can be controlled. Your personal stress management program will help you increase your chances for a healthy life in the years to come (see Figure 14). It guides you in deciding to pursue a course of action, in committing yourself to reducing health-threatening risks, and in living a health-enhancing lifestyle. Gaining control over stress-producing situations involves a number of procedures:

Identifying the stress
Appraising and developing commitment
Becoming more aware of behavior patterns
Developing an action plan
Trying out the plan
Evaluating how the plan is working

FIGURE 14. *Developing a stress reduction program.*

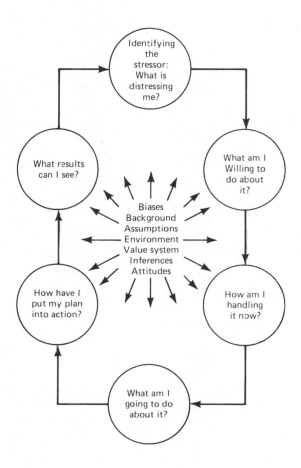

The success of a stress reduction program lies in the dynamic movement through these phases, continually recycling through its steps to develop skills that can be used across a variety of problems and situations for a more satisfying and productive life, finished performance, or perfection (see Figure 15). No one can be expected to solve all real-life difficulties. Some problems must, in some measure, be endured. Others require more active adaptation by summoning man's abilities to counteract difficulties. People will

FIGURE 15. *Plateaus of learning in developing competent coping methods for making positive use of stress.*

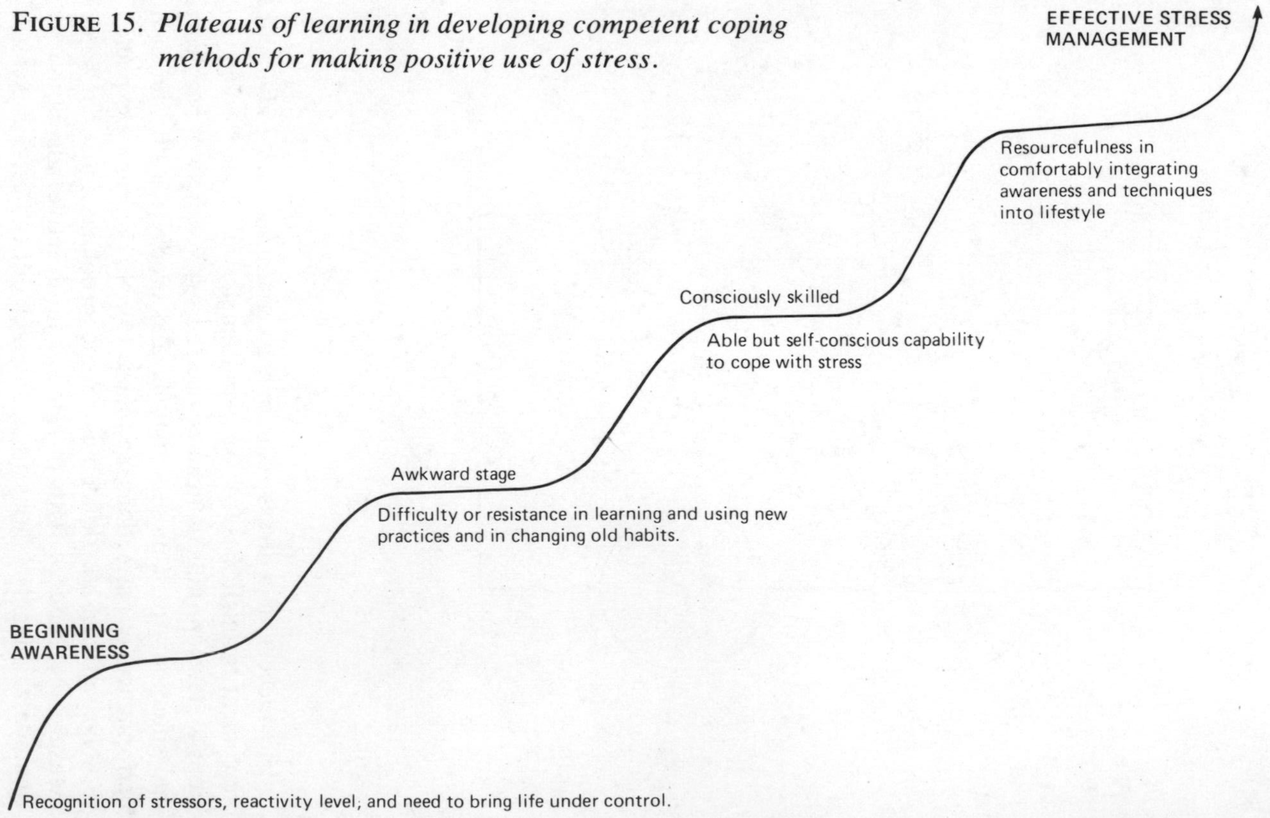

EFFECTIVE STRESS
MANAGEMENT

Resourcefulness in
comfortably integrating
awareness and techniques
into lifestyle

Consciously skilled

Able but self-conscious capability
to cope with stress

Awkward stage

Difficulty or resistance in learning and using new
practices and in changing old habits.

BEGINNING
AWARENESS

Recognition of stressors, reactivity level, and need to bring life under control.

have to use their skills to promote mature strategies of adaptation and mastery in the face of stress.

Identifying the Stressor

Events that you find intolerably stressful may not even be noticeable to another person. As we have pointed out, reactions to stress are highly individual and each person's vulnerability is unique to him alone.

Sometimes the obvious problem you face is not the real source of the distress. For instance, having to fire an employee is not generally a pleasant experience. Despite your awareness that this action must be taken for the best interest of the company, you are disturbed at having to be the one to discharge someone. You may consciously think that the reason lies in your anticipation of an angry or tearful scene or your concern that the employee may not be able to get another job or may suffer other negative personal ramifications.

More careful examination of the situation may reveal that the real reason your stomach is upset and your palms are sweaty is your fear that your act will be unpopular with others, that you will not be liked for carrying out the task, and you have a very strong need for approval from others. By being able to pinpoint what feelings are causing your distress, you are often in a much better position to handle your problems without feeling excessive stress. Look beyond the obvious to identify and understand what is perturbing you.

Appraising and Developing Commitment

In Part I, we focused on the social forces that tend to cause stress. Part II explained the mental and physical repercussions of stress on the individual. Conscious awareness of the powerful force of stress in your life should motivate you to take charge of your life and commit yourself to improving your health and well-being. This commitment requires daily recognition that you have a choice between self-enhancing and self-destructive behaviors. There is much you can do to improve the quality of your life. We have outlined many techniques, and you can creatively initiate additional methods that are uniquely your own. We have provided the tools; you must supply the labor.

Our experience has shown that being given the know-how to cope with stress is perhaps the biggest step in developing the self-confidence and enthusiasm to sustain commitment. The cliché "success breeds success" is certainly true in the overall impact of a stress reduction program. The increased vitality, productivity, and effectiveness experienced by successfully overcoming time, inter-personal, and environmental stressors on a daily basis increase the ability to cope with the stresses and strains of life in general. The rewards of a well-balanced life of work and family, companionship and solitude, challenge and ease, exercise and rest, rebound to reinforce a daily commitment to low-stress living and working.

Becoming More Aware of Behavior Patterns

Self-monitoring can reveal both constructive and destructive behavior patterns and can give you an indication of your coping abilities. For instance, do you eat, argue, or withdraw when faced with a problem? When confronted with an unpleasant task, do you procrastinate or get it done as soon as possible? Do you look for someone else to do it or refuse to take the responsibility? In order to eliminate the unpleasant stress feeling, do you try to anesthetize yourself with tranquilizers or liquor, or do you de-escalate the stress response through relaxation or reengineer the pressure situation by altering your perception of it or making a plan of action?

Record keeping can help you stop and look at your tension and what you do that contributes to or alleviates its effects. Many people have benefited from keeping a daily log of their stressors—thoughts, actions taken, and the results of their behavior on their sense of well-being. After two weeks of observing how you react to life's changes and challengers, you may be able to spot those coping behaviors that work for you and those that do not.

It is possible to neutralize stress, before it becomes an excruciating headache, without medication and without losing sleep. Perhaps the most helpful coping advice focuses on what you can do to change and develop yourself and reduce the stress in your life.

People who get along best in life are those who can respond to any given situation with a wide range of different coping behaviors. As pointed out earlier, these can either be positive and adaptive or maladaptive.

Take the time to reflect on how you react to undesirable or traumatic circumstances in your life. Are you prone to feelings of sadness, worthlessness, anger? Do you seek advice or comfort from a friend or professional, or do you bottle up your feelings, become petty and irritable, stop eating, or take a couple of tranquilizers?

Make a list of the last week's stressful situations and how you handled them. Were your responses constructive or destructive as you look back on your coping styles? Become aware of those you most frequently use and consciously set about to eliminate those habits that are counterproductive to your health and well-being. Concentrate on finding and using adaptive coping techniques. You already employ some creative mechanisms in dealing properly with situations. Build up your repertoire by learning from your family, friends, and others who successfully cope with stress.

Up to this point, you have received a great deal of information. One thing is apparent: No matter what you do, your health is affected one way or another. This is certainly not a new thought, but it is worth emphasizing.

Designing Your Stress Management Program
Identification of tension triggers is the first step in setting a course of action to control the stress in your life. Separate the stressors into two categories: the inevitable ones (those beyond your direct control) and those you can do something about.

Using accepted management techniques, you should know you can correct many stress-producing situations, such as being late for appointments, having too much to do, hating your job, having no confidants, and being overweight. In the chapter on effective time management, techniques were detailed. Among the solutions to the time/work problem, delegation of authority and setting of priorities were elaborated.

You have a few options in eliminating job-related stress as well. At the one extreme, of course, you can change jobs. Short of this or "suffering through," you can change departments, look for new challenges within your position, try to find some aspect of your work you do enjoy and focus on that, or take other positive steps. Other minor irritants may not be devastating by themselves, but if allowed to accumulate over a prolonged period of time, can be hazardous to your health.

We have mentioned the importance of maintaining a support network and having close friends in whom you can confide and to whom you can relate, whether it is about work or other matters of interest. The cultivation of warm, honest, interpersonal relationships is an integral part of maintaining balance in a person's life.

There are health risks and rewards attached to certain physical and emotional conditions and behavior patterns. For example, the health risks of smoking have been widely publicized. The habit increases the smoker's susceptibility to pneumonia, emphysema, lung cancer, heart attack, high blood pressure, and weakening of the arterial walls. The health benefits of breathing techniques include neuromuscular relaxation, increased oxygenation, reduced tension, and increased respiratory ability.

In addition to considering risks and rewards, taking stock of your health assets and liabilities is the first step in deciding what plan of action is appropriate to accomplish your health objectives. Become aware of the effects of your current lifestyle on your life expectancy. Risk factors influencing this projection were enumerated in the section on total physical checkup. Reviewing Part I will help you analyze your current lifestyle and identify stressful areas that must be addressed in your program to enhance your well-being.

In the following pages, several strategies are introduced to be responsive to your needs. An effective plan will incorporate several approaches: physical, spiritual, social, mental, and emotional, according to the unique circumstances. The approaches employed can be:

Generalized intervention techniques
Symptom-directed techniques
Individually oriented techniques
Stressor-directed techniques

These approaches are aimed at strengthening your capacity to cope with stress constructively by:

1. Managing the number of stressors you encounter by controlling the pace of your life.
2. Fortifying your stress filter through physical and mental conditioning to reduce the harmful effects of stressful events.
3. Directing your stress responses into positive attitudes and behaviors and personal effectiveness.

Chapter 16 will review the techniques of the four approach areas.

Trying Out the Plan

Considering the large dividends in your present and future health, the motivation for following through on your resolutions would seem implicit in your plan. Nevertheless, many people take better care of their pets and cars than of their own health. Good intentions or wishful thinking will not produce good health. Many people put off changing their behaviors, defending their ignorance by saying it is too much trouble or that there is not enough time to take care of themselves properly.

Indeed, trying to eliminate old habits and assume new ones is not easy. It often demands taking new attitudes, reeducating yourself, exercising self-discipline, and reassigning priorities. Taking deliberate steps to eliminate self-defeating conduct means waging an ongoing battle to overcome the natural tendency to do the familiar and revert to old ways. Therefore, enlisting the help of your physician, spouse, co-workers, relatives, and so on, can be particularly important to reinforce your goal of health enhancement.

In this chapter, we are specifically concerned with your personal effort, with what you do to channel the stress in your life into a positive, health-enhancing lifestyle.

Evaluating How the Plan Is Working

People who are able to handle stress effectively report a sense of harmony or balance in their lives. They awake refreshed after a night's sleep and seem alert, vigorous, and calm throughout the day. They are able to make decisions and generally cope with the demands made upon them.

When a person meets his needs for nutrition, exercise, and relaxation, he can feel the difference. Attention to low-stress communication techniques, active listening, and time management methods improve interpersonal relations. Improved relationships can, in turn, reduce mistakes, frustration, and anxiety.

These and other results indicate the effectiveness of your plan. A sense of control over yourself and your environment enables you to handle potential problems in an effective manner. This in turn builds confidence to meet new demands.

AWARENESS

Awareness of the life cycles explored in Part I may enable you to be sensitive to the changes taking place in your own life as well as in the lives of your fellow workers. No one can always avoid change, but it can often be predicted, and its negative effects can be controlled to a certain degree through preparation and understanding.

Foreknowledge seems to mitigate personal stress and lessen group crises. For instance, if you are given sufficient warning of an in-law's visit or a corporate restructuring, appropriate steps may be taken to prevent stress from building up to an intolerable level. Regulating the occurrence of self-initiated changes and allowing room for involuntary ones can provide the appropriate pace required to maintain physical and emotional well-being.

COMMON SENSE

Many commonsense approaches to combating hazardous stress can help if they are incorporated into your daily health regime. Nevertheless, although most people are aware of these approaches, relatively few people actually make them a daily way of life. Basic health-enhancing habits include the following:

Eat three meals a day, including breakfast.
Avoid sugar, salt, animal fats, and processed white flour.
Pursue a regular program of physical activity or other leisure pursuits.
Nurture and maintain friendships.
Get enough sleep (usually six to eight hours).
Practice abdominal breathing and relaxation.
Schedule time and activities alone and with others to maintain a well-rounded lifestyle of living and working.
Stop smoking.
Limit alcohol (one drink with meals) and caffeine intake.
Identify and accept emotional needs.
Pace yourself to allow for an even flow of demands.
Recognize the early behavioral or physical signs of stress and take action against the stressor.
Allocate your time and energy to allow for periods of rest and stimulation.
Take appropriate supplements if needed for proper nutrition.

Adherence to these basic health habits can prevent you from succumbing to a dangerous cycle of destructive behavior. It is not uncommon for someone to drink too much at night in order to unwind and sleep and then drink too much coffee in the morning to wake up and "get going." About 10:00 A.M. and then again at 3:00 P.M., he eats candy bars for quick bursts of energy. He also drinks heavily and has a late evening meal. The cycle goes on.

During the stress situation, there is often increased smoking, drug, alcohol, caffeine, sugar, or starch indulgences. Additionally, poor sleeping habits, erratic behavior and performance, depression or anxiety, and irritability are some of the stress-related problems that ensue from failing to practice a healthful regime as a way of life.

POSITIVE ATTITUDES TOWARD PERSONAL HEALTH

In most situations a person can control much of what happens to him. Planning ahead, you are more likely to find things getting done the way you expect. For many people, the limitations illness places on their activities are enough to get them to do things to keep healthy and enable them to do the things they want to do. People with a positive outlook characteristically do not let things they cannot change overwhelm them. They mentally decide to have a good day, no matter how other people are feeling. They take charge of and responsibility for their own feelings and actions. They are in control of their lives.

NEGATIVE ATTITUDES TOWARD PERSONAL HEALTH

For those people who believe that events usually take their own course no matter what they do, stress management is an uphill battle. Just hearing about some disease makes some people think they might get it. Unfortunately, rather than use this awareness of the possibility of disease to take preventative measures, they remain inert, passively waiting to see what will happen.

These people depend a great deal on the physician for taking care of health problems. They do not recognize that their health can be enhanced substantially by a cooperative interchange of the doctor's opinion and what they themselves do about their own health. They acquiesce in their health problems and absorb the negative feelings and stress in their environments. Their lack of responsible participation in creating a healthy atmosphere and condition contributes to their own stress and that of others.

If you want to strengthen your ability to stay well and improve the overall quality of your life, you will need to recognize and mobilize the resources available to you.

STRESS SEEKERS

Most often people think of damaging stress as more pressure than someone has resources to handle. There can also be life-damaging stress from too little challenge in life. But neither of these conditons explains the phenomenon of the stress seeker. Psychologist–sociologist Samuel Z. Klausner defines this type of person as one who deliberately immerses himself in stress. Sky divers, mountain climbers, and lion tamers are examples of people who deliberately court stress.

Why would anyone pursue such high-risk activities? The crowds who race the herd of galloping bulls at Pamplona, the artists struggling for aesthetic excellence, and the inventors pushing toward intellectual achievement all seek to prove their own worth or to achieve elusive "perfection." The emotional boost of public accolades, though the effort to attain them is always exhausting and often dangerous, motivates performers and politicians.

Whatever the nature of the stress sought, those who seek it share certain characteristics:

Their behavior is carefully planned.
They repeatedly return to the stressful situation (war, a mountain, a racetrack).
They need to conquer fear.
They struggle for perfection.
They refuse just to adapt or adjust to their environment.
They choose an adversary who poses no risk of destroying them.
They have the feeling of being intensely alive.

EXPRESSING FEELINGS

There are many people walking around or with whom you work who are suppressing medically dangerous amounts of hostility. When emotions are bottled up, people are more likely to suffer from stress illnesses of the heart, colon, arteries, and stomach.

Stress may lead to hyperarousal. Investigators have reported a significant correlation between the finding of breast cancer in women coming to biopsy for a lump in the breast and the suppression of anger as a behavior pattern. Additionally, psychological studies comparing lung cancer patients who were smokers with cancer-free smokers revealed that cancer patients were significantly more liable to denial and repression of their emotions. Lung cancer patients who smoke tend to be less self-assertive and less given to expressions of emotion than smokers in general.

Feelings cannot be controlled by ignoring them or eliminated by denying them. When you try, you give up control of your feelings and allow them to control you. If denied or suppressed, such feelings as hostility, resentment, fear, or anger will fester inside you and emerge in deceptive and destructive ways.

For example, feelings are commonly expressed through nonverbal behavior, either indirectly (staying away) and symbolically (buying a gift) or directly (laughing, crying, slamming doors). Nonverbal expressions of feelings often have high impact. Your actions demonstrate that something is going on inside you. However, without expressing directly and clearly what it is you are feeling, you can find that your behaviors are misunderstood and add stress. Trying to state your feelings may be difficult, but it is worth the effort in helping you to keep in touch with the gamut of emotions of your inner experience. It helps you to know yourself.

Increasing your awareness of yourself helps you identify your sources of stress and understand the choices for personal action. Identification of feelings can be very useful in helping you to understand a situation better or in clarifying your expectations in a situation. Self-awareness provides the basis for self-control and personal stress management.

SELF-ESTEEM/SELF-PRESERVATION

As you may have concluded from this chapter, your personality is a significant factor in the level of stress you experience. In Chapter 14 you learned the important role of your perception, the meanings and attitudes you give to occurrences in your life. The manner in which you define or interpret a life event is a function of your self-esteem.

The key to adopting a low-stress lifestyle is in accepting responsibility for the way you live and recognizing that you have the power to effect positive changes. Feelings of depression, anxiety, and helplessness are frequently manifestations of low self-esteem. Underrating yourself and focusing on the negative aspects of your life are two common sources of devaluating your own worth. The ability to enjoy life on the whole, to laugh at yourself, and to develop a good sense of humor can alleviate stress. The person with low self-esteem will tend to be overwhelmed by stressful conditions and experience a sense of frustration, with a probable decline in performance.

When a person understands the reality of his worth as a person, his sense of confidence in his ability to perform is enhanced and he can usually meet challenging circumstances more effectively. This mature ego is flexible, inner-directed, and assertive.

On the other hand, the stress-prone personality bases his sense of worth on external measurements, people, symbols, and material items. These outer-directed people are susceptible to a great deal of stress, since they are often crippled by criticism, the fear of failure, and the sense of an overpowering environment. They tend to repress feelings, take disagreements personally, and be socially inhibited or destructive.

Low self-esteem may also manifest itself in aggressively hostile behavior and lack of consideration for others. Both passive and aggressive postures are stress producing and disruptive to the person and to those with whom he comes in contact. An overactive ego can also be unhealthy if it leads to defensive, hostile behaviors.

Believing in yourself, your ability to order your life, and your positive characteristics can minimize the negative influence on you. Self-confidence and self-acceptance provide a strong base for implementing your stress management program and improving the quality of your life. Caring about yourself and valuing your health enough to make the right conscious choices will contribute to your overall well-being by helping you to understand yourself and stress.

CHAPTER 16

Intervention and Management Techniques

The cause-and-effect relationship between severe stress and illness is an accumulation of all the factors of a person's relationship with his environment and his society. In the face of the innumerable problems of everyday living and undefined worries and tensions, countless Americans reach for the familiar home remedies for the stress they experience—a martini or glass of wine, junk foods, cigarettes, pills. All are readily available to counteract or mask the distress temporarily but they do not provide long-term solutions to problems. In fact, they may compound the distress one experiences by initiating health and social problems.

Therefore, in the following pages, we shall present several techniques for modifying the personal and social–environmental interaction that can enable you to deal more effectively with stressful situations and increase your immunity to stress. After being exposed to a broad range of alternative actions and methods, you can formulate your own program, adopting those techniques and activities that seem most promising for you.

GENERALIZED TECHNIQUES

Generalized techniques are those health-enhancing habits that can ease the impact of stressors on mental and physical health. They are often commonsense approaches that provide a sound basis for effective, low-stress living. In the rush of daily living, we may overlook the basic guidelines of rest, regulation, and moderation to maintain health. There is no magic spell, injection, or shortcut to good health. Individual effort and responsibility are required for gaining and keeping a high level of wellness.

[257]

MAN'S PHYSICAL NATURE

In review, the "alarm reaction" inherent in man has historically enabled him to alter his behavior to accommodate to stress in his environment. The hormonal and nervous systems ready the body for the physical fight-or-flight response. The body does not discriminate between a tangible and intangible challenger but categorically increases heart and respiration rates, dilates the pupils for visual acuteness, and pumps sugar, fats, blood, and oxygen into the muscles to stimulate action. When there is no activity to use up the stress products, the overload can be destructive, as these forces go unrelieved and turn in on the individual. They then are likely to increase vulnerability to degenerative diseases such as cardiovascular disease or ulcers.

When the hormonal buildup of epinephrine and norepinephrine is not used for its intended physical purpose, inappropriate usages are manifest in the body's efforts to release the products. Free-floating anxiety, irritability, and other adverse emotions are frequently experienced by the stressed but sedentary executive. The physical nature of man cannot be ignored if he is to function effectively. Both mind and body require physical activity and programs to improve and maintain fitness. These can be highly successful in treating and preventing health breakdown.

Over 1,000 companies have invested in on-site physical fitness facilities supervised by company medical personnel. They have realized positive returns in terms of improved morale, lower sickness and absentee rates, increased alertness and energy, and greater productivity on the part of those employees utilizing the exercise machines and engaging in weekly workouts.

The sustained and dynamic activity of a regular exercise program has important implications for improved muscle tone and posture, weight control, and tension reduction. It also helps to prevent the serious diseases incurred in the absence of any such program. Overweight people are more susceptible to heart disease, arthritis, and diabetes than people whose weight is maintained within normal boundaries. The sedentary businessman runs the risk of his muscles deteriorating from disuse, and this condition may ultimately result in his bodily functions being adversely affected. Specifically, his circulatory, respiratory, digestive, and cardiovascular systems require exercise to keep in good working order. Also, exercise will burn off many of the stress-arousal products that are produced by the multiple stressors in our environment.

The enjoyment of exercise can transcend diversionary pursuits when the recreational pursuits are void of competitive performance comparisons and ego striving and focus on body awareness. Physical activity can provide a feeling of well-being and relaxation most effectively if entered into with a noncompetitive, self-enhancing attitude. When you compete physically against the clock, a record, or someone else, that exercise can create more stress through excessive critical performance analysis.

Although many people are highly motivated by a competitive spirit and keep it within healthy limits, some people are destroying themselves by it. For the most part, exercise requires eye, hand, and muscle coordination and concentration, which are achieved through mobilization of the stress response. However, the athlete must adapt carefully to the levels of stress engendered by physical exertion to remain just below the point of distress. When he exceeds his tolerance limits, injury, physical fatigue, or mental exhaustion results.

Your physican can help determine your maximal aerobic power and maximal attainable heart rate. Once these have been determined, the precise amount of exercise that is enough to achieve fitness but not exceed safe limits can be outlined.

Many people approach recreational pursuits so aggressively that they push themselves beyond their capacity. Their drive to win at any cost can push them into the danger zone and risk physical breakdown. Therefore, the hard-driving, time-conscious, aggressive individual is cautioned against setting highly competitive goals for distance, speed, tolerance, time, or scores. Rather, he is encouraged to enjoy his weekend tennis match for the sake of the outdoors, body–mind involvement, and social aspects. Freeing the mind of the competitive pressure experienced in the business world has a restorative, revitalizing quality.

Popular reports of employee fitness programs indicate that fewer days are lost to illness with active exercise programs. The primary health-related effect of exercising is conditioning of the cardiovascular system, rather than actually reducing stress itself. Nevertheless, some experts feel that exercise has both physical and emotional aspects. There is the physical release, increased lung efficiency, and increased endurance, but also, not infrequently, there is a reduction of anger, aggressiveness, and depression. Usually, the physical expenditure is followed by a relaxed, alert calmness and rejuvenated spirit.

Running, yoga, hiking, swimming, and bicycling are but a few of the activities that can aid in reducing distress and anxiety and help build a healthier body. The pure enjoyment, friendships, and fitness values of tennis, golf, skiing, bowling, and other physical activities also contribute to your total well-being over the long run. To summarize, regular physical exercise of the proper kind and amount can:

Improve muscle tone and posture
Control weight
Reduce tension by preventing stress buildup
Dissipate or use up the stress products of the hormonal and nervous systems
Decrease one's reactivity to stressors
Promote a feeling of well-being, tranquility, and transcendence
Delay the onset of or slow down degenerative diseases
Prevent boredom
Provide relaxation

PHYSICAL FITNESS PROGRAMS

Physical fitness through health clubs and gymnasiums is a popular choice for both muscular and cardiovascular development. Pulse rates can be elevated and controlled for precise periods for heart development and for visible muscular development. The heart gains in muscular strength during exercise. When it is strong, fewer beats are required to supply the body with blood. Thus, the heart gets more rest and relaxation time while efficiently meeting the body's need. Exercise enhances the vigor of the heart muscle and its subjection to nervous control.

Loss of fat can be achieved simultaneously through progressive weight-resistance exercises. These programs integrate diet and proper rest with exercise schedules based on an individual's intrinsic capacity. However appealing and potentially desirable various health club programs may be, the health spa industry should be approached with caution. To achieve the health benefits sought through corporate or private memberships, the following considerations deserve to be kept in mind.

Overcrowded facilities from swelled membership and high traffic times can be stress producing and discourage regular participation in the program. In addition, poor exercise supervision or inadequately trained instructors or staff members can result in muscle-strain backaches and other ailments. The facilities should also be made aware of any limitations or physical disabilities you may have so that they may tailor a health-enhancing regime to your particular needs and abilities.

Before joining a gym, spa, or health club, ask for a guest pass so that you can examine the facilities and try out the equipment. See what they offer as it relates to the achievement of your personal fitness goals. Ask questions. Because of the high employee turnover in this industry, you will have to look for a constant level of expertise rather than for an exceptional employee. Through questioning instructors about diet and exercise, you can evaluate their expertise. Staff members may be college-trained physical education majors, physical therapists, or self-educated lay persons. They can be well informed, with an ability to translate their knowledge into an effective personalized program for you.

If you cannot get satisfactory answers to your questions and the so-called "professional" lacks sufficient physiological and nutritional background, it is doubtful whether the best-equipped gym will offer any long-range benefits. Swimming pool, whirlpool, steam room, sauna, sunlamps, racquetball, jacuzzi, jogging track, yoga, and nutrition classes are some of the most popular offerings available.

Many executives combine physical conditioning with social or community activities at their local Boys' Club, YMCA, college, or university. Aside from the physical benefits, this can provide the social outlet and support system to which we have referred as contributing positively to a person's general well-being.

A person does not have to belong to any organization or enroll in any class to achieve his physical fitness goals. He can establish his own recreational regime, possibly receiving some direction from the myriad of books available. The key is self-awareness of your limitations, needs, and personal requirements. Jogging 10 miles a day may be invigorating for your neighbor but deadly or boring for you. Your medical history, body type and build, age, temperament, habits, physical location, and time schedule are factors influening the amount and kinds of exercise in which you engage.

NUTRITION AND DIET

Nutrition and exercise are closely linked, since a person's diet provides the body with fuel for activity and exercise circulates the nutrition in the blood to the brain cells and wherever else it is needed. Too much caffeine, sodium, refined sugar, or processed flour can lead to distress. Also, a deficiency of certain vitamins, minerals, and nutrients can upset body chemistry.

Poor dietary habits can make a person irritable, hyperactive, unattractive, anxious, sluggish, and disoriented. These results can impair an individual's ability to meet the demands of his job effectively and collaterally be disruptive to the climate of the workforce and general quality of life.

Malnourishment can lead to coronary heart disease, mental retardation and other birth defects, arthritic disease, and mental disease. Besides these medical problems, alcoholism, multiple sclerosis, dental disease, glaucoma, cataracts, muscular dystrophy, and cancer are affected by diet.

Many doctors, nutritionists, and self-appointed experts propound the benefits of fat-free diets, low-salt diets, vegetarian diets, sugar-free diets, or any number of other good restrictions or promotions for a longer or thinner or healthier life. In addition, a plethora of health food stores, vitamin advertisements, nutritional guides, classes, weight reduction clubs, and clinics have added to the layman's confusion. Which approach is the right one?

The selection is not easy. A lot of the regimens force you to make a radical change in eating habits, which is difficult for many people to do. Additionally, conflicting advice makes choices difficult. For example, there is little agreement on precisely what should be eaten and what should not, and in what amounts. For instance, eggs and meat have been enmeshed in the cholesterol and protein controversies. And no one disputes the need for vitamins, but the question is whether or not supplements are necessary in order to compensate for dietary deficiencies and meet body requirements.

The health and vitality of human systems depend on the external food supply of essential body chemicals such as manganese and zinc, in addition to a number of vitamins and other nutrients, the number of which is not precisely known. Individual nutritional needs, particularly those of people who have difficulty building or maintaining a suitable internal environment, are determined by many variables—body fat, musculature, neural and hormonal balance, metabolism, stress level, heredity, exercise, and special medical conditions.

Before you elect to go on any diet or decide what kind of change is necessary, ask a physician to assess your state of health. The physician can evaluate strategies for bioecological stress treatment and health enhancement such as noise abatement and nutritional control.

In spite of the variety of exhortations to eat or abstain from various foods, experts generally agree on the following nutritional recommendations, which the U.S. Senate Committee on Nutrition and Human Needs has endorsed:

Reduce salt, refined sugar, fat, and cholesterol consumption.
Increase fruit, vegetable, and whole grain consumption.
Limit meat consumption, substituting poultry and fish.

To a great extent, as health experts say, "we are what we eat."

Diet and stress have a feedback effect on one another. For instance, excessive stress can weaken the endocrine system and may result in hypoglycemia. This low blood sugar is due to insufficient production of the hormones that convert body starch into sugar. Salt is a contributing factor in the incidence of arteriosclerosis (hardening of the arteries) and of hypertension, as are hereditary and stress factors. These and other conditions, such as obesity and heart ailments, exemplify the interaction of stress, diet, exercise, and other variables on health. The human body is a delicate balance of the physical, emotional, and mental aspects of being.

A diet low in fats and high in nutrients can promote a more energetic lifestyle and aid in the prevention of cardiovascular disease and other diet-related diseases. Iron, potassium, or magnesium deficiencies can be causes of chronic fatigue, when you feel every cell of your body is dragging.

VITAMINS

Frequently vitamin supplementation to replace the depleted supply can eliminate morning exhuastion, increase physical work capacity, and enhance your overall ability to perform under the highest workload conditions.

In addition to problems of fatigue, other effects of pollution rob us of our optimum health. To counteract the by-products of twentieth-century urbanization—fatigue, crowding, noise, chemical pollutants—vitamin C can help improve appetite, sleep, and energy level. Vitamin B complex, magnesium and potassium, and calcium folate provide further relief from the fatigue, digestive disorders, depression, and insomnia of which many of us are victims.

Our concern for good nutrition is not to be confused with food faddism. We are not talking about zealously following a certain diet for a time. We are recommending an understanding of the series of processes by which man takes in and assimilates food for promoting growth, replacing worn or injured tissues, and generally enhancing health. An important component of any stress reduction program is sound nutritional habits, such as those enumerated as commonsense health habits earlier.

MODELING/IMITATION

We learn by imitation. In fact, virtually all of us developed from infancy through childhood and adolescence and into adulthood by copying the behavior of others and modeling ourselves after selected (conscious or unconscious) examples. Some of our maladaptive copying responses imitate an alcoholic mother or obese father, a hypochondriacal friend, or a suicidal movie star. We are not always aware of how we learned these responses to life's problems.

Your family or environment may not provide you with a wealth of learned coping behaviors. These are basically acquired either by observation or by experience. Many people have never been exposed to positive ways of dealing with life change and with stress. Consequently, it is perfectly natural for them to go to bed with a headache or to accept other forms of illness as their dominant behavior. They really don't know how to be well or what they would do if they were well.

Different situations call for different responses. Your ability to react with laughter, anger, sadness, or logic, taking time for orientation or preparation, or just delaying action and curbing the amount of change you encounter may save you from backache, ulcers, or worse.

BUILDING SUPPORT NETWORKS

Getting together with friends who will listen, share things with you, or offer light conversation can be therapeutic. Getting together in a candid exchange with fellow employees to work out minor frictions and more cooperative work arrangements can lower the collective stress level effectively.

People who are functioning members of their community, who are "socially healthy," also tend to have a higher degree of psychological health and physical well-being. Those people who have developed a source of social support, who have close friendships, strong family ties, and warm relationships with neighbors and fellow workers, generally deal more effectively with stressful events than those who are socially isolated.

Therefore, conscious efforts to expand social and personal contacts can be an effective coping device. People are an essential part of your life. They provide objectivity, reassurance, fun and warmth, and additional perspective. Furthermore, people you care for and who care for you can provide support, advice, comfort, and protection during troubled times. You can trust them enough to share your innermost thoughts, feelings, and opinions.

There are many ways you can expand your social network. Join a social organization, sports club, or church group. Broaden your range of interests and activities and invite others to join you. Look up old friends and keep in contact with your family. By demonstrating your interest in others—their ideas, activities, and feelings—you will provide the basis for establishing what can be a most fortifying relationship.

LIFE PLANNING

Set aside time for yourself to rediscover your feelings, your thoughts, your hopes, and yourself. This solitude provides a periodic break in routine in order to reevaluate your priorities and decide what activities, people, goals, and values are really important to you. Pinpointing sources of pleasure and pain and of satisfaction and frustration enables you to recognize the needless sources of stress in your work or personal life with which you should dispense to increase your state of well-being. Ask yourself exactly how important the thing you are worreid about is. Is it worth making yourself or others sick over?

Take control of your environment whenever possible. Curb demands and stress buildup (for example, limit the number of telephone interruptions). Schedule your appointments realistically, allowing enough time on your calendar so that you are not always rushing from one meeting to another. Each day, set your priorities in the morning and stick to that order. Take up a new task only when you finish your priority items.

Learn how to manage demands from others. Let them know how much time and effort you are willing to give them. Let them know, too, when you cannot accept their requests. Try to get the person who wants you to take on another task to help you evaluate the urgency of the request and determine where it fits among your priority items. Slow down. When you act rushed, you will feel pressure.

Other specific ways of planning your life by using your time more effectively were covered in Chapter 3. A review of that material will help you to identify objective, realistic, and obtainable goals; establish priorities; design an action plan; and generally get more out of life. Effective time management can relieve overload, burnout, frustration, and other distressful situations and enhance your general well-being.

SYMPTOM-DIRECTED INTERVENTIONS

When someone is troubled more by a specific symptom associated with a variety of stressors than by a few specific stressors, symptom-directed interventions are most appropriate. There are times when you cannot pinpoint what is bothering you; you only know you are upset. In situations where you cannot eliminate the causes of stress, you will have to content yourself with attacking the symptoms.

Some of the more common symptoms that are treated with these techniques include chest pain, low back pain, tension headache, and hypertension. Before employing any of these techniques, it is essential that your physician give you a medical examination, in case you have any organic disease that may require medical therapy.

Employees and their companies alike are discovering that a good break at the right time of day can be more effective in leading to the best solutions than plodding through when the brain is overloaded. An important step toward prevention of stress disorders is to take time to relax. The emergence of systematic, teachable relaxation techniques is an important breakthrough in health management. The realization that human beings are capable of relaxation through will has spawned a variety of techniques to lower the stress response threshold.

Autogenics and relaxation training by classical hypnotherapeutic techniques can reduce heart and respiratory rates to attain some stress relief. Even when confronted by an otherwise distressing event, situation, or person, you can learn to relax automatically by visualization therapy and other means.

This type of relaxation can also be facilitated by the use of physiological monitoring devices that enable a person to measure minute changes in the body's internal activities and check his level of relaxation. Biofeedback may involve self-regulation of circulation (through temperature control) or GSR (galvanic skin response) or training muscle relaxation (EMG) or alpha brain waves (EEG). All these techniques electronically monitor information to reveal maladaptive behavior responses.

The relationship between yoga and stress reduction has been known for thousands of years. Yoga and other meditation philosophies require extensive training in the mental and physical exercises practiced to achieve relaxation and increase mental efficiency. These practices can quiet the mind, steady the emotions, slow the respiration, make muscles supple, and regulate the organs.

Transcendental meditation provides another popular technique for gaining mental and muscular rest and renewal. Clinical tests show that this procedure can reduce heart rate and blood pressure and may improve work efficiency.

Listening to soothing instrumental music, letting yourself float with the melody, imagining yourself in a soothing environment, and allowing the music to relax your muscles may help relieve tension.

Deep muscle relaxation, alternately tensing then relaxing the muscles of your hands, biceps, face, shoulders, chest, stomach, legs, and feet, helps focus on the feeling of relaxation that follows the muscle tensing.

Once you learn to relax by one of these methods, use it in moments when you feel distress coming on. Take a break from the activity causing the stress, retire to a private spot, and relax. Let your mind drift from the pressure of daily activities. Remember how you felt when you relaxed, and relive those feelings.

Once you learn to relax quickly, use imagery to break the emotional reactions triggered by pressures you often encounter. First relax, then imagine yourself facing a situation that normally makes you tense, such as the pressure that builds up when you face a deadline. Repeat this several times, each time imagining yourself handling the situation calmly. Stop the stress-associated scene if it makes you feel more tense than relaxed. Repeat this until you can go through the entire scene without feeling any tension.

We will now look at some of these and other techniques more closely.

BIOFEEDBACK

Biofeedback offers an alternative to those suffering from functional disorders to drugs and surgery in some cases. Biofeedback techniques can be used alone or in combination with psychotherapy and physical therapy. There is a growing interest in the psychophysiological aspects of human dynamics. Research is being done on biofeedback techniques dealing with epilepsy, the control of heart rate, blood pressure, hyperkinesis, hypertension, and general clinical applications related to stress disorders and other complex physiological processes. Some insurance plans cover biofeedback treatments if ordered by a medical doctor.

Generally, biofeedback has three characteristics in common with older approaches to organic disease, such as meditation, yoga, and progressive relaxation. They all (1) emphasize providing the patient with a new self-perception of his body, (2) teach the patient techniques he can use for himself, and (3) encourage the patient to acquire more responsibility for his own health and its relationship to his life patterns.

The capacity to learn self-regulation to control the unconscious physiological processes of the heart, viscera, and brain is inherent in every human being. However, there are no shortcuts for a quick remission of muscle tension, acidic stomach, migraine headache, and other problems. Biofeedback mechanisms must be learned and applied through practice, usually under trained supervisors.

Patients learn to understand the relationship between the mechanical instrument monitoring responses and their neuromuscular reactions. This objective feedback information gives the patient cues to correlate his conscious feelings with the associated unconscious physiological processes of his body. The subject then is trained to integrate the two and control these processes mentally, eventually without the aid of instruments.

The implications for medicine of the individual voluntarily controlling such involuntary processes as blood pressure, muscle tension, skin temperature, heartbeat, and certain brain wave patterns (such as the alpha waves) are great for the treatment of certain psychosomatic illness processes. The effects are potentially permanent as the patient learns self-control over a variety of emotional and physical states.

PROGRESSIVE MUSCULAR RELAXATION

Progressive muscular relaxation is based on the assumption that as your muscles relax, your mind will too. It is physically impossible to feel nervous or fearful when every controllable muscle in your body is relaxed. The opposite is also true; a chronic state of muscle tension can increase stress and result in numerous psychosomatic disorders, including tightness in the throat and chest cavity, some eye problems, lockjaw, backache, spasms of the esophagus and colon, and perhaps rheumatoid arthritis.

Systematic muscular tension and relaxation increases the before-and-after sensations of relaxation. Once you are aware of these physical states, you will find it easier to recognize the symptoms of a mild tension state. This will enable you to employ relaxation techniques before muscular tension produces the mental anxiety that perpetuates a vicious cycle of ever widening stress manifestations.

Tensing and relaxing each muscle from head to toe takes only a few minutes, yet can provide you with renewed vitality for several hours.

AUTOGENIC TRAINING

Clinical results demonstrate that autogenic therapy can increase resistance to all kinds of stress in about 80 to 90 percent of all adults. Generally speaking, the physiological and psychophysiologically oriented effects of autogenic therapy may be considered as being diametrically opposed to changes elicited by stress.

This therapeutic approach consists in training people to exercise control over their own physiology to promote in themselves certain self-normalizing, recuperative processes that are directed and coordinated by the brain. In contrast to other medically or psychologically oriented forms of treatment, this methodology involves using mental and bodily functions simultaneously to achieve homeostasis. A passive spectatorlike concentration on a verbal autogenic formula is maintained during the practice of autogenic training. The content of the formula and the sequence of the different exercises are carefully designed to adapt to the particular disorders the patient is experiencing.

Insomnia, bronchial asthma, stuttering, writer's cramp, anxiety, and cardiospasms are a few of the problems that can be treated effectively. A number of approaches, verbal formulas, and training postures are possible. There are meditative exercises, organ-specific exercises, and intentional formulas designed to influence specific mental functions and behavior deviations. Combinations of the different autogenic approaches permit flexibility and precision of clinical and nonclinical application.

Autogenic methods can be adapted for the treatment of psychosomatic, behavior, and vasomotor disturbances as well as disorders of the gastrointestinal tract, immune system, and cardiovascular system and musculoskeletal disorders, and for other clinical applications.

This form of therapy requires the patient's active participation, seriousness of intention, and average intelligence. The method can be applied individually or in groups. Since it operates in a highly differentiated and delicate field of neural mechanisms, it must be emphasized that the clinical application of the method should be carried out by physicians who have learned the technique themselves under the guidance of an experienced colleague.

The benefits from autogenic training can be observed over periods ranging from a few days to a few months. These generally include an increase in emotional and physiological tolerance; less inhibited and more natural social contact; warmer, more intimate interpersonal relations; increased objectivity; and enhanced overall capacity to cope.

TRANSCENDENTAL MEDITATION

Transcendental meditation (TM) is one of the best-known techniques for eliciting the relaxation response. Many businessmen have graduated from the standard course by an authorized instructor and regularly meditate at least once or twice a day. They report increased creativity, memory, self-reliance, and productivity. In addition, studies verify that TM decreases anxiety, depression, and emotional disturbance.

RELAXATION THERAPY

As in transcendental meditation, relaxation therapy is based on the body's inherent capacity to elicit a reaction that is the reverse of the fight-or-flight response of the general alarm reaction. This relaxation response is common to hypnosis as well as many forms of meditation. In essence, it is a means of achieving a generalized decrease in sympathetic nervous system activity. Decreases in respiration, heart rate, and muscle tension are among the changes noted during the relaxation response.

It is an altered state of consciousness in which the mind and body are deeply relaxed, awareness of your surroundings diminishes, and you become especially receptive and respond to suggestions that are acceptable to you. In the self-hypnosis form you can return to a state of total awareness at will. While in this state of deep relaxation, your bodily functions slow down. In fact, it may be more restful than sleep, because the mind is not troubled intermittently by dreaming.

Typically, you sit or recline comfortably in a quiet area of your home or office. Then you close your eyes and imagine you are somewhere very pleasant, far from worries and responsibilities. Looking at that peaceful scene, you recall the relaxed, trouble-free feelings you experienced in that setting. Practice naming every detail of the scene until a key reference to your fantasy enables you to take a brief, free, mental vacation at will.

Studies have shown significant beneficial effects on psychological and somatic symptoms such as reduced apprehension, agitation, and anxiety and decreased blood pressure. In addition, incidences of illness were reduced and self-rated job performance and job satisfaction were augmented.

There are innumerable ways to utilize relaxation therapy, as it can be activated any time and any place. For instance, many athletes find that it aids in focusing concentration to improve their performance in competition. You can use it to wake up in the morning, to sleep at night, or to calm nerves before a sales presentation, a stressful interview, or a trip to the dentist.

Many tape recordings are available to elicit the relaxation response. These vary from recordings of natural sounds like the ocean to a soothing voice. Some people find taped instructions easier than the time and concentration inherent in autogenic training. However, at times this method leads to dependency on hearing the instructor's soothing voice on the cassette rather than on more self-reliant methods.

Other techniques that have been tried to reduce distress are acupuncture, acupressure, dietary therapy, and vitamin therapy. Their effectiveness has not yet been determined. Nevertheless, modern man is determined to explore every opportunity to bring stress under control as he faces new life-threatening challenges.

HYPNOTHERAPY

Hypnotherapy is an effective psychotherapeutic technique for resolving difficulties in adjusting to stress, tension, and anxiety. Many people have found that this form of relaxation can help them to readjust their integration of thought and cope with life more contentedly and effectively.

The vast majority of the population can learn to enter the hypnotic state of temporarily altered consciousness by properly instructed and qualified medical and psychological practitioners. A technique that attempts to go beyond the treatment of symptoms (specific etiological factors) to the psychic causes of a problem requires specialized training in psychotherapy.

All methods of hypnotherapy involve the use of one or another of hypnotic techniques and phenomena, such as hypermnesia or post-hypnotic suggestions.

There is scarcely any functional disturbance or psychosomatic syndrome that has not been treated successfully by the direct suggestion technique in hypnosis. Epilepsy, seasickness, multiple sclerosis, migraine, insomnia, asthma, and muscular rheumatism are only a sampling of the scope of therapeutic applications. The patient may obtain relief from his symptoms or experience disappearance of the attitudes underlying the symptoms, sometimes temporarily, often permanently.

Many people can be assisted in coping with stress by using the peace of mind achieved in the state of hypnosis. This form of relaxation enables the thought processes to slow down and become more orderly. The tranquility achieved can restore a patient's confidence as his anxieties, doubts, and fears dissipate. One of the principal benefits of hypnotherapy is that the calm serenity of the mind continues after wakening, becoming more prolonged with repeated inductions and sessions. This peacefulness of mind continues to build up, especially when the patient has been trained in autohypnosis.

STRESSOR-DIRECTED INTERVENTIONS

Stressor-directed interventions are useful when extreme stress reactions occur in response to a specific stressor (or phobia) such as fear of flying. Common stressors for which these interventions may be effective include speaking before a group of people, interaction with specific superiors or employees, and facing physically unpleasant working conditions each day.

These preventive techniques attempt to reduce or eliminate the stress response to the specific activities or conditions that are perceived by the individual as stressors.

DYNAMIC PSYCHOTHERAPY

This intervention technique reduces and frequently eliminates the stress response by providing information or insights about the stressor and/or about the person's reasons for perceiving the stressor as a threat. Many of the problems are rooted in childhood although some have more recent origins. A skilled therapist can mobilize your subconscious and bring your fears or other feelings to your conscious awareness. You can then deal with such stressors as your fear of dogs, hostility toward authority, or self-consciousness about meeting new people.

SYSTEMATIC DESENSITIZATION

Systematic desensitization is a behavioral therapy that attempts to substitute muscular relaxation directly for the tension response to stress. The desensitizing process is helpful in alleviating phobic anxiety or tension from the fear of a specific thing (such as flying or public speaking). This technique works through the "ordeal" by constructing a hierarchy of 15 to 20 items from the least frightening experience to the phobia.

You are helped to work your way from step to step in your imagination, while in a relaxed state. You look at the distressing item under nonthreatening circumstances in the doctor's office. As you become comfortable with an item, you gradually move on to each point on your list until you can deal with the phobic source of tension.

Concentrating on relaxing enables you to let distracting thoughts go, and you become more comfortable with yourself and your ability to handle situations. Your mind in this state of relaxation is most receptive to accepting a new outlook, and a change in perspective can help you cope even more constructively.

Systematic desensitization is currently the most widely studied of the stressor-directed intervention techniques. Through a sequence of progressive relaxation steps, the individual is gradually taught to substitute relaxation for the stress response. Such preconditioning can channel anticipatory stress into constructive behaviors and reduce the distress of actual confrontations.

In the end, everyone has to find his/her own best cure for job stress. Chuck Foster, director of the office that handles citizens' complaints about San Francisco's buses and streetcars, pounds out on his typewriter all the things he would like to have said to the caller; then he throws the paper away. For Chicago television reporter Susan Anderson, baking, knitting, and cleaning her house give her mind something uncomplicated to do as a change of pace from the anxiety of going on camera every day appearing knowledgeable and aggressive. For others, jogging or other hard regular exercise is the way to relieve the pressures caused by job stress.

Whether the best way to switch gears to give your mind and body a change of pace is swimming 20 laps in a pool or listening to Beethoven's Fifth Symphony is a matter of personal preference and experience. Some people react to stress mentally, some physically, and some with a combination of the two. Knowing which way to express stress overload can help you choose an appropriate response to relieve it.

Thus, in order for the complex nature of your life to work harmoniously for you, we strongly advocate a holistic approach to well-being. Because a multidimensional health-enhancement program offers more ways of relating to your inner and exterior environments, you have more chances of succeeding in your fitness goal. Adherence to an individualized stress management program encompassing meditation, exercise, diet, relaxation techniques, biofeedback, and other learned skills can help reduce and prevent life-threatening stress in your life.

The breadth of your repertoire of skills will provide you with the resources to help you feel healthier, increase your positive energy, and generally improve the quality of your life. Such a program promotes little changes in many aspects of your life without causing a major upheaval in any one area. Physicians, mental health care specialists, and other service professionals can be helpful in coordinating your efforts based on informed choice.

Good health in mind and body does not just happen without positive action. Understanding and learning to control stress by employing some of these techniques are important steps toward good health.

Healthy people know how to live with stress. They know how to pace themselves, to relax, and to recognize their own stress limits. Controlling stress and channeling it constructively are crucial to the full development of your potential in physical capabilities, mental powers, special talents, and abilities to give and receive love.

You can help determine the extent of your own fulfillment by the way in which you use your awareness and make your choices. If you continue to grow in awareness of yourself and the world around you, you are more likely to make stress a positive force in your life. Awareness of the nature of stress and how to handle it will help you to choose your actions wisely in meeting the challenges that arise and overcoming stressful conditions and situations.

Managing stress wisely means knowing what amount of stress is right for you—enough challenges to stimulate development, but not so many that you are overwhelmed. Part I illustrated how stress is connected with how you go about daily life, the kinds of pressures you face, how well you take care of your health, and how you may be a stress carrier or stress other people. Depending on how you handle the many problems of modern life, some of the stressful situations will rebound to your benefit or take their toll mentally and/or physically. If you fail to find effective solutions, stress will increase and persist to your disadvantage.

On the other hand, conscious awareness of yourself and the nature of stress can strengthen your general resistance to its detrimental effects. Your subsequent capacity to learn how to call on your repertoire of coping skills and master the pressures—without developing a stress reaction—will be enhanced.

We have presented a broad sampling of intervention and management techniques in this chapter and throughout the book. Because of the individual nature of stress, we do not presume to have mentioned all the methods available.

You have the choice of viewing a situation either stressfully and as a personal failure or nonjudgmentally, as a learning experience. If you choose the healthier information-gathering approach, you can begin to identify what you can use and learn from the situation to improve the quality and effectiveness of future encounters. Understanding what works for you and what does not enables you to come to terms with your present circumstances and to direct your life in a more productive and fulfilling manner.

CHAPTER 17
Developing a Corporate Stress-Reduction Program

The question is no longer whether organizations should institute stress reduction programs, but how. As was pointed out at the beginning of this book, there is substantial evidence that chronic stress is costly in terms of human resources and therefore of the overall economic stability that underlies the functioning of an organization.

Organizational stress may be one of the most devastating occupational hazards. It can be defined as the nonspecific response of the individual to any perceived demand made upon him by the organization. Each employee responds to the person–environment interaction through a pattern of individual alarm, physiological response, and behavioral patterns. Depending upon differences among people and environmental conditions, these alarm reactions may lead to adaptive, positive responses and relative health (eustress) or maladaptive responses, with their associated costs for both the employee and the organization (distress).

The stressors in the workplace were enumerated in Chapter 2, but it is helpful to reiterate those dimensions of a person's organizational environment that have the potential for creating damaging stress.

ORGANIZATIONAL STRESSORS

The major organizational stressors fall into at least four general categories:

Role-making dysfunctions and conflict
Job factors
Physical working conditions
Interpersonal relations

A variety of both direct and indirect costs must be recognized and assumed by the organization when employees are distressed on the job as a result of their maladaptive responses to these and other stresses. These consequences are undesirable and dysfunctional from an organizational perspective.

There are two levels at which management can intervene preventively to reduce the amount of distress for employees. The preventive interventions may be classified as either organizational interventions or individual interventions. In Chapters 15 and 16, we outlined the personal perspective and techniques for alleviating stress. The following interventions are those alternatives available to the corporation in order to provide a healthy working environment and therefore enhance the stability and success of the corporation.

DEVELOPING ORGANIZATIONAL INTERVENTIONS

Business organizations must increasingly deal with the problems of job-induced stress: alcoholism, drug abuse, and the increasing difficulties of employees in adjusting to the changes in society as a whole and in their personal lives in particular. The human costs of doing business are giving rise to the application of organizational problem-solving resources to improve the quality of working life by taking appropriate actions to bring this modern disease under control.

Developing a stress reduction program can involve six structural steps:

Identifying the stress
Appraising and developing corporate and individual commitment
Recognizing current behavior patterns
Developing an action plan
Trying out the plan
Evaluating how well the plan is working

As in the individual stress management program, careful planning can prevent potential problems, while intervention techniques can be employed in areas of specific weaknesses.

Implementing an effective stress reduction program requires conscious and sustained effort over time. Conflicting values, inconsistent feelings, and discouraging environments often make it difficult to sustain this effort. Corporate executives need to apply themselves, inspire their workforce, and mobilize their resources to maintain a health-enhancing work environment that encourages and stimulates productivity.

The amount of effort required to incorporate stress reduction techniques into corporate policy and personal habits may vary over time. At times, procedural and behavioral changes will be subtle and gradual. Under different circumstances, the adjustment will seem more abrupt. The procedures involved in instituting stress reduction strategies may require a continuing recycling through the six steps in the face of the ever changing dynamics of corporate life. New thoughts, feelings, and features of the physical, economic, political, and social environment constantly interact to add to the complexity of controlling stress in the business world.

Identifying the Stress

Recognizing that stress is inherent in the life of every individual and impacts on all his activities and human contacts is fundamental to developing strategies to minimize its potentially damaging effects. As explained in Chapter 2, denial of the stress problem is not uncommon by many people and organizations. However, in the face of substantial and impressive evidence to the contrary, this position is indefensible and can be costly and dangerous to all concerned.

Therefore, the first step in combating the hazards of chronic stress or stress overload is to recognize that the problem exists. This may be a clear-cut truth for some, but it represents a major stumbling block for many troubled organizations. Without this awareness, a company is not likely to expend the conscious effort, funds, or time required to control the problem.

Other companies may know a problem exists but are unable to formulate it. Identifying stress in the working environment demands that we specify its components as fully as possible. This means learning what is known about industrial/organizational stress as well as specific stressors indigenous to the work environment. Identifying which thoughts and behaviors of an employee interfere with efforts to reduce stress can also pinpoint areas that may need altering. This identification can be made by analyzing the employee's definition of the job (company, role, and so on) in terms of assessing his beliefs, expectations, and self-evaluation. His attributions are also important. For example, to whom or what does he attribute authority, his success or failure, eustress or distress, or boredom and dissatisfaction?

Chapter 14 discussed how influential a person's perception of a problem is on the amount of stress he experiences or generates. Whether a given situation is a threat or a challenge is largely a matter of personal impression. Sometimes the first step in controlling stress-producing behavior is learning to look at the causative problem from a different perspective.

The executive who must resolve conflicting and interrelated events into reasonably stress-free courses of action should recognize that "problem" is but a word; it is not a thing in itself. The section on general semantics in Chapter 14 elaborates on this distinction.

The stress problem in an organization cannot be separated from the background in which it is embedded and grows. It cannot be made to stand alone, unchanging and isolated from the remaining whole of the environment. It is an integral part. Like other business difficulties, the stress problem cannot be measured in its entirety, defined in all dimensions, frozen into its pattern of the moment—or solved in a vacuum.

For these reasons, we must recognize that any solution initiates change and is but the first of the adaptations created on the continuum of the dynamics of change. If you accept that there is no one technique that can eradicate distress from organizational life, you may become convinced that significant progress can be made in reducing the incalculable costs to your business through the implementation of overt stress reduction strategies.

The more pressure a problem generates, the less opportunity there is for an immediate solution. Some people seem to thrive on pressure situations and are able to make decisions with relative calm and confidence. Most people, however, show confusion, disorientation, or distortion of reality when overloaded with stress. They show signs of fatigue, anxiety, irritability, and general tension. They are also unable to think clearly or remember well, which causes a general decline in performance and personal effectiveness. Consequently, excessive pressure can cause a breakdown in problem-solving and decision-making abilities.

The more pressure a problem generates, the more probability of error in using stop-gap measures rather than problem-solving techniques. On the other hand, the more appropriate the solution, the less the pressure generated by the problem. The solution almost never fully erases the problem. Again, stress reduction requires constant vigilance.

Commitment: Deciding to Act

A valid commitment emphasizes that organizations and people will do what is necessary to improve their ability to follow through with a desired change. It is a decision to change together, with some action taken to help implement that decision. Simply recognizing the presence of distress in the work environment and deciding to "make some changes" in policies, structure, or behavior are sufficient indications of commitment.

Commitment requires us to act, to engage in processes and use procedures that will ultimately bring about and maintain a concerted thrust toward improving the quality of day-to-day work. It is aimed at restructuring our mental and physical environments to support our decision to change. It is a necessary step in promoting organizational change, but it may not be enough in terms of long-range cost and personal effectiveness.

Therefore, we need to look at two phases of commitment: assessment and development. When beginning a corporate stress reduction program, it is important to assess the following: (1) How willing is the corporation to keep working on the problem? (2) What actions are being taken to support the decision to change?

As we have pointed out, the assessment is closely bound with the company's conceptualization of the problem. Some ways of looking at a problem make for easier commitment than others. For example, if management believes that participatory opportunities positively affect employee involvement, motivation, and dedication, commitment to instituting a participation policy is strong. On the other hand, if management holds strict autocratic beliefs, commitment to such a program is weak. In this case, the feelings of job dissatisfaction and alienation can be aggravated by illusory or lip-service programs. The lack of commitment to policy substance and follow-through can have a negative impact on company operations, morale, and the stress problem.

The function of the assessment phase in determining corporate commitment is to identify the thoughts, feelings, behaviors, and features of the mental and physical environment that can make it difficult to initiate and implement a stress reduction program. We alluded to several of these in Chapter 2; for instance, poor lighting, noxious fumes, lack of privacy, tyrannical supervision, a ruthlessly competitive climate, mistrust, and lack of authority. A stress reduction program in the work situation can bring about substantial improvements in morale, health, and personal well-being. And these improvements can lead directly to improved job performance and other benefits to organizational effectiveness, including a tangible increase in profitability.

Dedication on the executive and upper managerial levels sets the pace for the entire organization. The people on these levels are the policymakers seen by employees as having the overall vision and authority to make things happen. Therefore, they are in the best position to be models and provide significant avenues for stress relief. Without this level of commitment, the program will have a short-lived contribution or no contribution at all to make toward the goals of organizational and personal effectiveness. Participation increases the ownership of change and the accountability. The backing of the major decision-making group can be the most effective agent of planned change in improving the health of the organization.

Corporate commitment is strongest when employee health is considered as important as such other work-related events as job performance. There is a growing corporate awareness that the more than $10 billion in organizational costs of stress-related problems derive directly from the collective individual costs of physical and emotional illness.

Since social, psychological, and physical factors on the job may have important influences on the employee's well-being and therefore on the overall corporate health, a three-pronged approach is advocated. Both individual and corporate stress reduction programs should include education, application, and evaluation.

Educating the program participants in the nature, sources, and repercussions of stress increases their consciousness of the very real need for such a program. The application of skills learned helps them control the stress in their own lives and alleviate it in others. Knowing what kinds of action to take when affected by stress can develop an almost automatic sense of control over themselves and the situations they encounter. The relief and increased effectiveness experienced strengthens commitment to the program. Lastly, on-going evaluation of the progress made in changing and creating conditions that are health enhancing can build and provide the energy necessary to engage in other steps of stress control.

Determining what works for you and what does not enables you to tailor your program to your specific needs, situation, and abilities. Because commitment may wane at any point, because it is difficult to change habits and familiar procedures and processes, constant monitoring, observing, and reinforcing are essential.

Most corporations are deeply concerned with improving management and executive behavior. Over the years a great many companies have been spending substantial funds in training and development programs. If managers fail to subscribe to the dictates of good management practices in their leadership supervisory roles, what happens to the people they supervise and the overall effectiveness of their programs? Real learning with measurable recall and accomplishment requires an intensive program and strong participatory commitment.

Recognizing Current Behavior

In order to lower the level of stress experienced in the work environment and to channel it into a positive organizational force, it is advisable to do an overall health profile of the corporation. Such a profile can be very revealing. It analyzes the rate of employee turnover, absenteeism, leadership ability, level of satisfaction, sense of reward, physical working conditions, needs, values, and behavior patterns. Responses in any or all of these areas can signal chronic levels of stress, tending toward a breakdown in the corporation or the people who direct it. Careful analysis of these and other risk factors will indicate those areas requiring special attention.

In Chapter 2, we discussed eight major risk factors that impact on overall job satisfaction, stress loading, and performance. In review, these factors are:

Workload	Assignment diversity
Physical conditions	Interpersonal relations
Job importance	Physical demands
Accountability	Mental stimulation

Lack of dedication, anxiety, frustration, ennui, or hostility may be the result of uncomfortable physical surroundings, monotonous tasks, lack of positive feedback, or indecisive leadership, to name only a few possibilities.

A review and appraisal of organizational values can provide valuable insight into executive planning, policymaking, and receptiveness to programs of planned change. In order to discover what prevailing norm guides, directs, or constrains the behavior of members of the organization, you need a sensitive awareness of different points of view at all levels of the organization.

Informal interviews with employees, managers, and executives can reveal as much from what they say as from what they select not to say. How do they perceive the relationship between profit requirements and the quality of working life within the organization? What are the real corporate priorities? What are the respective responsibilities of the various levels within the organization to one another, to the corporation, and to the community at large?

Surveys and interviews can be important investigative tools to find out what kinds of health problems prevail, how people view their jobs and co-workers, what stress levels are experienced by people, and how they are being manifest in their behaviors. Assessment of communication lines, levels of dissatisfaction, common complaints, and areas of employee dissatisfaction aid in diagnosing activities and policies of the organization requiring change.

Careful examination of this information helps to develop increased awareness of the people, attitudes, feelings, actions, and places that may be triggering or breeding distress in the organization.

The observations gained can give a new slant on the stress problem experienced in the company and reveal relationships not recognized before. Analysis of this detailed information may make possible more informed decisions about what to change, what to address first, and how to begin.

Developing an Action Plan

Developing a stress reduction program can involve the following steps:

1. Specifying the particular areas to work on.

2. Observing behaviors, policies, procedures, and conditions to increase awareness of their overriding control.
3. Generating specific techniques to help reduce distress.
4. Evaluating the alternative courses of action available in terms of short- and long-term consequences; the effort, resources, and attention required to implement them; and the likelihood of following through (amount of tenacity) on them.
5. Assigning priorities to the actions that will be taken.

The program utilizes traditional problem-solving, decision-making, and organization development models. It recognizes that there are actually three bottom lines in the business world—financial, social, and human. Therefore, our efforts are directed toward improving both the effectiveness of the system itself and the people within the system. The aim is to make the corporation humanistically and economically viable. What detracts from one eventually exacts a price from the other. The necessity and desirability of creating a practical program to deal with the fact of stress are obvious enough to motivate more and more organizations to implement action plans incorporating some of the processes enumerated in this chapter.

Trying Out the Plan

Implementing a corporate stress reduction program means setting a number of procedures into motion simulteneously. There needs to be a continuous recycling through the stages. The work requires determination, self-evaluation, a willingness to expend the necessary amount of energy and attention, and creativity. You might need to try out a number of plans before you find one that is practical and effective for your company. The rationale for various approaches and "how-to" techniques for each are outlined to provide you with a reservoir of possibilities for lowering the stress experienced in your company.

Organization of the workplace. The effects of the work environment on employee health, levels of personal satisfaction, and opportunities for self-development can lead to physical and emotional distress if the workplace is not organized to minimize stress-producing factors. Excessive routine, conflict of role expectations, chronic overload, autocratic supervision, and lack of support from superiors and co-workers are a few of the most common causes of distress. A climate of low satisfaction with high employee turnover and the absence of cohesive work groups is another example of a stress-producing environment.

In developing a corporate stress-reducing program, attention to specific working conditions can make a difference. For example, adequate lighting, comfortable seating, good air and heat circulation, and pleasant surroundings are important to the person spending the majority of his day there. Backaches, headaches, and anxiety can be significantly reduced in many cases by changing the stress-producing agent—harsh or dim lighting, loud or grating noises, extremes in air conditioning or heating, or uncomfortable seating.

The obvious is frequently overlooked in trying to find solutions to problems in the work setting. Actually, attention to such basic or simple factors can remedy irritability, poor concentration, and low productivity to a significant degree. Standard office management and record-keeping procedures may be so routine that they are forgotten or put off by more pressing matters until they themselves become stressful. A review of Chapter 3 on time management brings to light other factors that impinge on a person's effectiveness.

One of the greatest sources of job stress is ambiguity. When an employee cannot develop a clear picture of his job and responsibilities, he may become anxious, disgruntled, fearful of making any decisions or taking action on his own initiative, insecure about his contribution, and lacking in overall job satisfaction. Therefore, carefully defining the job, tasks, performance criteria, and desired results can help eliminate many of the stressors of confusion, uncertainty, and lack of direction. With clear and specific objectives toward which to work, there is a consistent basis for work planning and motivation for reaching those objectives.

Role analysis and restructuring. The restructuring or redefinition of roles and jobs in an organization is a fundamental process in organizational intervention. This is done in order to establish patterns of interaction that buffer the employee from such organizational stressors as outmoded job definitions, functions, and roles.

Also, this intervention technique tries to clarify the role for the employee in order to reduce ambiguity and the potential for conflict. It is aimed at avoiding interrole conflict, intrarole conflict, person–role conflict, and/or role overload. Perceived role ambiguity correlates with job-related tension and employee withdrawal from work. This may be manifest in absenteeism, turnover, or psychological withdrawal. The latter can mean lower job involvement and less identification with the organization, and it may be linked to other undesirable organizational consequences.

The technique is a form of job engineering that merges the behavioral and technical aspects of the job. It utilizes an integrated sociotechnical approach that clarifies by definition the specific, tangible objectives as well as the creative objective of the job. By defining the role the employee is to play in terms of accomplishing something of recognized value, you can measure performance and what the job is worth and then match the job and the person for greatest total effectiveness. Furthermore, by defining the job objectives, conditions, processes, equipment, and materials, you can optimize the relationship between production and job satisfaction, mobilizing stress to maximize personal effectiveness and reduce distress.

Work redesign is linked to role analysis and restructuring. Its aim is to diagnose categories of jobs and redesign them to trigger and direct employees' motivation. Since behavior is goal directed toward need satisfaction, work redesign can effectively enhance employee performance by providing work situations with opportunities for actual achievement, feelings of accomplishment, challenge, a sense of importance, and personal growth.

The way in which the job is defined and the work is designed will place demands upon the person. Therefore, every job needs to be retested and reevaluated from time to time to ensure against job or employee obsolescence. Other potential sources of job stress include underutilization of skills, physical overload, interpersonal contact overload, and absence of positive feedback.

Job enrichment. The importance of building such motivational factors as recognition and responsibility into the job is a major aspect of this technique. The thrust is to elicit eustress from the employee. This can be accomplished, for example, by clarifying job goals on both objective and creative levels and by deciding under what circumstances the work is to be done. It integrates human needs into the task structure in order to optimize the load factors related to productivity and satisfaction. Job design elements might have to be added, deleted, or modified to reach that goal.

Performance planning. A careful analysis of the responsibilities inherent in a job will clarify expectations and reduce the distress commonly experienced when performance standards are not understood. In addition, evaluation standards set forth before the work is begun further enhance the employee's sense of security. He knows what he has to do, so he can plan his course of action—what course to follow to succeed. He may experience eustress by virtue of the control he feels. Knowing the proper direction to take, he can focus his efforts on attaining the goal.

Occupational category. Some occupations and career paths are potentially more stressful than others. For instance, an air traffic controller is exposed to more stressful situations than a librarian. A person who does not have ample resources and capabilities for meeting a variety of demands would be wise to choose an occupational field in which the amount of stress encountered is limited.

The essence of social engineering is to seek alternatives or modifications of a position to reduce personal stressors; that is, to follow the path of least resistance. In Chapter 15, "stress seekers" were profiled and the innate personality of a "racehorse" and a "turtle" were highlighted. We are reminded that people perform most effectively and with a higher level of satisfaction when their skills, personality, growth potential, and needs interface compatibly with the job tasks and performance expectations.

Conversely, when the job makes demands on the employee beyond his level of competence, training, or temperament, feelings of inadequacy, frustration, restlessness, and/or a desire for escape hamper productivity and positive feelings. The accumulation of these distressing feelings can lead to a crisis situation for the employee and/or for the business. Stress is a part of all jobs, but distress need not be.

We often think of the high-pressured situations in the course of a business career as the debilitating culprits. However, as we pointed out earlier, studies have found that understimulation, a job devoid of challenges or change, can produce many of the same physiological symptoms as overwork.

Diminishing distressful workloads. Work overload results not only when others place innumerable demands on someone but also when he makes high demands on himself and goes after more than he can handle. There are several techniques that can reduce chronic overload and prevent it from leading to the breakdown of a system, whether biological or corporate.

Structures that allow for work delegation or sharing work with others can relieve overload. Also, someone should be able to ask for more work or responsibility if he or she is underloaded.

The overload situation can also be alleviated by developing employee skills to work more efficiently, more effectively, and faster. This can be done through in-house training, procedure manuals, films, courses, and classes.

Sometimes work overload is caused by difficult working hours because of personal commitments and needs. In selected situations, flexitime offers new freedom from the traditional nine-to-five work-day and has been used with good results. There are a number of variations to the system, depending on the needs and type of work of the particular company. Some companies have established "core hours" when everyone must work. In certain cases, the employee is assigned a particular task to be performed by a certain deadline with no other time requirement. Other companies establish a weekly or monthly hour requirement, the satisfaction of which can be determined by the employee's initiative. That is, the work of a full 40-hour week can be done in three or four days.

It will not be possible or desirable for every company to utilize this innovative program. There are an estimated 3,000 American firms and half a million employees now on the system. Employees are responding with efficiency and responsibility to meet deadlines and perform satisfactorily.

Some of the more significant contributions the utilization of flexitime has made include notably increased productivity; decreased turnover, tardiness, and absenteeism; greater efficiency and responsibility; and mutual trust between management and employees. The beneficial health implications are obvious.

Low-stress communication. We have talked about many techniques that rely on communication skills. Clarifying roles, task requirements, areas of responsibility, and work evaluation are only a few of the benefits.

To diffuse potentially highly stressful situations, low-stress communication is essential. In Chapter 14, perception, listening, and communication skills were explained at length. Here we shall draw on this background as it relates to improving the organizational climate.

When management consciously develops low-stress communication skills, it can significantly reduce the levels of stress felt by employees. Poor communication behaviors can add to a problem situation and produce more conflict, hard feelings, and stress for everyone involved. Helping others to keep their own stress levels down will help you keep yours down and increase everyone's productivity.

The basis of low-stress communicating is positive reinforcement—that is, making the majority of your interpersonal transactions friendly, positive, and rewarding. When you affirm another's self-esteem by sincere compliments, expressing respect for his or her opinions and constructive criticism, he or she generally reacts positively. On the other hand, if you are accusing, quick to anger, and belittling, others are more inclined to be uncooperative, no matter how much truth or important information there is in what you say.

We are all familiar with situations in which a strong stance must be taken, despite the uneasiness the recipient will experience. We are not suggesting a coddling approach; rather, we remind you to use the social skills you have acquired over the years in a way commensurate with getting the job done. We often tend to forget what we know about the human ego, body language, and voice quality when we are in difficult business situations or are feeling moody.

We suggest that you inventory your punishing and rewarding behaviors in dealing with colleagues and employees to see if there are better, more mutually productive ways of communicating and relating. Frequently, it is not so much what you say, but how you say it—your tone of voice, physical posture—and in whose presence that makes the difference in getting your message across effectively.

If you want a receptive audience for your stress reduction plan, how you communicate the program, information, and techniques will have a great deal to do with gaining participants or adversaries. As with other stress-reducing skills, communication skills can create an enjoyable, achievement-oriented climate that ultimately is reflected on the organization's bottom line.

In-house services. Seminars and workshops on how to anticipate and deal with the complexity of changing social, economic, technological, and organizational forces with more flexibility, creativity, and responsiveness can help develop health resourcefulness. A basic understanding of the mechanics, sources, and consequences of stress, as set forth in Parts I and II, is perhaps the most significant aspect of any stress reduction program.

Intensive workshops might also include assertion training, role playing, relaxation, and breathing techniques to combat distressing experiences.

Throughout Part I, references are made to the stresses produced by change. The changing nature of the adult life cycle—marriage, career, aging; society at large; and politics, community affairs, economics, and technology—requires constant adjustment.

Some companies are helping their personnel cope with twentieth-century life on a variety of fronts. They are making available in-house or referral services for consultation, testing, and/or guidance in such areas as vocational and career planning and development, technical seminars, and personal development workshops.

Large companies will pay for relocation expenses and aid in house hunting. A few will even buy an executive's home or cover any loss in the sale. There are relocation services to help the newcomer locate schools, doctors, and other community resources and help the uprooted family get established in a new area. In addition, special attention is given to the termination process, retirement and transitional counseling, conflict resolution, promotion, work–family interplay, and other potentially troublesome and distressful areas.

Health care. The medical examination was discussed in Chapter 16, but special programs may also be set up within the company's medical department, or employees may be urged to take a physical by an outside preventive medicine clinic. One-to-one stress counseling and training in stress management techniques can be provided by a stress specialist.

With the company behind him, a medical director can implement changes to make it a healthier place to work. For instance, the typical company's cafeteria food is often processed, high-calorie fare—soft drinks, potato chips, sandwiches on white bread. Arrangements with the cook, or even the catering truck company, can be made to make available natural foods like fresh fruit, yogurt, and avocado sandwiches on whole wheat bread.

Reducing noise by soundproofing, space planning, sound shields, machine adjustments, and so on also reduces stress. Space planning for workflow, privacy, and cutting down on the crowded feeling helps. Lighting and temperature control are two more potentially stress-producing physical variables. Harsh light or not enough light can influence an employee's general level of functioning, and extreme fluctuations in temperatures can be discomforting and distressful.

The temperature comfort zone for human beings is between 65°F and about 80°F. Of course, everybody has his own preference within that range. However, it is safe to say that when temperatures rise or fall beyond the comfort zone, people are adversely affected. Their behavior, mental alertness, dexterity, and other physical capacities are somewhat diminished. Prompt attention to temperature deviations and restoration of a comfortable climate can improve morale and productivity greatly.

Proper adjustment of equipment and furniture such as typing tables and chairs, workbenches, and shelving can alleviate back pain, eyestrain, and headaches. These are only a few of the most common stressors in the work environment that can be alleviated swiftly and easily. But they are commonly overlooked in favor of the day-to-day rush of business operations.

To be effective, a company health program must be tailored to individual needs, as enumerated in Part I. Needs vary with the person and his or her circumstances. For instance, an assembly-line worker doing very fine eye–hand work, putting copper wire onto resistors, could use an eye care program of simple exercises to reduce eyestrain and headaches. On the other hand, an executive may need a forum to express feelings, regular exercise, and/or quiet time alone, during which he can give his thought processes a rest from decision making and other pressures and responsibilities routine to his position.

People can learn when and how to use different tools for cutting down stress. For one person, it might be to take a walk every day. For another, it might mean doing a relaxation exercise or listening to a tape to aid in meditation. For a third, a yoga class or a hobby could be the answer. To get and stay healthy, a person needs to make the connection between what he does in his daily life and its effects on his ability to function at optimum levels.

A company gym or health club privileges can aid the sedentary businessman's circulation and general health, raise morale, and increase productivity. Lack of physical fitness can be prevented. The organization can draw on a variety of possibilities, ranging from simple encouragement to providing programs and facilities for employees. However, each person holds the principal responsibility for lowering his own cholesterol, maintaining his weight, stopping smoking, and enhancing his own health and well-being.

Evaluating the Plan

To some extent, we all evaluate how well we are doing in the course of everyday activities. A more conscious awareness becomes an important factor in maintaining both commitment and lower stress levels in ourselves and others.

Evaluation involves comparing your progress with realistic and useful standards and testing results of the plan in terms of specific developments and accomplishments. For instance, incidence of stress diseases and occupational health problems and human resources accounting can provide useful measures. They can indicate what effects job conditions may be having on employee well-being.

Improved attitude scores, reduced absenteeism, fewer infirmary visits, and lower turnover statistics can prove the cost effectiveness of specific actions and conditions resulting from the organization's plan. Testing, evaluation, and feedback procedures can show an increased tolerance to stress.

SUMMARY

Organizational stress is engendered not only for the reasons explored throughout this book but also for reasons in everyone's experience. Because of its multifaceted nature, stress must be fought from a multidimensional perspective. Providing a meditation room for employees for some mind-clearing peace and quiet is not the panacea for all stress-related ills; nor are "aggression" rooms and devices. A one-day seminar identifying the stress problem and discussing diet, exercise, and relaxation without follow-up opportunities does not allow real learning to take place by reinforcement and feedback.

The important health (mental and physical) implications of each one of these measures are many. They can all interface to bring about a healthier, more effective employee and organization. Stress is personal; that is, what works for one company is unique, as are the people who make up the company. Tailoring a corporate stress reduction program to your company's specific needs, resources, and level of commitment requires broad perspective, flexibility, creativity, and responsiveness to social forces.

Once the plan has been drawn up, management awareness and involvement are essential. Successful execution of the plan may depend on how prepared both management and employees are to change and how they relate to others and to the job. With today's drive to improve the quality of life, a stress reduction program inspires commitment. It is clearly within each person's and company's interest and control to reduce stress.

CHAPTER 18
Professional Assistance

As an experienced professional yourself, you know that when you need novel, specialized, or merely fresh or more objective views or help, you can easily justify the cost of going elsewhere for special services in finance, architecture, advertising, personnel, construction, engineering, research, law, and so on. This chapter is about professional assistance in stress management. When is it necessary, warranted, or desired? Who are the professionals? How is one chosen rather than another?

A professional may be defined as a person with specialized knowledge acquired after intensive academic and experiential training in behavior and health modification. We mention several different kinds of programs as alternative means of achieving good health. In the first chapter of Part III, we covered several ways of helping yourself. In this chapter we are going to look at how others can assist you in achieving your health goals. We will also discuss some of the signs of various problems that may indicate that help is needed.

With the increased health consciousness of this decade, the development of a wealth of commercial enterprises and health specialties has made the selection of services difficult. As in the section on development of a stress reduction program, identification of the problem is the first step. We will discuss how certain behaviors (habits, practices) can be harmful and what can be done to change them.

Corporations can and do offer in-house programs, outside referrals, and/or encouragement for employees to pursue a health-enhancing lifestyle. We shall explore several of these approaches.

[295]

PROFESSIONAL ASSISTANCE

Although many stress-related disorders clear up when the stressor is removed or the emotional difficulty subsides, chronic problems may require the attention of a physician or stress specialist. Your personal or company doctor may also recommend psychological counseling to help you plan a lower-stress lifestyle and better, more health-enhancing habits.

A counselor will not tell you how to live your life, but he can provide guidelines to follow in evaluating your situation. Therapy can help you gain perspective with regard to the complexities. Having a professional to talk to about your particular difficulties in getting and staying well is conducive to achieving these goals and is sound business practice. Developing a stress-coping strategy that conforms with your particular temperament and lifestyle will help you maintain a sense of well-being and confidence.

Through tests and questionnaires administered by a skilled professional in the area of stress, you can learn what health hazards loom large in your life and, through counseling, you can learn how best to reduce those hazards. In selecting a stress specialist, look at his basic professional credentials. He should be a psychiatrist, a well-informed internist, or a behavioral or clinical psychologist. All of these must have special training and experience in the field of stress and disease. Parenthetically, we need to decide who is going to determine the appropriateness of the credentials. A good source is the American Institute of Stress.

Seeking professional guidance follows the basic problem-solving model outlined in Chapter 17. The first step toward starting on the road to recovery is to be aware of the problem. In this chapter we will follow the outline of the previous chapters. In that regard, we will identify some of the symptoms and signs of such problems as alcohol and drug abuse, obesity, malnutrition, disease, and emotional and mental malfunctioning, including behavioral aberrations. From this awareness base, we suggest various avenues of professional intervention that can help build personal and corporate health and well-being.

MENTAL HEALTH

Many people who go to a psychiatrist or psychologist have been stigmatized as weak, unable to solve their own problems, or mentally ill. These stereotypes have been the antithesis of the strong, independent, competent, driving business person. This dichotomy has practically made seeking the help of mental health professionals and executive aspirations mutually exclusive. Many people with such spartan views have died of stroke or heart attack.

However, the situation is turning around or opening up. Increasing numbers of major corporations are enlisting the services of psychiatrists and psychologists, in consideration of the effect of the total stress milieu on a person on duty from nine to five. There are several reasons for providing counseling or other forms of therapy. It permits people to:

Ventilate feelings from the distant or recent past
Learn to adjust to a demanding situation
Gain insight into feelings or actions
Learn new ways of experiencing self
Make major life decisions wisely

Different kinds of help are available:

Psychiatrist
Psychologist
Marriage and family counselor
Social worker
Minister, priest, or rabbi

Each of these therapists or counselors has a particular background and training as well as an individual style, and can follow a wide range of theoretical and practical approaches:

Gestalt therapy
Transactional analysis
Psychoanalysis
Behavior alteration or modification
Jungian dream analysis
Rational–emotive therapy
Conjugal family therapy
Crisis counseling and intervention
Spiritual advice and counsel

Events and conditions that cause change are often very stressful and demand adjustment. A qualified counselor with whom you feel comfortable can draw from his wealth of experience and training to help you function more effectively and achieve the relief or the quality of life you desire.

DRUG ABUSE

The problem of drug abuse—both legal and illegal overuse—is legion. Overprescribing of mood-altering drugs is a national health problem. Each person, in the last analysis, will have to make the ultimate decisions for himself or herself regarding the use of drugs. However, there are some constructive approaches that can be utilized to ameliorate the problems of drug abuse.

Unfortunately, there are no simple answers and there's no panacea for the apparently epidemic proportions of this and other health concerns in our society. But professional means are available to stem the tide and help people avoid and cope with such high-risk, low-gain behaviors as drug abuse.

The very qualities that help a man get ahead in the business world—self-reliance, competitiveness, self-sacrifice, denial of feelings, and singleness of purpose—may produce distress and inhibit a sufferer of that stress from seeking help. All too frequently the climb to the top of the executive ladder is a lonely effort. Socially isolated people are more likely than socially integrated people to fall back on a destructive coping mechanism, such as eating or drinking too much, and to ignore normal health practices when overstressed.

Drug abuse foundations, centers, self-help support groups, educational programs, magazine articles, hot lines, television specials, and rehabilitation hospitals are but a few of the information and treatment resources to which a person can turn for assistance.

Common Symptoms

If a manager sees that an employee or co-worker is having or causing an inordinate amount of problems on the job, he may look for signs of potential drug abuse. A poor, unkempt physical appearance, increased absenteeism, withdrawal from responsibility, and a general change in overall attitude can indicate something is wrong. Excessive activity or lethargy, chain smoking, and irregular eating and/or sleeping habits are additional signs of a troubled person.

These symptoms are not in themselves definite indications that the problem is drugs. As we have pointed out in prior chapters, uncoped-with stress in a person's environment or personal life may manifest itself in the same way. How, then, can you seek appropriate guidance from such general observations?

Obviously, you cannot. As a manager you can recognize a problem exists and refer the person to a physician or counselor, hoping that an examination or consultation will reveal the cause or causes. We are not suggesting that any lay person take it upon himself to make a medical or psychiatric diagnosis. Rather, we are asking you to be in tune with the people with whom you work and be aware that discernible, unexplained changes in behavior can indicate a potentially explosive problem to which attention should be paid.

In the area of drug dependency, there are more specific signs to look for than those mentioned above.

Barbiturates

Barbiturates act as a depressant to the central nervous system and have a calming, sedating effect. If someone is taking barbiturates, he or she may display symptoms of alcohol intoxication, but will have no odor of alcohol on the breath. That person may appear drowsy or disoriented, have thick speech, be quarrelsome, and stagger or stumble frequently. The physical and psychic addiction to these sedatives or hypnotics makes withdrawal extremely difficult. An overdose can cause a coma and death due to respiratory failure. Combined with alcohol, these drugs are especially dangerous.

Glue Sniffing

The glue sniffer also displays poor muscular control, drowsiness, and sometimes unconsciousness. His breath or clothes may carry the odor of the substance inhaled and he may have excessive nasal excretions and watering of the eyes.

Amphetamines

Amphetamines stimulate the central nervous system and temporarily increase alertness and energy and reduce symptoms of fatigue. They are usually prescribed to reduce depression, appetite, or fatigue. The amphetamine abuser has dilated pupils and may wear sunglasses at inappropriate times to hide this fact. He is characteristically irritable, argumentative, and nervous and has difficulty sitting still. He may lick his lips frequently and rub and scratch his nose because of the dryness experienced. Excessive use of breath fresheners is common to mask the side effect of bad breath. Chain smoking, hyperactivity, incessant talking, poor eating and/or sleeping habits, paranoia, and hallucinations may plague the stimulant abuser. Dangerous side effects also include high blood pressure, weight loss, aggressiveness, and abnormal heart rhythms.

Narcotics

Most people are familiar with the telltale paraphernalia of the narcotics abuser: syringes, bent spoons, bottlecaps, eyedroppers and nasal aspirators, cotton, and needles. Inhaling cocaine or heroin in powder form leaves traces of white powder around the nostrils, causing redness and rawness. Injecting heroin leaves needle marks on the inner surface of the arms and elbow. These may be covered up by wearing long-sleeved shirts most of the time or by injecting the drug in other areas of the body, where the scars will not be seen as readily. On the job, the addict is lethargic and drowsy. His pupils are constricted and fail to respond to variations in light levels.

Marijuana

Marijuana users are difficult to recognize unless they are observed under the influence of the drug. The sweetish odor of burning marijuana cigarettes or pipes resembles that of burning weeds or rope and may be detected on clothing shortly after usage. In the early stages, the person may appear animated and hysterical, with rapid, loud talking, and bursts of inane laughter. While under the influence, his depth perception is distorted, making driving or operating other machinery dangerous. In addition, the distinction between reality and fantasy may become blurred, and the smoker is oblivious to anybody else's point of view.

In the later stages, the person becomes sleepy, lethargic, very relaxed, or stuporous. The effect on each person varies from time to time. Although the user is usually docile, on some occasions he may become violent. The eyes may become red and the face puffy, and appetite is depressed. As with glue sniffing and hallucinogen use, marijuana smoking is usually a group activity.

Hallucinogens

The odorless, tasteless, colorless drug LSD is often added to sugar cubes, cookies, or crackers. It may be injected, but is generally taken orally. The drug primarily affects the nervous system, producing changes in mood and behavior and perceptual changes involving the senses, body image, and time that can last for several hours.

Users generally sit or recline passively in a dream or trancelike state. Paranoia and terror may cause someone under the drug's influence to flee from an imagined threat. The user loses contact with reality and cannot make realistic judgments, which could lead to serious accidents. Hallucinations may recur without warning at any time after taking the drug, and mental functions may be damaged permanently.

Furtive behavior, association with known drug abusers, suspected theft, and appearances in odd places such as closets and storage rooms may be signs of drug abuse.

Hidden Addictions

Prescription drug abuse is sometimes more difficult to detect because the symptoms are not as easily identifiable and there is little, if any, social opprobrium or criminal association, as there is with alcohol or street drugs like heroin.

The problem of drug dependency is not limited to hard-core "junkies." It is widespread among the highly educated and successful professions and classes of both sexes. In 1979, more than 68 million prescriptions were written for Valium and Librium alone.

Studies by the FDA Substance Abuse Treatment Centers indicate that the number of tranquilizer prescriptions has surpassed that of antibiotics, to make it the most frequently prescribed class of drugs in the United States. This in itself may point to serious abuse. On the other hand, it may simply reflect the real extent to which a broad segment of the population is neither managing nor dealing with the stressors in its lives.

The excessive use of prescribed drugs accounts for more than 90 percent of the tranquilizer market. Not surprisingly, Valium is the most frequently prescribed drug in America. It is prescribed by physicians to relieve pain from muscle spasms, overall feelings of apprehension and anxiety, and insomnia, to make patients feel more in control when under stress, or simply to allow patients to get through the day.

All tranquilizers like Valium and Librium, including such sleeping pills as Dalmane, are psychotropic drugs acting on the part of the brain known as the limbic system, which controls the central nervous system. "Mood elevators" and "pain killers" are also in this group. Valium and Librium belong to the chemical class of benzodiazepine tranquilizers. These drugs carry the risk of having disturbing side effects on both mind and body and creating potential daily dependency.

The drugs do have legitimate benefits. They relieve short-term specific physical symptoms and some major psychological disorders. However, unlike a drug like penicillin, which you stop taking after it has cured what was ailing you, a mood-altering drug has the potential not only of relieving pain but also of giving pleasure or a mental high.

Consequently, many people reach for a pill to help them cope with the ordinary stresses of life. Therefore, most specialists on drug dependency believe that prescriptions should be given only for relatively short periods of time. Many patients get around their physicians' control by obtaining prescriptions from more than one doctor in order to meet their increasing dependency on tranquilizers. Warnings of danger do not appear to be sufficient.

Overcoming the tranquilizer or other drug habit is not easy. Withdrawal symptoms may include chills and fever, insomnia, violent itching, pain, acute anxiety, and hallucinations requiring hospitalization.

When people recognize their pattern of drug abuse, they usually cite specific situations—for example, deadlines or public speaking—rather than their entire lives as triggering the anxiety or escape mechanism. Pinpointing the stressors that made them reach for the drug(s) can help people to start working on specific things in specific areas of their life to help them do a better job of coping.

Getting Help

Physicians. If you feel that your life or that of someone close to you is being impaired by the use of drugs, consult your physician immediately or recommend that he see his. The doctor may not be aware of the drugs being taken or, in the case of prescribed drugs, may have underestimated the effect of the dosage. Follow up, to see whether your advice was taken. If you can, and if it is necessary, exert some pressure—moral or bureaucratic. You would stop a friend from suicide. Drugs can be equally serious.

Psychotherapy. Psychotherapy on a personal or a group basis can help a person face and deal with the emotions the drugs have been masking. Sometimes it is the only solution for people who want to end their dependence on drugs. University medical schools and some hospitals have experimental therapy programs for different categories of drug habits.

Organizations. Pills Anonymous is one group whose chapters are branching out from New York City to help "pill" addicts and their families. Alcoholics Anonymous also makes some attempt to deal with the dual addict, the problem drinker and pill taker, though alcohol is the primary concern of that organization.

Community services. Community mental health centers, hospital emergency rooms, clergymen, crisis "hot" lines, and other drug rehabilitation services are listed in the Yellow Pages under "Drug Abuse and Addiction—Information and Treatment." In a crisis, call the police or the emergency room of a general hospital.

Reporting the Problem

It is not always easy to identify a drug problem within an organization, and few people are willing to talk about it, let alone acknowledge it. People who strongly suspect or know of the problem are often reticent to disclose this information to the medical director, personnel office, or management for fear of jeopardizing the user's position (or their own job, in the case of a superior's addiction) or social acceptance.

This protective behavior is self-defeating, because the distress grows from covering up the problem or trying to work around it. As in the problem of alcoholism, early recognition is a vital factor in heading off a crisis situation. Employees and co-workers are in a position to spot the problem at an early stage, before the person's work performance and reputation are irretrievably damaged.

Corporate Response

As part of an early detection plan, some corporations are having specialists train their supervisors and managers to evaluate job performance, noting any drop below standards or change in work habits that cannot otherwise be explained.

Employees seeking treatment on their own initiative are guaranteed confidentiality and provided with either on-site medical assistance or outside referrals. The threat of discharge is made only for failure to follow through with treatment, if job performance does not improve, and/or if the employee endangers himself or others on the job,

Finally, companies are increasingly offering stress reduction programs with instruction in more positive coping techniques that can be substituted for the chemical controllers.

Laboratory Detection

Sophisticated laboratory equipment is available to verify or eliminate the suspicion of drug abuse. The equipment is sensitive enough to pick up one-trillionth of a gram of amphetamine in a urine sample. It can detect other stimulants and painkilling narcotics taken 72 to 96 hours before the test.

Gas chromatographs separate out constituent elements one by one. For example, amphetamines come out in three minutes, narcotics in about 20. Their presence is signaled by a "spike" in a pengraph tracing of the machine. When there's no spike, no drugs are present in the system.

However, if the test is positive, the drug can be identified by the mass spectrometer. This device, by bombarding the drug molecules with ions, produces a pattern, or "fingerprint," of the unknown chemical. Like human fingerprints, each drug's pattern is unique, and the chemical is readily identifiable.

If an illicit drug is detected by the medical examiner, he can then take appropriate action and make referrals to professionals to help discourage the person from using drugs and help him kick the habit.

Breadth of Problem

Millions of Americans are heavily dependent upon drugs for dieting, sleep, alertness, relaxation, heightened consciousness, euphoria, or pleasure. Rather than employing the positive coping techniques detailed in this book to achieve these ends, a lot of people use counterproductive methods. Many people become drug dependent on legally prescribed drugs that were initially intended to help alleviate another problem but have since created a new one through prolonged or excessive self-medication.

A person may be under the care of several physicians for a variety of medical problems, and a lack of control over the number and/or types of drugs being used can be deadly. Though the individual medications may not be lethal, several of the drugs taken in conjunction can interact with each other to produce a fatal or at least debilitating synergistic or incompatible effect. Despite the inherent danger of mixing drugs and alcohol, increasing numbers of "dual addicts" are appearing in emergency rooms and Alcoholics Anonymous meetings. For those who took lethal doses, it is too late, but for others there is still hope through continuing group and self-help effort.

Drug usage has increased yearly. The percentages of the different categories of drugs used with varying frequency may not seem high, but collectively they add up to a great deal of drug use in any given organization. Heavy reliance on tranquilizers, pep pills, sleeping pills, diet pills, and others represents a clear and present danger to safety and health in the work environment. The problem must be met head-on through a cooperative effort between professionals and clients.

ALCOHOLISM

Another widespread form of escape from stressful reality is excessive drinking. It is the number one form of stress escape, and the most expensive in many ways. Americans spend over $11 billion annually in retail purchases of alcoholic beverages alone, not counting bar and restaurant consumption. About 5 percent of the general population, one out of 20 adults, is harmfully addicted to alcohol—over 10 million people! The cost in terms of life, health, property, and productivity is astronomical.

The cocktail hour may provide pleasant warmth, relaxation, and euphoria, but reliance on alcohol consumption to achieve these effects can produce one of the most devastating diseases known.

The fact that alcoholism afflicts some people and not others has led to much confusion in selecting the method of preventing or treating compulsive drinking. Physiological and biochemical factors, such as endocrine imbalances and poor nutrition, may have led to the problem. Heredity may genetically predispose someone to become an alcoholic. Children of alcoholics are about 50 percent more likely to have some biochemical susceptibility to alcohol than children of nondrinkers. Mental or emotional difficulties resulting in acute anxiety or self-indulgence can cause people to feel that they cannot cope with life while sober.

Alcoholics Anonymous defines an alcoholic as "any person whose indulgence in alcohol continuously or periodically results in behavior disruptive to normal relations with his or her work, family, or society." We are not speaking solely about the quantity of alcohol consumed, but about the mental compulsion to drink and the effects it has as well. Not all heavy drinkers are alcoholics, and vice versa.

Whereas a normal person (nonalcoholic) can stop drinking at will, the alcoholic cannot stop for long without help. He is unable to limit his drinking. Once he introduces alcohol into his system, he loses all control, and drunkenness inevitably follows because of his physiological susceptibility. Fatigue, drowsiness, poor balance, loss of sex drive, blackouts, and other incidents of unusual sensitivity to moderate alcoholic intake, plus otherwise unmanageable anxiety, are some of the most common side effects. Therefore, only complete abstinence will afford an alcoholic a normal life and good health. There is an Alcoholics Anonymous saying that "One drink is too many, and a thousand are not enough."

Over 80 percent of the drinking alcoholics in America become hospitalized or die before they can effectively undergo treatment. In addition, at least 40,000 of the nation's traffic fatalities per year—nearly half—involve alcohol. Other destructive effects include damage to the functions of the liver, impaired ability to produce antibodies against infections, malnutrition, and heart problems. Alcoholism is regarded as incurable except by abstinence, according to Alcoholics Anonymous and many other groups fighting it.

Alcohol is hazardous both to physiological and psychological well-being. Chronic drinking affects one's peace of mind as dependency develops. Behavior may become sneaky and dishonest, both to oneself and to friends and family. One would like to think of oneself as merely a social drinker, but then why lie about how much one drinks and why gulp drinks and sneak extras?

The mildly tranqulizing effect moderate drinking may evoke eludes the alcoholic. Instead, mental alertness, coordination, speech, and judgment are impaired. He finds himself doing and saying things that he would otherwise be too inhibited or self-controlled to do. In fact, alcohol is a contributing factor in 50 percent of all homicides and 25 percent of all suicides.

Business and industry lose about $15 billion a year on alcohol-related problems—absenteeism, accidents, insurance benefits paid out, and reduced performance at work. Innumerable government-sponsored treatment programs, scientific centers, Alcoholics Anonymous groups, and private hospitals are working on the illness of alcoholism.

As in the case of drug abuse, early detection of the problem drinker is a vital factor in bringing the problem under control. Many corporations have come to recognize and accept alcoholism as a disease and offer in-house programs or obtain professional treatment and outside referrals. Alcoholism is now recognized by federal law as just as much a handicap as blindness or paraplegia.

Supervisors and co-workers can be helpful in recognizing blood-shot eyes, loss of memory, trembling, alcoholic breath, abnormal skin tone, and lack of coordination. If treatment can be implemented before rule violations or unsatisfactory work performance and disruptive behavior go too far, the troubled employee may be able to keep his job.

Fear of being fired if discovered often prevents an employee from seeking help even when he knows he needs it and when his need is obvious to his friends. A particularly insidious difficulty is that the alcoholic's family will (understandably) cover up for him or even deny the problem. Experts counsel these families to remove all such props and protections and let the full weight of the alcoholic's behavior fall on him—to hasten his waking up and taking steps to save himself—while standing ready to help when such awareness comes.

Therefore, some companies include hospital care for alcoholism in their insurance plans, provide confidential counseling, and let employees know that these and other support systems are at their disposal without fear of automatic dismissal.

The New York offices of both the National Council on Alcoholism and the Corporate Headquarters Alcoholism Project, the National Clearinghouse for Alcohol Information in Rockville, Maryland, and your local chapter of Drinkwatchers and of Alcoholics Anonymous can all provide further information on alcoholism to help overcome the cost of problem drinking to the company and its employees. Alcoholics Anonymous is listed in every major telephone directory in the United States, and in most cities it maintains a free 24-hour switchboard for emergencies.

CIGARETTE SMOKING

Another popular stress reliever exacting a tragic long-term price is cigarette smoking. Cigarette smoking can result in adverse physical and psychological reactions for both the smoker and the nonsmoker.

The evidence that smoking is hazardous to everyone's health is incontrovertible. Nevertheless, millions of Americans spend $6 billion per year on tobacco. Mountains of statistics attribute heart ailments, chronic bronchitis, and emphysema and lung and throat cancer in part to smoking.

The nicotine in the tobacco can stimulate the adrenals, releasing epinephrine and norepinephrine. That hastens the blood-clotting process and damages the arterial walls. Chronic smoking elicits the stress response and keeps the body in an aroused physiological state, with increased heart rate, elevated blood pressure, raised respiration rate, and stimulated release of glucose and fatty substances like cholesterol into the blood. Although the body can adapt initially to the nicotine, the constituents of the smoke wear down the tolerance and can precipitate ventricular fibrillation, resulting in heart attacks and increased chances of a stroke or coronary artery thickening, to name a few of the physiological effects.

Not to be discounted is the fact that the nonsmoker is also affected by a smoky environment. The nonsmoker has not developed a tolerance to nicotine and his respiratory system is adversely affected by repeated exposure to cigarette smoke. In addition, a smoky working area can cause nausea, headaches, and irritation of the eyes and nose of the nonsmoker. These may affect his work performance; the irritation makes it difficult for him to concentrate or do finely detailed work. The adverse physical and psychological reactions may cause increased absenteeism, requests for transfers, or even elective severance if the working conditions become intolerable to the nonsmoker.

In response to this problem, some companies have designated smoking and nonsmoking areas and removed cigarette machines and substituted gum and fruit machines for breaks. They also have paired smokers or nonsmokers on projects and sponsored Smokenders and similar programs. Some insurance companies—but too few—offer preferred rates for the nonsmoker as an incentive to avoid or quit the habit. Some employers simply prohibit smoking on the premises, and others advertise specifically for nonsmokers.

Recognizing that such a change in behavior is a personal choice, companies are encouraging employees to cut back or quit smoking entirely by making publications, group programs, and medical supervision available to them. Reinforcement in the work environment by health-conscious management of the climate will add multiple benefits to all concerned.

CHAPTER 19
The Road Ahead

The different approaches suggested to control your stress can be as productive as some of your current behavioral patterns—but less stressful. As we have stated throughout this book, each person can live more effectively with the unavoidable stresses that are a continuous part of twentieth-century life and work. Many of the most common stressors in life—or in the organization, family, environment, personality—that must be faced in the future have been identified. Rather than resist new challenges, people (and corporations) should regulate the changes in their lives and try to keep them from becoming too intense or too pressing by pacing themselves and planning ahead whenever possible.

Life is presumed to supply pleasure and have worth. When we begin to be unsure of our capacity to enjoy life, to feel satisfaction and a sense of achievement, we may experience deep anxiety. The prevalence of existential anxiety in contemporary America signals a threat to the meaning and quality of life. In a predominantly middle-class society such as the United States, few are struggling for mere existence, simply to earn food, shelter, clothing, and comfort. For most, basic survival needs have been met.

The contemporary concept of survival is tied to the question of emotional meaning in our lives. Many people are waging a fight against a seemingly meaningless round of diversionary activities, devoid of psychological involvement, variety, challenge, status, significance, or accountability. The problem is that when life is stripped of the mechanisms that make a person feel worthwhile, anxiety, boredom, and general dissatisfaction set in. The devices that in previous ages gave a sense of pride, stability, and creativity—religion, family, work—have changed in significance or weakened.

The twentieth century seems to have conspired against modern man. Most of our entertainments have been reduced to diversions. We have become observers rather than participants. By the same token, heretofore rewarding work has become a mechanical, unremitting chore. Boredom is creeping beyond the assembly line and into the professional offices.

Increasing specialization demands mastery of a specific skill, procedure, or area of expertise that in turn demands a limited focus to achieve. The excitement and challenge inherent in perfecting a special technique or discipline is soon reduced to myopic concentration of effort and daily repetition of the same problem or types of problems. The work inevitably becomes boring.

Stripped of stimuli, a person begins to feel alienation, agitation, impatience, or resentment. The fidgety, special kind of restless anxiety that disrupts the homeostasis of modern man is a warning signal that all is not well and something must be done. This phenomenon alerts us that active attention must be paid to seeking another level of experience in our daily activities to improve the quality of our lives.

If we do not learn to understand, anticipate, and guide the great forces of change at work on our world today, we will suffer immeasurably by the vast upheavals in both our personal and business lives. So swift is the acceleration of change that trying to make sense of all the difficulties and opportunities in order to steer them in the right direction for the future is our biggest challenge. Fortunately, we are not simply at the mercy of these events. As we have seen, there are ways of meeting the challenge and handling the concomitant stress.

JOB-STRESS RESEARCH

Business-related stress research is in its infancy. There are many areas in which further evidence is needed to identify, clarify, and validate the apparent relationship between organizational stress and disease. Up to now, studies of strictly job-related stress have concentrated primarily on peptic ulcer and heart diseases. Data need to be developed by which an organization can assess its impact on other diseases as well as on the total health of the employee. Further research is expected to uncover many of the same relationships between work-related stress and health problems that exist between other life stressors and disease.

Intervention techniques need to be tested and evaluated in actual work settings. That way organizations can judge correctly which approaches they should offer or support. For instance, continued research needs to be done in the area of the detection and treatment of risk factors. Specifically, we need to know what the correlation is between coronary disease and coronary risk and relevant dimensions of job performance and job satisfaction. Parts I and II illustrated how prolonged distress can cause other structural and functional damage when there is an imbalance between demand and the ability to cope.

Another potential problem worthy of the attention of researchers is the theory that people become ill when some crisis forces them to abandon social rules or values that have hitherto provided them with a sense of security. In fact, the roots of aggression and antisocial behavior are in the thwarting of the basic human needs for love, security, new experiences, praise, and recognition.

Further research is needed into the employees' assignment of responsibility for stressful situations and for the results of attempts to alleviate stress. Perhaps the application of theories of causality and locus of control in the area of job stress would prove fruitful.

Another area of stress research that needs further study is in the field of psychological processes. What is the link between the physical and psychological processes? How are specific physical events such as high blood pressure related to specific decision-making strategies? Are irrational decisions the result of high blood pressure, or does high blood pressure lead to irrational decision making? Learning, personality, attribution, perception, and motivation are a few of the areas that cognitive and social psychology could explore.

Combining performance and health measures in a longitudinal study would help in gaining a more comprehensive understanding of the sequential consequences of job stress. It would also seem fruitful to study the effects of stress on the employee and on the organization simultaneously and multidimensionally. And, of course, we should not omit investigations of the possible beneficial human consequences of stress.

Stress is not an easy or simple subject to explore. By their very nature the stress response and general adaptation syndrome are complex and variable. They do not lend themselves to definitions that are simplistic and clear-cut. To simplify the subject by drawing sharp lines of distinction and making broad generalizations that must be qualified is to provide only the most basic understanding of this highly complicated subject.

We recognize that the exact mechanism of the hormonal reactions to stressors, the use of the generic term "stress," and other areas in the stress field need to be clarified. The means by which the same stressor can produce diverse manifestations or even different diseases in different people needs to be explored and documented carefully.

Another fruitful area of research is of the stress-resistant person—the one who seems to show no symptoms of stress-related maladies, though exposed to the same stressors. Is his or her resistance constitutional or genetic, or is it the result of learning, or of fortunate circumstances in his or her formative environment?

In this book we discussed various internal and external conditioning factors that enhance or inhibit sensitivity or proneness to disease. We have also tried to increase the employee's and the company's conscious awareness of these potent conditions in our daily lives. (An overview of their interelationship is depicted in Figure 16.) However, doubt, confusion, and controversy still exist in the continuing efforts to understand the functional aspects of man and society. The search may help man develop a personal philosophy that will enrich the quality of life for all living things.

THE LIMITS OF ADAPTATION

Man is more than a machine made of interlocking systems. He is a living organism, continually adjusting to and interracting with his external surroundings. His mode of living may be altered or stopped by even a slight change in the environment or in his relation to it. The ways in which an organism reacts is an absorbing biological process. It receives the signal of change and transfers the information to appropriate internal systems, which then provide the adjustment. As we have seen repeatedly, when the demands for adjustment are too great, the adaptive machinery breaks down,

FIGURE 16. *Interrelationship of factors in the dynamics of stress.*

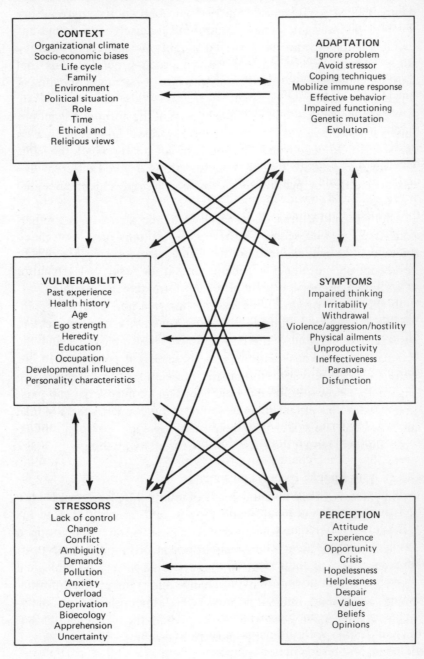

selectively affecting predisposed body areas and disrupting the body's homeostasis. The consequences may be physical, emotional, and/or behavioral.

EVOLUTION AND CHANGE

Just as a person adjusts to changes, so does the corporation of which he is a part. The doctrine of evolution has itself evolved slowly with man's greater and greater understanding of the world that he inhabits and of the other living things that inhabit it with him. In the same way, management theory has evolved slowly over the decades with a greater understanding of the dynamics of business and of the people and groups that make it run. The forces of change are so swift and so widespread that it becomes impossible to believe that what is happening in this decade is anything like the "normal" progress we have experienced in the past.

About 25 percent of all the people who ever lived are alive today. Ninety percent of all the scientists who ever lived are living now. The amount of technical information available doubles every ten years. In order to deal with the forces of change on a human level, we can no longer ignore the related stages of human activities on and off the job. The functional relationship of people to the organization as a whole cannot be overlooked. Various factors cooperate in the process of natural selection, by which variants appropriate to the environmental situation are preserved.

Corporations, like people, are challenged to adapt in order to survive. Modern management has to work out strategic adaptations to the problems of corporate accountability, women and minorities, stress, and other changes in processes and practices enumerated earlier in the book. In order to maintain the economic stability of their business, executives need to program their organization into constructive paths of planned change.

Evolution is a dynamic and unpredictable process. Consequently, it is likely that in the development of any group there are plateaus of adjustment separating periods of change.

Over the centuries, the concept of work has evolved from individual physical toil for survival into a cooperative effort with monetary and psychological rewards. Survival in today's world goes beyond dealing with the physical threats of nature to the intangible elements of job satisfaction, personal dignity, respect, and opportunities for personal growth and self-expression. Work has become such a psychological and emotional necessity for modern man and woman that research repeatedly indicates that the majority of people would continue working despite eligibility for retirement, windfall fortunes, or the satisfaction of material needs. In fact, forced retirement has been said to lead to premature deaths in many instances.

In addition to this evolution in attitudes toward work has come an evolution in management theory. Many organizational structures have evolved from the authoritarian or autocratic approach to the human relations approach. Corporate policies, interrelations, and/or personnel decisions are becoming more democratic when appropriate to the task at hand. Flexibility and creativity are essential in dealing effectively with the uncertainty, unpredictability, and accelerated changes in today's world.

American business is marshaling the technology and organizational know-how that have made this country an economic leader among nations to effect socioeconomic change. It has also raised the quality of work life by alleviating the distressful by-products of our "success." Contrary to many expectations, technology has not decreased the value of the human component in business. It has altered its value, just as it has created whole new classes of personnel, but mankind is still the most essential and valuable component in business and industry.

The financial, social, and personal bottom lines of corporate life are inseparably linked. The apparent human and organizational costs resulting from job stress warrant the application of personal and organizational strategies. Their purpose is to enable employees to enjoy good physical and mental health by reducing unnecessary stress in the work environment.

SUMMARY

In review, we have presented some strategies aimed at changing the person's:

- Psychological characteristics or condition by meditation, relaxation response, autogenic training, self-hypnosis, development of a philosophy of life, and cognitive behavior modification.
- Physical/physiological characteristics or conditions by proper

diet, regular exercise, biofeedback, aggression-release rooms, and meditation.

- Behavior by time management, active listening, low-stress communication, emotional desensitization, self-expression, assertion training, social support systems, withdrawal, occupational change, recreational activities, and overt behavior.
- Work environment by changed routine, personalized environment, changed organizations, changed route/means of travel, delegation or sharing of tasks, flexitime, and time management.

In addition, we suggested deliberate organizational strategies for managing job stress and improving the physical and mental health of employees aimed at changing:

- Organizational processes, structures, programs, and so on by design and management of roles, identification of stressors, reward systems, communication, job enrichment, shift patterns, transfers and relocation, selection and placement procedures, education, and performance evaluation.
- Role characteristics or conditions by redistribution of workload, role definition, and employee participation.
- Task/job characteristics or conditions by training opportunities, improving job fit with abilities and preferences, individualization, job focus rather than occupation, workload, responsibility, organization of work, job redesign, leadership development, and physical alterations.

And lastly, we suggested various professional services available to ameliorate a person's stress load and relieve its organizational impact on such problems as:

- Psychological/emotional, with the help of the minister, marriage and family counselor, psychiatrist, psychologist, social worker, and physician.
- Drug abuse, with the help of the physician, rehabilitation hospital, educational program, friend, support group, detection training center, psychotherapist, and laboratory specialist.
- Alcohol problem, with the help of those named above, plus Alcoholics Anonymous and Drinkwatchers.
- Cigarette smoking, with the help of incentive programs, restricted areas, Smokenders, and educational programs.

- Physical fitness, with the help of health club membership, on-site gym facilities, recreational activities, and physical examination.
- Nutrition/diet, with the help of cafeteria control, physical examination, vitamin and mineral supplements, and educational programs.

CONCLUSION

In view of all the information presented in this book, it is evident that job stress–employee health phenomena are very complex. There is no single cause or single effect. Rather, there are many factors and cumulative effects. People may react differently to the same stressor under different circumstances or on different occasions. They also cope differently with the same stressor under different circumstances or on different occasions.

There does not appear to be a single formula or point of intervention that will deal effectively with stress for all people in all organizations under all circumstances. Therefore, a combination of strategies and resources needs to be developed to help people and organizations to deal selectively with the stress of today's world. As Siegfried Giedion says in *Mechanization Takes Command:*

> Our period demands a type of man who can restore the lost equilibrium between inner and outer reality. This equilibrium, never static, but, like reality itself, involved in continuous change, is like that of a tightrope dancer who, by small adjustments, keeps a continuous balance between his being and empty space. We need a type of man who can control his own existence by the process of balancing forces often regarded as irreconcilable: Man in equipoise.

Our intent is to share more than concern with you about the stress in life, and especially in the business world. Once having identified the sources and disseminated background information, we set forth "how to" descriptions and programs of what you can do to improve your health and well-being. We are aware that even reading about stress can be distressing and leave one with a feeling of helplessness and hopelessness. Perhaps worst of all, many people just accept chronic stress as the price man has to pay for progress and existence in the twentieth century. We do not accept this acquiescent position. We believe you can actively pursue avenues of planned change and utilize methods to alleviate the damaging effects of destress and to use eustress. Stress is not the enemy; man is his own worst enemy. He must take control of and responsibility for his actions, health, and life.

We have learned a great deal about stress, what variables are important, and how we may develop a stress reduction program for the benefit of all concerned. Both the person and the organization play important roles in taking up the challenge to improve the quality of life. The synergism of such concerted effort has the potential to guide us into a new century of personal well-being and corporate health, all of which will come back to our credit on the bottom line.

Bibliography

Achterberg, Jeanne, Carl Simonton, and Stephanie Matthew-Simonton. *Stress, Psychological Factors, and Cancer*. Fort Worth, Tex.: New Medicine Press, 1976.

Albrecht, Karl. *Stress and the Manager*. Englewood Cliffs, N.J.: Prentice-Hall, 1979.

Anderson, Carl R. *Locus of Control, Coping Behaviors, and Performance in a Stress Setting: A Longitudinal Study*. College of Business and Management, University of Maryland, 1976.

Argyris, Chris. *Integrating the Individual and the Organization*. New York: Wiley, 1964.

Aronson, Elliot. "Reconsidered: The Nature of Prejudice," *Human Nature*, July 1978.

Barber, Theodore, et al., eds. *Biofeedback and Self-Control* (series of annuals). Chicago: Aldine-Atherton, 1970–1974.

Bensman, Joseph, and Robert Lilienfeld. "Friendship and Alienation," *Psychology Today*, October 1979.

Benson, Herbert. "Holistic Approach Utilizes Relaxation Response, Biofeedback," Roche Report, *Frontiers of Psychiatry*, January 1, 1979.

———. *The Relaxation Response*. New York: William Morrow, 1975.

———. "Your Innate Asset for Combating Stress," *Harvard Business Review*, July–August 1974.

Berland, Theodore. *Rating the Diets*. New York: Signet Books, 1979.

Berne, Eric. *Games People Play*. New York: Grove Press, 1964.

Bieler, G. Henry. *Food Is Your Best Medicine*. New York: Random House, 1965.

Blakeslee, Alton. *Your Heart Has Nine Lives*. Englewood Cliffs, N.J.: Prentice-Hall, 1973.

Bloomfield, Harold H., Michael Peter Cain, Dennis T. Jaffe, and Robert B. Kory. *TM: Discovering Inner Energy and Overcoming Stress*. New York: Delacorte Press, 1975.

Bogen, Joseph. "The Giant Walk-Through Brain," *Human Nature*, October 1978.

Bois, J. Samuel. *The Art of Awareness*. Dubuque, Iowa: William C. Brown, 1975.

————. *Breeds of Men*. New York: Harper & Row, 1969.

————. *Explorations in Awareness*. New York: Harper & Brothers, 1957.

Boshear, Walton, and Karl Albrecht. *Understanding People: Models and Concepts*. La Jolla, Calif.: University Associates, 1977.

Bove, Alfred A. "Cardiovascular Response to Stress," *Psychosomatics,* October 1977.

Brenman, Margaret, and Merton M. Gill. *Hypnotherapy*. Josian Macy, Jr., Foundation, 1944.

Bresler, David. *Hurting*. New York: Simon & Schuster, 1978.

Brown, Barbara. *Stress and the Art of Biofeedback*. New York: Harper & Row, 1977.

————. *New Mind, New Body*. New York: Harper & Row, 1974.

Brozek, Josef. "Personality Differences Between Potential Coronary and Noncoronary Subjects," *Annals of the New York Academy of Sciences,* pp. 1057–1065.

Brunvand, Jan Harold. "Urban Legends: Folklore for Today," *Psychology Today,* June 1980.

Burke, Ronald J., Tamara Weir, and Richard E. DuWors, Jr. "Type A Behavior of Administrators and Wives' Reports of Marital Satisfaction and Well-Being," *Journal of Applied Psychology,* October 1979.

Cannon, Walter B. *The Wisdom of the Body*. New York: W.W. Norton, 1932.

Caplan, Robert D., et al. *Job Demands and Worker Health: Main Effects and Occupational Differences*. Washington, D.C.: U.S. Department of Health, Education and Welfare, 1975.

Carter, C. Sue, and William T. Greenough. "The Brain Sending the Right Sex Messages," *Psychology Today,* September 1979.

Cartwright, Dorwin, ed. *Group Dynamics*. New York: Row, Peterson, 1956.

Charlton, Randolph S. "Divorce as a Psychological Experience," *Psychiatric Annals,* April 1980.

Chase, Stuart. *Power of Words*. New York: Harcourt, Brace, 1954.

————. *The Proper Study of Mankind*. New York: Harper & Row, 1948.

————. *The Tyranny of Words*. New York: Harcourt, Brace, 1938.

Coelho, George V., David A. Hamburg, and John E. Adams, *Coping and Adaptation*. New York: Basic Books, 1974.

Cole, Michael. "How Education Affects the Mind," *Human Nature,* April 1978.

Colligan, Michael J., and William Stockton. "Assembly-Line Hysteria," *Psychology Today,* June 1978.

Colligan, Michael J., M.D. Smith, and J.J. Hurrell. "Occupational Incidence of Mental Health Disorders," *Journal of Human Stress,* September 1977.

Cooper, Gary L., and John Crump. "Prevention and Coping with Occupational Stress," *Journal of Occupational Medicine,* June 1978.

Cooper, Gary L., and Judi Marshall. "Occupational Sources of Stress: A

Review of the Literature Relating to Coronary Heart Disease and Mental Ill Health," *Journal Of Occupational Psychology,* March 1976.

Cooper, Kenneth H. *Aerobics.* New York: Bantam Books, 1969.

"Coping Style Linked Inversely to Marital Stress, Depression," *Frontiers of Psychiatry,* November 1, 1978.

"Coping with Anxiety at AT&T," *Business Week,* May 28, 1979.

Coser, Lewis A.: "Reconsidered: The Lonely Crowd: A Study of the Changing American Character," *Human Nature,* September 1978.

Cousins, Norman, *Anatomy of an Illness.* New York: W. W. Norton, 1979.

"Cracking Under Stress: How Executives Learn to Cope," *U.S. News & World Report,* May 10, 1976.

Derdeyn, Andre P., "Divorce and Children: Clinical Interventions," *Psychiatric Annals,* April 1980.

DeSilva, Regis A., and Bernard Lown. "Ventricular Premature Beats, Stress, and Sudden Death," *Psychosomatics,* November 1978.

Diamond, Marian C. "The Brain/Uppers and Downers in the Air," *Psychology Today,* June 1980.

Dinman, B. D., R. R. Stephenson, S. M. Horvath, and M. O. Colwell. "Work in Hot Environments: 1. Field Studies of Work Load, Thermal Stress and Physiologic Responses," *Journal of Occupational Medicine,* Vol. 16 (1974), pp. 785–791.

Dlin, Barney M. "Risk Factors and Life Style," *Psychosomatics,* October 1977.

Dorfman, Wilfred. "Depression: Its Expression in Physical Illness," *Psychosomatics,* November 1978.

Dranov, Paula. "Stress Tests Getting to the Heart of the Controversy," *Family Weekly,* 1980.

Drinkwater, B. L., and M. M. Flint. "Response Speed and Accuracy During Anticipatory Stress," *Journal of Motor Behavior,* Vol. 1 (1969), pp. 220–232.

Drinkwater, B. L., P. B. Raven, S. M. Horvath, J. A. Gliner, R. O. Ruhling, N. W. Bolduan, and S. Taguchi. "Air Pollution, Exercise, and Heat Stress," *Archives of Environmental Health,* Vol. 28 (1974), pp. 177–181.

Drinkwater, B. L., M. M. Flint, and T. S. Cleland. "Somatic Responses and Performance Levels During Anticipatory Physical-Threat Stress," *Perceptual Motor Skills,* Vol. 27 (1968), pp. 539–552.

Drinkwater, B. L., T. S. Cleland, and M. M. Flint. "Pilot Performance During Periods of Anticipatory Physical-Threat Stress," *Aerospace Medicine,* Vol. 39 (1968), pp. 994–999.

Drucker, Peter F. *The Age of Discontinuity.* New York: Harper & Row, 1968.

Dubos, René. "Health and Creative Adaptation," *Human Nature,* January 1978.

———. *Man, Medicine and Environment.* New York: Mentor, 1968.

———. *Man Adapting.* New Haven, Conn.: Yale University Press, 1965.

Dudley, Donald L., and Elton Welke, "How to Live with Stress," *Penthouse Forum,* November 1977.

Dunbar, Flanders. *Psychosomatic Diagnosis.* New York: Harper & Brothers., 1943.

Dychtwald, Ken. *Bodymind.* New York: Pantheon, 1977.

Ehrlich, Paul R., and Anne H. Ehrlich, "What Happened to the Population Bomb?" *Human Nature,* January 1979.

Engel, George. "Emotional Stress and Sudden Death," *Psychology Today,* November 1977.

Fabun, Don. *The Dynamics of Change.* Englewood Cliffs, N.J.: Prentice-Hall, 1967.

Farber, Seymour M., and Roger H. L. Wilson. *The Challenge to Women.* New York: Basic Books, 1966.

Fischer, H. Keith. "Management of Emotional Factors," *Psychosomatics,* October 1977.

Flach, Frederic F.: "Introduction: Divorce and the Psychiatrist," *Psychiatric Annals,* April 1980.

———. *A New Marriage, A New Life.* New York: McGraw-Hill, 1978.

———. *Choices: Coping Creatively with Personal Change.* Philadelphia: Lippincott, 1977.

Forbes, Rosalind. *Corporate Stress.* New York: Doubleday, 1979.

Frank, Benjamin S. *No Aging Diet.* New York: Dell, 1976.

Fredericks, Carlton. *Psycho-Nutrition.* New York: Grosset & Dunlap, 1976.

Freedman, J. L. *Crowding and Behavior.* San Francisco: W. H. Freeman, 1975.

Friedl, Ernestine. "Society and Sex Roles," *Human Nature,* April 1978.

Friedman, Arnold P. "Characteristics of Tension Headache: A Profile of 1,420 Cases," *Psychosomatics,* July 1979.

Friedman, Meyer, and Ray Rosenman. *Type A Behavior and Your Heart.* New York: Alfred A. Knopf, 1974. [For a report on Friedman and Rosenman's original research, see Ray H. Rosenman, et al., "Coronary Heart Disease in the Western Collaborative Group Study: Final Follow-Up Experience of 8½ years," *Journal of Human Stress,* September 1977.]

Friedman, Milton. "Holistic Health: Is Washington Listening?" *Nutritional Journal,* Fall 1978.

Gagnon, John H. "Reconsidered," *Human Nature,* October 1978.

Galbraith, John Kenneth. *The Age of Uncertainty.* Boston: Houghton Mifflin, 1977.

Garfield, Charles A. *Stress and Survival.* St. Louis, Mo.: C. V. Mosby, 1979.

Gaze, Samuel B., ed. "Life Events and Illness," *Psychiatric Capsule and Comment,* February 1979.

Geba, Bruno. *Breathe Away Your Tension.* Random House: New York, 1974.

————. *Vitality Training for Older Adults*. New York: Random House, 1974.

Geer, J. H., G. Davison, and R. Gatchel. "Reduction of Stress in Humans Through Nonveridical Perceived Control of Aversive Stimulation." *Journal of Personality and Social Psychology*, Vol. 16 (1970), pp. 731–738.

Gessel, Arnold H. "Biofeedback Aided Relaxation and Meditation in the Management of Hypertension," *Psychosomatics*, June 1978.

Gibson, John E. "Attitudes About Work," *Family Weekly*, November 26, 1978.

Giedion, Siegfried. *Mechanization Takes Command*. New York: W. W. Norton, 1969.

Glass, David C., and Jerome E. Singer. *Urban Stress*. New York: Academic Press, 1972.

Goldberg, Herb. *The Hazards of Being Male*. New York: Nash Publishing, 1976.

Goldberg, Philip. *Executive Health*. New York: McGraw-Hill, 1978.

Goldstein, Joseph. *The Experience of Insight*. Santa Cruz, Calif.: Unity Press, 1976.

Goleman, Daniel. "Why Your Temples Pound," *Psychology Today*, August 1976.

————. "Matter over Mind: The Big Issues Raised by Newly Discovered Brain Chemicals," *Psychology Today*, June 1980.

Gottschalk, Louis A., and Goldine C. Gleser. *The Measurement of Psychological States Through the Content Analysis of Verbal Behavior*. Berkeley and Los Angeles: University of California Press, 1969.

Gottschalk, Louis A., Carolyn N. Winget, and Goldine C. Gleser. *Manual of Instructions for Using the Gottschalk-Gleser Content Analysis Scales: Anxiety, Hostility, and Social Alienation-Personal Disorganization*. Berkeley and Los Angeles: University of California Press, 1969.

Green, Richard, ed. *Human Sexuality: A Health Practitioner's Text*, 2nd ed. Baltimore: Williams & Wilkins, 1979.

Greenspan, Kenneth. "Biologic Feedback and Cardiovascular Disease," *Psychosomatics*, November 1978.

Grinker, Roy R., and John P. Spiegel. *Men Under Stress*. Philadelphia: Blakiston, 1945.

Guthrie, Robert R. "When an Executive Reaches the Top Early in His Career, What Does He Do for an Encore?" *The Executive of Orange County*, December 1979.

Hall, Judith A., Robert Rosenthal, Dane Archer, M. Robin DiMatteo, and Peter L. Rogers. "Decoding Wordless Messages," *Human Nature*, May 1978.

Hall, Richard C. W., William P. Gruzenski, and Michael K. Popkin. "Differential Diagnosis of Somatopsychic Disorder," *Psychosomatics*, June 1979.

Hall, Richard C. W., Earl R. Gardner, Mark Perl, Sondra K. Stickney, and

Betty Pfefferbaum. "The Professional Burnout Syndrome," *Psychiatric Opinion,* April 1979.

Hamburg, David A. *This Question of Coping.* Nos. 1–14. Nutley, N.J.: Roche Laboratories, 1973.

Hamner, Clay W., and Dennis W. Organ. *Organized Behavior: An Applied Psychological Approach.* Dallas: Business Publications, 1978.

Hartung, G. Harley, and Emile J. Farge. "Personality and Physiological Traits in Middle-Aged Runners and Joggers," *Journal of Gerontology,* Vol. 32 (1977), pp. 541–548.

———. "Your Innate Asset for Combating Stress," *Harvard Business Review,* July–August 1974.

Hayakawa, S. I. *Language in Thought and Action.* New York: Harcourt, Brace, 1939.

———. *Symbol, Status and Personality.* New York: Harcourt, Brace and World, 1963.

———, ed. *Language, Meaning and Maturity.* New York: Harper and Brothers, 1954.

Henry, James P., and Daniel L. Ely. "Emotional Stress: Physiology," *Primary Cardiology,* August 1979.

Hertzberg, Frederick. *Motivation to Work.* New York: Wiley, 1959.

Hinkle, L. E. "The Concept of 'Stress' in the Biological and Social Sciences," *Science, Medicine and Man,* 1:43, 1973.

Hirschowitz, Ralph G. "Consultation to Changing Organizations," *Psychiatric Opinion,* December 1978.

———."The Human Aspects of Managing Transition," Personnel, May–June 1974.

Hirst, William, Ulric Neisser, and Elizabeth Spelke. "Divided Attention," *Human Nature,* June 1978.

Hittleman, Richard. *Yoga.* New York: Workman, 1969.

Holmes, Thomas H. "Life Situations, Emotions, and Disease," *Psychosomatics,* December 1978.

Holmes, Thomas H., and T. Stephenson Holmes. "How Change Can Make Us Ill," *Stress,* Woodland Hills, Calif.: Blue Cross of Southern California, 1974.

Holmes, Thomas, and Richard Rahe. "The Social Readjustment Rating Scale," *Journal of Psychosomatic Research,* Vol. 11 (1967), pp. 212–218.

Horney, Karen. *Our Inner Conflicts.* New York: W. W. Norton, 1945.

Horowitz, Mardi J. *Stress Response Syndromes.* New York: Jason Aronson, 1976.

Horvath, S. M. "Cardiac Disease in the Context of the Future Environment," *Environmental Research,* Vol. 2 (1969), pp. 470–475.

Horvath, S. M., T. E. Dahms, and J. F. O'Hanlon. "Carbon Monoxide and Human Vigilance: A Deleterious Effect of Present Urban Concentrations," *Archives of Environmental Health,* Vol. 23. (1971), pp. 343–347.

Horvath, S. M., P. B. Raven, B. L. Drinkwater, J. F. O'Hanlon, and T. E. Dahms. "A Brief Literature Search Regarding the Influence of Air

Pollutants on Work Capacity and Psychophysiological Responses of Man," *Project Clean Air Task Force Assessments*, 1970.

"How to Deal with Stress on the Job," *U.S. News & World Report*, March 13, 1978.

Howard, John H. "Management Productivity: Rusting Out or Burning Out?" *The Business Quarterly*, Summer 1975.

———. "To Reduce Stress Get Yourself a Senior Manager's Job," *The Canadian Banker & ICB Review*, November–December 1975.

———. "What Is Our Capacity to Cope with Stress?" *The Business Quarterly*, Winter 1973.

Howard, John H., P. A. Rechnitzer, and D. A. Cunningham. "Stress Inoculation: For Managers and Organizations," *The Business Quarterly*, Winter 1975.

Howard, John H., Peter A. Rechnitzer, and D. A. Cunningham. "Coping with Job Tension—Effective and Ineffective Methods," *Public Personnel Management*, September–October 1975.

Huffer, Virginia. "Biofeedback: A Flexible Approach," *Psychosomatics*, June 1979.

Human Nature, April 1978, June 1978, October 1978, and January 1979.

"Hypertensive Adolescents React Intensely to Stress," *Frontiers of Psychiatry*, May 1, 1979.

Ilfeld, Frederic W., Jr. "Age, Stressors and Psychosomatic Disorders," *Psychosomatics*, January 1980.

Imparton, Nicholas, and Oren Harari. "Five Myths About Stress," *San Francisco Business*, October 1979.

Jacobson, Edmund. *You Must Relax*. New York: McGraw-Hill, 1957.

———. *Progressive Relaxation*. Chicago: University of Chicago Press, 1938.

Jacoby, Susan. "The Tranquilizer Habit," *McCall's*, January 1980.

Jeffrey, D. B., and R. Katz. *Take It Off and Keep It Off*. Englewood Cliffs, N.J.: Prentice-Hall, 1977.

Jenkins, David. "Recent Evidence Supporting Psychologic and Social Risk Factors for Coronary Disease," *New England Journal of Medicine*, April 29 and May 6, 1976.

Johnson, Harry J. *Executive Life-Styles: A Life Extension Institute Report on Alcohol, Sex and Health*. New York: Thomas Y. Crowell, 1974.

Johnson, Virginia E., and William H. Masters. "Why Working at Sex Doesn't Work," *Redbook*, April 1973.

Johnson, Wendell. *Your Most Enchanted Listener*. New York: Harper & Brothers, 1956.

———. *People in Quandaries*. New York: Harper & Brothers, 1946.

Kahn, Robert L., and Robert P. Quinn. *Role Stress. Mental Health and Work Organization*. Chicago: Rand McNally, 1970.

Kanfer, F. "The Many Faces of Self-control, or Behavior Modification Changes Its Focus." Paper presented at Eighth International Banff

Conference on Behavior Modification, University of Alberta, Calgary, Canada, March 1976.

Kasch, Fred W., and John L. Boyer. *Adult Fitness*. Palo Alto, Calif.: National Press Books, 1968.

Kelly, Joe. *Organizational Behavior*. New York: Richard D. Irwin, 1974.

Kennedy, Joseph A. *Relax and Live*. New York: Prentice-Hall, 1953.

Kibbee, Joel M., Clifford J. Croft, and Burt Nanus. *Management Games*. New York: Reinhold, 1961.

Kiley, John Kantwell, *Self-Rescue*. New York: McGraw-Hill, 1977.

Klausen, K., E. D. Michael Robinson, Jr., and L. G. Myhre. "Effect of High Altitude on Maximal Working Capacity." *Journal of Applied Physiology,* Vol. 21 (1966), pp. 1191–1194

Klausen, K., D. B. Dill, E. E. Phillips, Jr., and D. McGregor. "Metabolic Reactions to Work in the Desert," *Journal of Applied Physiology,* Vol. 22 (1967), pp. 292–296.

Korzybski, Alfred. *Science and Sanity*. Lime Rock, Conn.: The International Non-Aristotelian Library Publishing Co., 1948.

———. *Science and Sanity. Introduction to Non-Aristotelian Systems and General Semantics*. Lancaster, Pa.: Science Press, 1933.

———. *Manhood of Humanity*. Lime Rock, Conn.: The International Non-Aristotelian Library Publishing Co., 1921.

Kostrubala, Thaddeus. *The Joy of Running*. Philadelphia: Lippincott, 1976.

Kostrubala, Thaddeus, Jamie B. Kotch, Karen D. Crassweller, and Martha M. Greenwood. "Historical and Clinical Considerations of the Relaxation Response," *American Scientist,* July–August 1977.

Kreitner, Robert, Steven D. Wood, and Glenn M. Friedman. "Productivity and Absenteeism Relative to Coronary Risk," *Arizona Business,* May 1978.

Kroger, William S. *Clinical and Experimental Hypnosis*. Montreal, Can.: Lippincott, 1963.

Krumboltz, J. D., and C. E. Thoresen, eds. *Counseling Methods*. New York: Holt, Rinehart and Winston, 1976.

Kryter, K. *The Effects of Noise on Man*. New York: Academic Press, 1970.

Kubler-Ross, Elizabeth. *On Death and Dying*. New York: Macmillan, 1969.

Kudrow, Lee. "Managing Migraine Headache," *Psychosomatics,* Vol. 19 (1978), pp. 685–693.

La Brecque, Mort. "On Making Sounder Judgments: Strategies and Snares," *Psychology Today,* June 1980.

Lakein, Alan. *How to Get Control of Your Time and Your Life*. New York: Wyden, 1973.

Lamott, Kenneth. *Escape from Stress*. New York: Berkley Medallion Books, 1976.

Laragh, John Henry. "Conquering the Quiet Killer," *Time,* January 13, 1975.

Larsen, Robert, and Virginia Kaiser. "The Self-help Process in a Group of

Cancer Patients," *Current Concepts in Psychiatry,* September–October, 1978.

Lazarus, Richard S. "Psychological Stress and Coping in Adaptation and Illness," *International Journal of Psychiatry in Medicine,* 1974, pp. 321–333.

———. *Psychological Stress and Coping Processes.* New York: McGraw-Hill, 1966.

Lecker, Sidney. *The Natural Way to Stress Control.* New York: Grosset & Dunlap, 1978.

Lee, Irving J. *The Language of Wisdom and Folly.* New York: Harper & Brothers, 1949.

———. *Language Habits in Human Affairs.* New York: Harper &-Brothers, 1941.

Leonard, Jon N., J. L. Hofer, and N. Pritikin. *Live Longer Now.* New York: Grosset & Dunlap, 1974.

Levi, Lennart. *Society, Stress and Disease.* New York: Oxford University Press, 1971.

Levinson, Harry. *Executive Stress.* New York: Harper & Row, 1966.

———. *Emotional Health and the World of Work.* New York: Harper & Row, 1964.

Lindemann, Hannes. *Relieve Tension the Autogenic Way.* New York: Wyden, 1973.

Lubin, Joann S. "Age of Anxiety: Stress Research Seeks Clues to Why Children Can't Cope with Life," *Wall Street Journal,* April 10, 1979.

Luthe, Wolfgang. *Stress and Self-Regulation: Introduction to the Methods of Autogenic Therapy.* Quebec, Canada: International Institute of Stress- —Center for Applied Studies, 1977.

———, ed. *Autogenic Therapy, Vols. 1–6.* New York: Grune & Stratton, 1969.

Mahoney, M. J. and Thoresen, C. E. *Self-Control: Power to the Person.* Monterey, Calif.: Brooks-Cole, 1974.

Manuso, James. "Executive Stress Management," *Personnel Administrator,* November 1979.

———. *Stress Management Training in a Large Corporation.*

Margolis, B. L., William H. Droes, and Robert P. Quinn. "Job Stress: An Unlisted Occupational Hazard," *Journal of Occupational Medicine,* October 1974.

Marrow, Alfred J., ed. *The Failure of Success.* New York: AMACOM, 1972.

Marston, William Moulton. *Emotions of Normal People.* Minneapolis: Persona Press, 1979.

Martin, M. J. "Psychosomatic Medicine: A Brief History, *"Psychosomatics,* November 1978.

Martindale, Davis. "Sweaty Palms in the Control Tower," *Psychology Today,* February 1977.

Marx, Jean L. "Stress: Role in Hypertension Debated," *Science,* December 2, 1977.

Maslow, Abraham. *Motivation and Personality.* New York: Harper & Brothers, 1964.

———. *Toward a Psychology of Being.* New York: D. Van Nostrand, 1968.

May, Rollo. *The Meaning of Anxiety.* New York: Ronald Press, 1950.

McCay, James T. *The Management of Time.* Englewood Cliffs, N.J.: Prentice-Hall, 1959.

McGregor, Douglas. *The Human Side of Enterprise.* New York: McGraw-Hill, 1960.

McKeown, Thomas. "Determinants of Health," *Human Nature,* April 1978.

———. "What Determines a Society's Health?" *National Journal of the Nutritional Academy,* Fall 1978.

McManus, B. M., S. M. Horvath, N. Bolduan, and J. D. Miller. "Metabolic and Cardiorespiratory Responses to Long-Term Work Under Hypoxic Conditions," *Journal of Applied Physiology,* Vol. 36 (1974), pp. 177–182.

McNerney, Walter J. *Stress.* Blue Cross Association, U.S.A., 1974.

McQuade, Walter. "What Stress Can Do to You," *Fortune,* January 1972.

McQuade, Walter, and Ann Aikman. *Stress.* New York: Dutton, 1974.

"Medicine Is Stressful, Psychiatrist Asserts," *American Medical News,* October 17, 1977.

Meichenbau, D. *Cognitive Behavior Modification.* New York: Plenum Press, 1977.

Melnick, Norman. "Could a Nice Guy Like You Have a Heart Attack?" *Psychology Today,* December 1976.

Michael, E. D., Jr., and S. M. Horvath. "Psychological Limits in Athletic Training." International Congress of the Psychology of Sport. Rome, 1965.

Miller, William H. *How to Relax.* New York: A. S. Barnes, 1944.

Miller, W., and R. Munoz, *How to Control Your Drinking.* Englewood Cliffs, N.J.: Prentice-Hall, 1976.

Minteer, Catherine. *Words and What They Do to You.* New York: Row, Peterson 1953.

Minter, Richard E., and Chase Patterson Kimball. "Life Events and Illness Onset: A Review," *Psychosomatics,* June 1978.

Mirkin, Gabe. "How to Cope with Job Stress," *Nation's Business,* January 1979.

"Mood Swings," *Drug Therapy,* June 1979.

Morano, Richard A. "How to Manage Change to Reduce Stress," *Management Review,* November 1977.

Morgan, W. P., P. B. Raven, B. L. Drinkwater, and S. M. Horvath. "Perceptual and Metabolic Responsivity to Standard Bicycle Ergometry Following Various Hypnotic Suggestions," *Inst. Journal of Experimental Hypnosis,* Vol. 21 (1973), pp. 86–101.

Mossfeldt, Folke, and Mary Susan Miller. "How to Keep Fit—While You Sit," *Reader's Digest,* September 1979.

Mulry, Ray. *Tension Management and Relaxation.* Glendale, Calif.: Griffin Printing and Lithograph, 1976.

Myers, David G. "How Groups Intensify Opinions," *Human Nature,* March 1979.

Naranjo, Claudio, and Robert E. Ornstein. *On the Psychology of Meditation.* New York: Penguin, 1971.

National Aeronautics and Space Administration. *A Clinical Investigation of the Effect Improved Physical Fitness Has on the Tolerance of Job Stress* (abstract), 1968.

"New Leads on Brain Functioning: How to Speak, Hear and See," *Medical News,* February 16, 1979.

Nichols, Ralph G., and Leonard A. Stevens. *Are You Listening?* New York: McGraw-Hill, 1957.

Norman, Donald A. "Post-Freudian Slips," *Psychology Today,* April 1980.

Ogden, C. K., and I. A. Richards. *The Meaning of Meaning.* New York: Harcourt, Brace, 1953.

O'Hanlon, J. F., K. M. Skinnarland, and S. M. Horvath. "Neuroendocrine Changes and Symptoms of Stress in Perceptually Deprived Men." *Proceedings of Fourth International Congress of Psychoneuroendocrinology.* Los Angeles: University of California, Brain Information Service Report No. 35, February 1974.

Ornstein, Robert E. *The Mind Field.* New York: Grossman, 1976.

Osofsky, Joy D. "Pregnancy Held Stressful for Couples Even if Planned," *Clinical Psychiatry News,* May 1979.

Oyle, Irving. *The Healing Mind.* Millbrae, Calif.: Celestial Arts, 1975.

———. *Time, Space and the Mind.* Millbrae, Calif.: Celestial Arts, 1976.

Page, Robert Collier. *How to Lick Executive Stress.* New York: Cornerstone Library, 1977.

Parkington, John J., and Benjamin Schneider. "Some Correlates of Experienced Job Stress: A Boundary Role Study," *Academy of-Management Journal* (1979), pp. 270–281.

Parlee, Mary Brown, and the editors of *Psychology Today.* "The Friendship Bond, a Survey Report," *Psychology Today,* October 1979.

Pelletier, Kenneth R. *Mind as Healer, Mind as Slayer.* New York: Delta, 1977.

Pelletier, Kenneth R., and Charles Garfield. *Consciousness: East and West.* New York: Harper & Row, 1976.

Peter, Laurence J., and Raymond Hull. *The Peter Principle.* New York: William Morrow, 1969.

Peters, Ruanne K., and Herbert Benson. "Time Out from Tension," *Harvard Business Review,* January–February 1978.

Plumb, Louise. "Managers React to Stress," *The Canadian Banker and ICB Review,* November–December 1975.

Pribram, Karl: "Holographic Memory," *Psychology Today,* February 1979.
———. *Languages of the Brain.* Monterey, Calif.: Brooks/Cole, 1971.
Proctor, Pam. "How to Survive Today's Stressful Jobs," *Parade,* June 17, 1979.
Profant, Gene R. "Stress Testing," *The Executive,* June 1979.
"Psychiatrist Advised on Coping with Terrorism," *American Medical News,* June 2, 1978.
Rama, Swami, and Rudolph Balletine. *Yoga and Psychotherapy.* Himalayan Institute.
Rapoport, Anatol. *Operational Philosophy.* New York: Harper & Brothers, 1953.
———. *Science and the Goals of Man.* New York: Harper & Brothers, 1950.
Raven, P. B. "Physiologic Monitoring of Heart Rate, Sweating, Body Temperature, and Metabolic Cost During the Work Situation," *Standards for Occupational Exposures to Hot Environments—Proceedings of Symposium.* Cincinnati, Ohio: National Institute for Occupational Safety and Health, 1976.
Raven, P. B., B. L. Drinkwater, S. M. Horvath, R. O. Ruhling, J. A. Gliner, J. C. Sutton, and N. W. Bolduan. "Age, Smoking Habit, Heat Stress, and Their Interactive Effects with Carbon Monoxide and Peroxyacetylinitrate on Man's Aerobic Power," *International Journal of Biomedia,* Vol. 18 (1974), pp. 222–232.
Raven, P. B., J. E. Wilkerson, S. M. Horvath, and N. W. Bolduan. "Thermal, Metabolic and Cardiovascular Responses to Various Degrees of Cold Stress," *Canadian Journal of Physiological Pharmacology,* Vol. 53 (1975), pp. 293–298.
Restak, Richard M. "The Other Difference Between Boys and Girls," *Reader's Digest,* November 1979. [Condensed from *The Brain: The Last Frontier.* New York: Doubleday, 1979.]
Reuben, David. *The Save Your Life Diet.* New York: Random House, 1975.
Ringer, Robert J. *Winning Through Intimidation.* Los Angeles: Los-Angeles Book Publishers, 1974.
Rogers, Carl. *On Becoming a Person.* Boston: Houghton Mifflin, 1961.
Rosch, Paul J. "Stress and Cancer: A Disease of Adaptation," in *Cancer, Stress and Death.* Jean Tache, Hans Selye, and Stacy B. Day, eds. New York: Plenum, 1979.
———. "Stress and Illness," *Journal of the American Medical Association,* Vol. 242 (1979), pp. 427–428.
———. "Holistic Medicine: Self-Care of the Future," in *Strategies for Public Health.* L. K. Y. Ng and D. Davis, eds. New York: Van Nostrand Reinhold, in press.
Rosenthal, Stuart. "A Clinical Perspective of Work Organizations," *Psychiatric Opinion,* December 1978.
———. "Expression of the Emotions in the World of Work," *Psychiatric Opinion,* December 1978.

Rossi, Alice S. "Essay: The Biosocial Side of Parenthood," *Human Nature,* June 1978.

Roth, June. "Executive Stress: How to Help Him Relax," *Harper's Bazaar,* October 1979.

Rowan, Roy. "Keeping the Clock from Running Out," *Fortune,* November 6, 1978.

———. "That Filing System Inside your Head," *Fortune,* August 28, 1978.

Royal Canadian Air Force Exercise Plans for Physical Fitness. New York: Pocket Books, 1962.

Rubenstein, Carin. "Vacations," *Psychology Today,* May 1980.

Rubin, Irwin, and Earl Rose. *The Power of Listening.* New York: McGraw-Hill 1978.

Rubin, Theodore Isaac. *The Angry Book.* New York: Macmillan, 1969.

Rubin, Zick. "Seeking a Cure for Loneliness," *Psychology Today,* October 1979.

Ruesch, Jurgen, and Gregory Bateson. *Communication: The Social Matrix of Psychiatry.* New York: W. W. Norton, 1951.

Ruesch, Jurgen, and Weldon Kees. *Nonverbal Communication.* Berkeley: University of California Press, 1956.

Russell, Bertrand. *The Conquest of Happiness.* New York: Liveright, 1930.

Sales, S. M. "Differences Among Individuals in Affective, Behavioral, Biochemical and Physiological Responses to Variations in Work Load," Doctoral dissertation, University of Michigan, 1969.

Samuels, Michael. *Seeing With the Mind's Eye.* New York: Random House, 1976.

Samuels, Michael, and Hal Bennet. *The Well-Body Book.* New York: Bookworks/Random House, 1973.

Scarr, Sandra, and Richard A. Weinberg. "Attitudes, Interests and IQ," *Human Nature,* April 1978.

Schaffer, Walt. "Stress, Distress and Growth," Davis, Calif.: Responsible Action, 1978.

Schiefelbein, Susan. "The Female Patient," *Saturday Review,* March 29, 1980.

Schnarch, David M., and John E. Hunter. "Migraine Incidence in Clinical vs. Nonclinical Populations." *Psychosomatics,* Vol. 21 (1980), pp. 314–325.

Schultz, Terri. "Does Marriage Give Today's Women What They Really Want?" *Ladies' Home Journal,* June 1980.

"Secrets of Coping with Stress." *U.S. News & World Report,* March 21, 1977.

Selkirk, Mary. "Reclaiming Our Health Rights," *Nutritional Journal,* Fall 1978.

Selye, Hans (interviewed by Laurence Cherry). "On the Real Benefits of Eustress," *Psychology Today,* March 1978.

———. "They All Looked Sick to Me," *Human Nature,* February 1978.

———. *The Stress of My Life.* Toronto: McLelland & Stewart, 1977.

———. *Stress in Health and Disease*. London: Butterworth, 1976.

———. *From Dream to Discovery: On Being a Scientist*. New York: Arno Press, 1975.

———. *Stress Without Distress*. New York: Lippincott 1974.

———. *In Vivo*. New York: Liveright, 1967.

———. *The Stress of Life*. New York: McGraw-Hill, 1956.

———. "A Syndrome Produced by Diverse Nocuous Agents," *Nature*, July 4, 1936.

Senders, John W. "Is There a Cure for Human Error?" *Psychology Today*, April 1980.

"Sex Differences Seen in Brain Asymmetries," *Brain Mind Bulletin*, June 2, 1980.

Shaffer, Laurence F., and Edward J. Shoben Jr. *The Psychology of Adjustment*. New York: Houghton Mifflin, 1956.

Shealy, C. Norman. *The Pain Game*. Millbrae, Calif.: Celestial Arts, 1976.

Sheehy, Gail. *Passages*. New York: Dutton, 1976.

Shevrin, Howard: "Glimpses of the Unconscious," *Psychology Today*, April 1980.

Simonton, Carl, Stephanie Matthew-Simonton, and James Creighton. *Getting Well Again*. Los Angeles: J. P. Tarcher, 1978.

Simonton, Carl, and Stephanie Simonton. "Belief Systems and Management of the Emotional Aspects of Malignancy," *Journal of Transpersonal Psychology*, Vol. 7 (1975), pp. 29–48.

Singer, Jerome E., and David C. Glass. "Making Your World More Liveable," *Stress*. Chicago: Blue Cross, 1974.

Slobogin, Kathy. "Stress," *The New York Times Magazine*, November 20, 1977.

Slovic, Paul, Baruch Fischhoff, and Sarah Lichtenstein. "Risky Assumptions," *Psychology Today*, June 1980.

Sobel, David S. *Ways of Health*. New York: Harcourt Brace Jovanovich, 1979.

Solomon, G. F., A. A. Amkrant, and P. Kasper. "Immunity, Emotions, and Stress," *Annals of Clinical Research*, Vol. 6 (1974), pp. 313–322.

Spiegel, David, and Herbert Spiegel. "Hypnosis in Psychosomatic Medicine," *Psychosomatics*, January 1980.

Stauth, Cameron. "Non-Specific Therapy," *National Journal of the Nutritional Academy*, Fall 1978.

Staver, Sari. "Parallel to Executive Stress Medicine Is Stressful, Psychiatrist Asserts," *American Medical News*, October 17, 1977.

Straus, Nathan, III. *Addicts and Drug Abusers*. New York: Twayne Publishers, 1971.

Stressin, L. "When an Employer Insists," *The New York Times*, April 3, 1977.

"Study Reveals Sex Roles with Cohabiting Relationships," *Frontiers of Psychiatry*, November 1, 1978.

Sugarman, Daniel A. "Male Impotence: What Every Woman Should Know," *Reader's Digest,* September 1973.

Suinn, Richard M. "How to Break the Vicious Cycle of Stress," *Psychology Today,* December 1976.

Tanner, Ogden, et al. *Stress.* Alexandria, Va.: Time-Life Books, 1976.

Taylor, Alex. "Stress Taking Toll of Top-level Execs," *Detroit Free Press,* November 14, 1978.

"Tensions of Executive Life." New York: Research Institute of America, 1958.

"The Corporate Problem That Didn't Go Away," *Behavioral Sciences Newsletter* (special report), 1977.

"The Executive Under Pressure," *Business Week,* May 25, 1974.

"The Fad Disease," *Time,* April 7, 1980.

"The 'Gamesman' Plays for Success, May Go Home with Depression," *Frontiers of Psychiatry,* June 1, 1977.

Thomas, Lewis. "The Strangeness of Nature," *New England Journal of Medicine,* Vol. 298 (1978), pp. 1454–1456.

Thoreson, C. E., and T. J. Coates. "Behavioral Self-Control: Some Clinical Concerns." In M. Hersen, P. Eisler, and P. Miller, eds., *Progress in Behavior Modification.* New York: Academic Press, 1976.

Thoreson, C. E., Kathleen Kirmel-Gray, and Peggy Crosbie. "Processes and Procedures in Self-Control: A Working Model," *The Canadian Counselor,* 1977.

Thorpe, Janet. "The Secret Formula of 'Dr. Stress'," *US,* September 6, 1977.

Toffler, Alvin. *Future Shock.* New York: Random House, 1970.

Townsend, Robert. *Up the Organization.* New York: Alfred A. Knopf, 1970.

Travis, John, and James Fadiman, eds. *Wellness Inventory.* Wellness Resource Center, 1975.

"Types of Distress Which Threaten Marriage," *Medical Aspects of Human Sexuality,* January 1980.

Ubell, Earl. *How to Save Your Life.* New York: Penguin, 1976.

Ursin, Holger, Eivind Baade, and Seymour Lerin. *Psychobiology of Stress.* New York: Academic Press, 1978.

Varela, Jacobo A. "Solving Human Problems with Human Science," *Human Nature,* October 1978.

Vayda, Eugene. "Keeping People Well: A New Approach to Medicine," *Human Nature,* July 1978.

Viscott, David. *Risking.* New York: Simon & Schuster, 1978.

Watts, Alan W. *The Wisdom of Insecurity.* New York: Pantheon Books, 1951.

Weiman, C. "A Study of Occupational Stressors and the Incidence of Disease/Risk," *Journal of Occupational Medicine,* Vol. 19, pp. 119–122.

Weisman, Avery D., and Harry J. Sobel. "Coping with Cancer through

Self-Instruction: A Hypothesis," *Journal of Human Stress*. Vol. 5 (1979), pp. 3–7.

Welford, A. T. *Man Under Stress*. New York: Wiley, 1974.

Whorf, Benjamin Lee. *Language, Thought, and Reality*. Cambridge, Mass.: MIT Press, 1956.

Williams, Roger J. "The Wonderful World Within You," *Executive Health*, December 1977.

———. "Nutritional Individuality," *Human Nature*, June 1978.

———. *The Wonderful World Within You*. New York: Bantam Books, 1977.

———. *Physician's Handbook of Nutritional Science*. Springfield, Ill.: Charles C Thomas, 1975.

———. *Nutrition Against Disease*. New York: Pitman Publishing, 1971.

Wise, Thomas N. "Abstracts," *Psychosomatics*, June 1978.

Wolf, Stewart G. "The Digestive System in Psychosomatic Perspective," *Psychosomatics*, November 1978.

Wolff, Harold G. *Stress and Disease*. Springfield, Ill.: Charles C Thomas, 1968.

"Women Discuss 'Groundbreaking' Careers," *Business Community Journal*, April 1980.

Woodworth. *The Nature and Technique of Understanding*. Vancouver, B.C.: Wrigley Printing, 1949.

Woolfolk, Robert L., and Frank C. Richardson. *Stress, Sanity, and Survival*. New York: Monarch, 1978.

———. "Physicians and Stress: How to Cure Yourself," *Current Prescribing*, 1979.

"Workshop Addresses Problems of Two-Career Couple," *Business Community Journal*, April 1980.

World-Wide Medical Press. "Personality Traits and Autonomic Controls in Borderline Hypertension," Roche Report, *Frontiers of Psychiatry*. April 1, 1980.

———. "Ventilation Is Not Enough," Roche Report, *Frontiers of Psychiatry*. April 1, 1980.

Wright, Nicholas, ed. *Understanding Human Behavior*. New York: Columbia House, 1974.

Yates, Jere E. *Managing Stress*. New York: AMACOM, 1979.

Yeager, Robert C. "Doctoring Isn't Just for Doctors," *Medical World News*, October 3, 1977.

Young, David R. "Are You Listening?" *TMM & I*, Spring 1979.

Ziegler, Dewey K. "Headache Syndromes: Problems of Definition," *Psychosomatics*, July 1979.

Index

[336]